Russian Mafia in America

Advisor in Criminal Justice

to Northeastern University Press

Gilbert Geis

JAMES O. FINCKENAUER

ELIN J. WARING

RUSSIAN MAFIA IN AMERICA

IMMIGRATION,

CULTURE,

AND CRIME

Northeastern University Press

Boston

Northeastern University Press

Copyright 1998 by James O. Finckenauer and Elin J. Waring

Library of Congress Cataloging-in-Publication Data

Finckenauer, James O.
  Russian mafia in America : immigration, culture, and crime / James O. Finckenauer, Elin J. Waring.
    p. cm.
  Includes index.
  ISBN 1–55553–374–4 (cloth : alk. paper)
  1. Russian American criminals—United States.
  2. Organized crime—United States. I. Waring, Elin J.
  II. Title.
HV6446.F56 1998
364.1´06´0899171073—dc21   98–23540

Designed by Bessas & Ackerman
Composed in Times by Coghill Composition in Richmond, Virginia.
Printed and bound by Edwards Brothers, Inc., Digital Book Center, in Ann Arbor, Michigan. The paper is EB Natural, an acid-free sheet.

Manufactured in the United States of America
05 04 03 02 01   7 6 5 4 3

to Linnea Abernathy and Margaret Finckenauer

CONTENTS

TABLES AND FIGURES

Tables

Figures

PREFACE

Our aim in *Russian Mafia in America* is to examine Russian organized crime in the United States. Accomplishing this aim has entailed a rather long and far-reaching research process. The idea for our study first began to germinate in 1990 when Finckenauer had discussions concerning organized crime with Russian colleagues at the then Soviet Academy of Sciences in Moscow. Nothing much came of the idea, however, until 1993, when, through the extraordinary efforts of Lois Felson Mock, the National Institute of Justice agreed to finance a study of crime committed by Soviet émigrés in the United States ("Soviet Émigré Organized Criminal Networks in the United States," 93-IJ-CX-0019). In addition to Ms. Mock's advocacy, our study was facilitated by two other factors—a collaborative partnership that we had arranged with the (New York, New Jersey, and Pennsylvania) Tri-state Soviet Émigré Organized Crime Project and our proposed use of a relatively new analytical tool called *network analysis*. Ours was to be the first use of this analytic method with criminal networks like those that were allegedly associated with the Russians.

The Tri-state Project was organized by the New York State Organized Crime Task Force, the New York and New Jersey State Commissions of Investigation, and the Pennsylvania Crime Commission. Its charge was to investigate Soviet émigré organized crime in the member's respective states. We worked with the Tri-state Project for four years. During that time we had access to every report, document, and piece of information the Project compiled. We also had total access to the attorneys, investigators, and intelligence analysts working for the Project. This collaboration produced a gold mine of information.

We additionally surveyed more than 400 law enforcement agencies from across the country, analyzed indictments and trial transcripts from their major criminal cases involving Russians, and collected virtually every article, book, and report written on the subject. Still more information came from our in-depth interviews with a wide variety of persons. We interviewed a number of figures in American law enforcement, journalists and writers in both the United States and Moscow, and law enforcement officials in Russia and in the former Soviet Republic of Georgia (in Tbilisi). We also did extensive interviewing with émigrés from the former Soviet Union who are now living in the United States. The result, we believe, is the most complete picture of the Russian émigré crime situation yet drawn.

Following the precept of describe, compare, and then explain, we first describe the phenomenon of crime among Russian émigrés to the United States. We then compare this phenomenon across time and place to gain historical perspective and context, contrasting our findings with commonly accepted notions of organized crime. Finally and most important, we explain what we think our examination reveals.

After a brief introduction and a statement of propositions in Chapter 1, we consider the issue of organized crime and the mafia in Chapter 2. What is organized crime, and what is the mafia? What do they do? Why do they exist? How are they different? Among the various theories about why some people engage in organized crime is the thesis that they have a mindset or worldview that attracts them to the "crooked ladder" of social mobility that organized crime can provide. Related to the crooked-ladder hypothesis and essential to an understanding of American organized crime are the ethnic dimensions of crime and crime's connection to the immigrant experience. Russians, therefore, need to be viewed in a context and tradition that includes Italians, Irish, Chinese, Colombians, and others. Beyond any general similarities that ethnic immigrants to the United States may share, we examine the special effects of growing up under the strange circumstances that characterized the former Soviet Union—circumstances that encouraged a talent for schemes and scams. We contend that a sucker mentality is especially evident among those most extreme people produced by the Soviet system—the ones known as *Homo sovieticus.*

Chapter 3 describes early Russian Jewish immigration to America, especially New York City, to glean lessons from this history about what is happening today. For some of these early immigrants, crime was a one-generation phenomenon that flourished in the late nineteenth and early twentieth centuries. For others—including well-known historical figures such as Arnold Rothstein, Waxey Gordon, Marm Mandelbaum, and, later, Meyer Lansky—crime was a ladder to wealth and power. In Chapter 4 we continue this history into the present and develop links between life in the USSR and the motivations of those who gravitate to organized and white-collar crime and corruption.

The setting for Chapters 5 and 6 is Russia itself. In Chapter 5 we describe the unique patterns of organized crime in the former Soviet Union—the old Soviet mafia, the so-called thieves-in-law or *vory v zakone,* the black market, the shadow and second economies, and the rampant corruption that characterized Soviet life. Inevitably, the amorality that was engendered among average Russians who broke the law to survive has had societal repercussions. Chapter 6 focuses on the current organized crime scene in Russia and examines both the symbiotic relationship among organized crime, business, and government in Russia and the threats this presents both at home and abroad. The transnational implications of potential Russian organized crime involvement in alien smuggling are also discussed.

In Chapters 7, 8, and 9, we return to the United States. Studying American organized crime has always been a specially vexing problem for criminologists and others; its ethnic dimensions and secretiveness make it difficult and dangerous to penetrate. Cooperation between law enforcement and the research community is critical in coping with these difficulties. But a certain wariness between researchers and law enforcement practitioners complicates the necessary collaboration. We believe we have successfully overcome these kinds of roadblocks in our work with the Tri-state Project. The fruits of that work are detailed in Chapters 7 and 8. Chapter 7 presents our overall findings, including those from our national survey. Our conclusion is that Russians in the United States demonstrate a distinction between organized crime and crime that is organized. This distinction has a variety of implications, as we show.

Our "crime that is organized" conclusion is reiterated by the network analyses reported in Chapter 8. Drawing on the extensive database compiled by the Tri-state investigators, we explore the intricate network structures in which Russian émigrés participated. These structures do not resemble those commonly associated with conventional organized crime, but they seem to be responsive to the particular criminal opportunities that Russians have engaged in.

Chapter 9 looks at the Russian mafia through the eyes of ordinary Russian Americans. The residents of the largest Russian community in the United States tell us what they think is going on with Russian organized crime, what they think about it, who is involved, who is victimized, as well as about their personal experiences with organized crime.

We revisit in Chapter 10 the propositions outlined at the starting point. Our conclusion—which may be startling to some—is that the Russian organized crime in America widely known as the Russian Mafia is first, not Russian; second, not a mafia; and third, not even organized crime. *Russkaya mafiya? Nyet!*

ACKNOWLEDGMENTS

The work we are presenting here was accomplished with the assistance of a great many people. We recognize a risk by attempting to name them all, and if we do overlook someone, please accept our sincere thanks and apologies. We begin by acknowledging those persons without whose help or support the research would have been literally impossible—those who were most critical and to whom we owe a special debt. They include Tom Abernathy, Emmanuel Barthe, Marilyn Cichowski, Ronald Goldstock, Helene Gurian, Paul T. (Pete) Haskell, Wilda Hess, Frederick Martens, Lois Felson Mock, James Morley, Donald T. Sobocienski, Marina Solomyanskaya, and Gregory Stasiuk. Tom's programming knowledge and computer skills rescued us on countless occasions. Manny did network analyses for two years, as well as anything else we asked him to do. It was Marilyn with her own study of Soviet émigrés who first opened the door to the possibilities of this larger study. Ron Goldstock, Helene Gurian, Fred Martens, and Jim Morley were the respective heads of the Tri-state Project collaborators who agreed to take us in and work with us. Wilda, Don, and Gregg from the New York Organized Crime Task Force staff in White Plains bridged the gap between the world of the theoretical and hypothetical and the world of the practical and operational. Marina, a Rutgers student, did a terrific job of interviewing émigrés in Brighton Beach. Finding Pete Haskell was like finding a gold mine. Starting literally from scratch, he built a disparate collection of information into a usable database—and he also knows a lot about cars! Finally, Lois Mock secured for us essential resources, without which this book never would have happened. She then for years listened to our excuses about where her report was. We hope that you find the final product to be worth it.

Other persons also made important contributions for which we are profoundly grateful. Phyllis Schultze of the Rutgers criminal justice collection found whatever books and articles we were looking for as well as many we did not know existed. Richard Mosquera of the Federal Bureau of Investigation supported our National Institute of Justice proposal and linked us with the FBI's Russian team. Leila Litvinova arranged interviews in Moscow and acted as interpreter. Alexander Nikiforov sustained our interest in Russian organized crime and provided invaluable materials. Edward Riley of the Drug Enforcement Administration in Miami was a helpful sounding board as well as a source of keen insights. Joseph Albini, Kólin Chin, and Lydia Rosner critically read the manuscript and offered numerous suggestions.

Help big and small also came from the following: Nathan Adams, Helene Berkholcs, Ella Boguslavsky, Linda Bryant, Tim Cadigan, Al Campagnola, Joel Campanella, Tony Cartusciello, Gary Dickinson, Joe Doherty, Jim Fox, Bill Friedlieb, Robert Friedman, Sophia Geyfetsman, Jeanette Gonzales, Alexandra Gorlig, Peter Grinenko, Bill Handoga, Adrian Kitzinger, Glen Ridgeway, Edfra Roman, Artie Schwartz, Eric Seidel, Bill Sousa, Ted Stanny, and Sondra Wright. We thank you all.

In the last but certainly not least category, we want to thank Bill Frohlich of Northeastern University Press. Bill stimulated our interest in doing the book and then patiently and quietly shepherded it through the creative process.

Russian Mafia in America

CHAPTER 1

INTRODUCTION

This is a story of Russian crime and criminals. Most of it takes place in the contemporary United States, especially in the Brighton Beach area of Brooklyn and in parts of New Jersey and Philadelphia. Some of it takes place in California and Florida.

To truly understand the Russians who have come to America—old and new, criminal and not, honest and not—we are compelled to look at who they are and where they have come from. Their roots are in czarist Russia, the Russia of the former Soviet Union, and the Russia of today. The most important lessons that immigrants learned were about survival under the novel and difficult conditions that marked Soviet life. For all Russians, being especially adaptive and innovative often meant putting aside morality and legality, and this outlook—characterized by rationalization, hypocrisy, and a double standard of morality—to varying degrees shapes the thinking and behavior of almost all Soviet Russians who have come to America. This is especially so for some of the most recent arrivals—those referred to as the new Russians—whose worldview was shaped in the declining years of a Soviet Union that was reaching its nadir of corruption and decadence.

Our story has additional roots in the prisons of Russia, especially the notorious prison camp system known as the Soviet gulag. Those prisons were the birthplace for a class of ruthless professional criminals, a number of whom have since turned up in the United States. They too are a significant part of the story.

Other roots reach into the neighborhoods where Russian immigrants have settled when they arrive in the United States, beginning with the late nineteenth- and early twentieth-century Russian Jewish immigrants who settled in New York City. A second wave arrived after World War I, and a third after World War II. More recently, a fourth wave of Russians came to the United States between roughly mid-1970 and 1991, and a fifth arrived after the collapse of the Soviet Union in 1991. Each of these immigrant groups has distinctive characteristics, yet they are linked by a common language and common origins. The economic experiences of Russian immigrants, and their dealings with crime and corruption, are part of that common origin.

Why should anyone be interested in this story? After all, haven't enough books (fiction and nonfiction) and articles on crime and organized crime been published? For the serious student of the subject, there are a host of government reports to be digested, as well. But apart from works of fiction and textbooks written mostly for undergraduate students, only a handful of original, book-length studies of organized crime can be found.[1] If one further excludes the works focused on Italian American organized crime, the list becomes considerably shorter. We know very little—and in some cases nothing—about the involvement of non-Italian groups that are becoming major perpetrators of organized crime in this country.

Only a few works deal with crime and organized crime in Russia, even though Russian immigrant crime (generally referred to as the *Russian mafia*) has received considerable media coverage. In fact, only one other book examines crime among Soviet émigrés to the United States.[2] Enormous changes have occurred since that book was published more than ten years ago, including the arrival of the fifth wave of Russian immigrants.

For Americans, this is more than just another story of organized crime among yet another group of ethnic immigrants. The relationship between Russia and the United States, both before and after the demise of the USSR, is unique. For half a century the Soviet Union was viewed as an arch enemy and superpower rival of the United States. Its economic, political, and social systems were very different from those of the United States, and it alone rivaled the United States in the extent of its international spheres of influence, nuclear arsenal, and space program. Since 1991, though, supporting the struggle for democracy in Russia has become a principal American foreign policy goal, and that struggle is thwarted and threatened by rampant organized crime and corruption.

Nowhere else in the world has organized crime so infiltrated the highest echelons of the state as in Russia today. Organized crime has power and control in Russia whose scope far exceeds the criminal control exercised by drug cartels in countries such as Colombia. Beyond its own borders, Russian organized crime is a global concern. Arms trafficking, alien smuggling, money laundering, trafficking in vital materials such as oil and timber, and (potentially) nuclear trafficking are among the Russian criminal enterprises on the international scene.

Focusing on ethnic identity (in this case Russian but also Chinese, Irish, or Italian) means wrestling with the idea of ethnicity, which plays a major role in our story. This is complicated by the popular characterization as *Russian* of anyone from any of the regions that were part of imperial Russia, the former Soviet Union, or contemporary Russia. In reality, such immigrants come from many regional groups (including Ukrainian, Uzbek, Armenian, and Byelorussian) and religious groups (such as Jewish and Russian Orthodox). Despite this diversity, people who lived in the Soviet Union share certain defining characteristics, the most important of which are the experiences of having been a Soviet citizen and of speaking the Russian language. Based on our study of the relationship between ethnicity and crime, it is clear that no ethnic group is criminal and that indeed most members of any ethnic group (including Russians) are not criminals.

Just what does being Russian mean? Our specific interest is in Soviet Russians, who are a somewhat special category. Are the Soviet Russians of the 1990s different from their Russian immigrant ancestors of a century ago, a half century ago, or a generation ago? Are these differences reflected in their experiences on our shores? Most important, do these differences have anything to do with Russians' involvement in crime?

In spite of the notoriety of the Italian word *mafia,* it has no common, universally accepted meaning. Our principal purpose here is to understand how and why this term has come to be associated with Russian criminals, both here and in Russia itself. To do so, we look at mafias and mafiosi—and also the role of mafia myths—as these relate to organized crime and the organization of criminal activities among Russian immigrants.

Whatever else it may invoke, *mafia* has connotations of organized crime, which leads us to consider the very idea of organized crime and how it differs from other crime. For example, one of the elements of organized crime is the conspiracy—that is, two or more people planning and carrying out criminal acts. *Conspiracy* also can be used in a broader sense of a fanciful explanation for otherwise unexplained phenomena that rely on the coming together of seemingly malevolent forces. Russians, mafias, and organized crime all seem to be attractive subjects for those who have a propensity for promulgating conspiracy theories.

In addition to ethnicity, Russians, mafias, and organized crime, a fifth major idea that plays a prominent role in our discussion is that of networks. The word *network* is used by criminal investigators and the press to characterize criminal organizations said to be engaged in organized crime. As we use the term, *network* means connections between individuals, organizations, or other entities. These networks may engage in joint, reciprocal, preferential, and mutually supportive actions. They may be complex or relatively simple, large or small. Trust is usually an important element in the operation of criminal and other networks. The networks that we analyze are made up mostly of Russians in the New York, New Jersey, and Pennsylvania areas where our primary research took place. The network activities we are mainly interested in are criminal.

We need to say a word about our research and its concentration in one particular geographical area. Organized crime is a difficult and even dangerous subject to study. One cannot approach it as one might approach juvenile delinquency or other types of crime. The typical tools of the criminologist—observation, surveys, interviews, samples, and questionnaires—are either extremely difficult or impossible to use when studying organized crime.

In light of these obstacles, we were fortunate to be permitted to join with the Tri-state Joint Soviet Émigré Organized Crime Project—a joint intelligence, investigative, and prosecutorial effort by the New York State Organized Crime Task Force, the New York State Commission of Investigation, the New Jersey State Commission of Investigation, and the Pennsylvania Crime Commission. The goal of the Project was to identify the nature and extent of Russian émigré crime within the tristate region of New York, New Jersey, and Pennsylvania to assist area law enforcement officers in their efforts to combat organized crime. For four years (1992 to 1995) the Project gathered and analyzed intelligence information by researching crimes, investigating crimes, and creating an information database.

Relying on teams of investigators, attorneys, and analysts from the collaborating agencies, the Tri-state Project employed all the tools traditionally used to investigate organized crime—including surveillance, informants, undercover investigation, intelligence reports, telephone records, and public information such as indictments and newspaper reports. Through our link with the Tri-state Project we were able to gain access to otherwise confidential information, which gave us a unique opportunity to learn about the organization of criminal activity among Russian immigrants in this region.

As is true with any research that depends on secondary data sources, problems can arise concerning the reliability and validity of the data, and these are compounded when the data are obtained from raw intelligence files. We describe the steps we took to deal with these issues. In addition to the information obtained by the Project, we collected a considerable amount of primary data and information using interviews and surveys, some of which would have been impossible to amass without our affiliation with the Tri-state Project. This combination of sources has given us the best of both worlds. We believe the results justify the research risks we have taken, but our readers will have to judge our methods for themselves.

To avoid being limited to the tristate region and the concerns of the Tri-state Project, we collected additional information through interviews with law enforcement officials, journalists, and other experts on Soviet crime, Soviet émigrés, and organized crime. We also surveyed prosecutors and law enforcement officials who are specialists in organized crime by simply asking respondents, "To your knowledge, has your agency ever investigated, prosecuted, or otherwise had contact with any criminals or suspected criminals who are from the former Soviet Union within the last five years?" Of course, an affirmative response could mean one or many contacts and one or many crimes. Nevertheless, this question was a useful starting point. Overall, about one-third of the respondents reported some contact with such criminals or suspects.

The following propositions are either supported or refuted by our research:

◆ Russian Mafia is actually a misnomer and perhaps even an oxymoron. The Russian Mafia is neither Russian nor mafia. There is no Mafia—Russian or otherwise—in the United States, nor is there one in Russia itself.

◆ The idea of an American-based Russian Mafia is largely a creation of the media and law enforcement. The symbolism and romance attached to the term *mafia*—and the level of law enforcement response it seems to call for—have given this idea a receptive audience in the United States; but it has little basis in fact.

◆ Although individual crimes that are highly organized are committed by Russians, there is no Russian organized crime as such in the United States.

♦ In Russia, on the other hand, organized crime is so pervasive as to be unlike anything experienced in the United States.

♦ Organized crime may have provided a "crooked ladder of social mobility" for Russian Jewish immigrants clamoring to enter the middle class a century ago, but this is not so with Russian immigrants today.

♦ Crime—often of a highly organized and complex kind—is a matter of choice for the minority of Russian immigrants who engage in it. This choice is shaped by many factors, among which are attitudes shaped by their Soviet experience.

This provocative set of statements provides the framework for the discussion in the chapters that follow. Because it is the overarching idea that each of the other major ideas of this work relates to, we begin our discussion in the next chapter with the idea of organized crime.

CHAPTER 2

ORGANIZED CRIME: MAFIAS, MYTHS, AND ETHNICITY

Much effort—by governmental commissions, law enforcement experts, and academics—has been devoted to trying to define *organized crime*. Despite these efforts, no clear and simple definition is universally accepted, which tells us something about the ambiguity and complexity of the topic. The absence of a common understanding makes it difficult to know what police, journalists, and scholars mean when they use the term *organized crime* to describe a criminal network. The same can be said about the term *mafia*. We begin, therefore, by defining how we use these terms in this work.

What Is Organized Crime?

As was pointed out by criminologist Thorsten Sellin more than thirty years ago, the difficulty in defining *organized crime* is not with the *crime* part but with the *organized* part.[1] We mostly bypass an unnecessary diversion into the thorny theoretical question of what organized crime is and, instead, focus on the more practical issue of what organized crime does. This, we believe, will be more fruitful in understanding the Russian crime situation. We start by briefly considering what a criminal organization is.

Criminal Organizations

Crimes can be committed by individuals acting alone or together with others. Any time two or more persons come together to commit a crime, they make up a network. These networks are often small, informal, and short lived. In some cases, however, a criminal network resembles the kind of formal organizations with which we are all familiar—for example, a work group in a business, office, labor union, or military unit. The commonalities are a hierarchy of authority, a division of labor, and continuity. Criminal networks that have these characteristics are called *criminal organizations.*

The nature of the crime, the characteristics of the situation, and the availability of crime partners determine whether individuals act alone or as members of a network in a particular instance. We can use a burglary to demonstrate the differences. A single individual acting alone can commit a burglary. But consider the following scenario. Three young, unemployed males hang out together. They are on the lookout for opportunities to get money. One of these young men gets a temporary job as a deliveryman. On one of his deliveries to the home of an elderly, frail couple, he observes their vulnerability as well as the fact that they have a number of valuable items in their home. The three arrange to break in and steal these items. At that moment they are acting as a criminal network exploiting a criminal opportunity, but they do not make up a criminal organization. They did not come together to create a professional burglary ring. They have not organized themselves to commit crimes and do not consider themselves to be members of a criminal organization. Their criminal network lacks the continuity over both time and crimes that would make it a criminal organization.

The chief goal of most criminal organizations is money. But besides financial gain, such organizations may perform a number of related functions for their members.[2] These can include sharing information about suitable criminal targets, new problems, and new techniques; providing contacts with like-minded others and what McIntosh refers to as "congenial sociability"; offering information about where to sell stolen or otherwise ill-gotten goods; providing protection from detection and law enforcement; and helping fellow members through hard times.

Criminal organizations come in many shapes and sizes, including burglary and car theft rings, street gangs, outlaw motorcycle gangs, drug posses, international drug cartels, and the groups that make up what is known as La Cosa Nostra. We can array them across a spectrum according to the degree to which they share certain defining characteristics, including the following:

♦ *Criminal sophistication* Criminal sophistication is determined by the degree of planning required to carry out the crimes, how long the individual criminal ventures last, and the amount of knowledge or skill required to carry them out.

♦ *Structure* A division of labor, clearly defined lines of authority and leadership roles, and stability over time and over criminal ventures are the marks of a highly structured criminal organization. *Division of labor* refers to the assignment of different roles to different people in the organization, such as organizers or specialists in certain tasks, like driving or safe cracking. There is usually a pecking order of authority, with some members having more and others less. *Stability* means that the organization does not come together on one occasion for one crime and then dissipate but continues over time.

♦ *Self-identification* Self-identification means that participants see themselves as members of a defined organization. Criminal organizations often create bonds between the members and the organization by having members wear special colors or special clothing, such as is seen with motorcycle gangs and street gangs, or by performing ritualistic initiation rites.

♦ *The authority of reputation* The capacity to force others, whether criminals or not, to do what the organization wishes without resorting to actual physical violence can be obtained only over a period of time. Having a reputation that by itself generates fear and intimidation means that the organization can operate much more efficiently and effectively than it could if it had to resort to actual violence all the time.

These characteristics are related to each other and appear in varying degrees in different networks. Some criminal networks, even ongoing ones, may have relatively low levels of these traits: that is, they have unsophisticated criminal operations, few participants, an amorphous or formless structure, and little or no reputation. The more sophisticated, larger networks are true criminal organizations that are involved in multiple criminal enterprises and have members who see themselves as an identifiable group having a reputation.

Less formal and simpler criminal networks do not necessarily develop into more formal and more complex criminal organizations.[3] As long as simpler organizational forms are able to get the job done, and the main activities do not diversify, then the simpler form is likely to remain intact.

The specific character assumed by a criminal network at any time is governed by the social context in which it operates, which, in turn, is comprised of a number of elements. One element is consumer demand for particular goods or services, such as drugs or prostitution. An organization has to be able to deliver to people what they want, when they want it, at an acceptable price. Increased police activity, another element, may require laying low, shifting locales, changing products, or operating with greater caution. The ability to recruit new members and thus maintain the viability of the organization is a third element, and it depends on a ready supply of potential recruits who are street smart, tough, and willing to take risks. Attracting new members hinges on the reputation the criminal organization has in the community. Finally, what the organization looks like and how it functions also is shaped by competition from other criminal organizations.

Actual and Potential Harms Caused by Organized Crime

Crime committed by criminal organizations results in more harm than crime committed by individuals or momentary groups. This does not mean that there is not harm, even considerable harm, to the victims of individual or group crimes, but the totality of the harm over time from the crimes of a criminal organization is much greater.

Because criminal organizations differ in size, sophistication, structure, self-identification, continuity, and reputation, they have different capacities for harm. Thus, another characteristic—we contend it is a key characteristic—for classifying criminal organizations is their capacity for harm. This capacity is actually a function of the other characteristics outlined.

Harm from crime occurs in a variety of forms, including economic, physical, psychological, and societal.[4] Economic harm includes the monetary losses by victims, the illicit gains by criminals, and the detrimental effects that criminal organizations have on particular marketplaces. An example of the latter is the control of certain industries and unions (such as the construction industry, building trades unions, and trucking industry) by criminal organizations. Because of this control, normal business practices, such as bidding on building contracts, are distorted by being fixed, and customers then have to pay higher costs for construction, shipping, garbage removal, and other services.

Physical violence is used to attain and retain monopoly control over criminal ventures. Targets of this violence may be extortion victims or persons who are assaulted or killed for other reasons. The reputation of a criminal organization comes, to a great extent, from a demonstrated willingness to use violence in this manner.

The psychological harm caused by crime involves the creation of a climate of fear and intimidation and a perception that a criminal organization can avoid apprehension by law enforcement. This particularly insidious form of harm deters people from reporting crimes to the police, spurs them to avoid jury duty or otherwise cooperate with law enforcement, and creates a climate of cynicism about the legal and political systems that might then be used as a rationalization for their own violations of the law.

Crime also undermines society's legal and political systems, compromises the political process, and corrupts law enforcement and other institutions. Some criminal organizations, with their enormous illicit wealth, can buy the services of police, prosecutors, judges, and elected officials through bribes and substantial campaign donations. In its most extreme form, these corrupt practices result in de facto control of the government by criminal organizations: the rule of law is replaced by the law of the jungle.

The magnitude of actual or potential damage caused by each of these types of harm is determined by the characteristics of the criminal organization involved. The most sophisticated criminal organizations usually provide illegal goods and services, thereby both subverting the political system that outlawed them and feeding the addictions and habits of the consumers of these illegal products. Others provide legal goods and services but in an illegal fashion. The harm attendant in the latter is in the undermining of the licensing requirements, regulations, and tax policies that have been created by the government to control the supply and distribution of these particular goods and services.

The harms that can be caused by the most complex criminal organizations are best exemplified in the United States by the groups of families comprising La Cosa Nostra, a group regarded by many practitioners and scholars as the epitome of organized crime in America. There is considerable difference of opinion about whether the Cosa Nostra is a national organized crime monolith but little disagreement about whether it is capable of producing great criminal harm to American society. Given that harm is the best basis for assessing the impact of criminal organizations, we compare and contrast

La Cosa Nostra to the organization of Russian émigré crime in the United States.

This requires first looking for certain key characteristics in the criminal organization of Russian émigrés. Do the Russians have the kind of structure, rationally designed to maximize profits, that Cressey says characterizes the Cosa Nostra?[5] The clues to the presence of this type of structure include rules of conduct, emphasis on respect and honor, recruitment procedures and initiation ceremonies, a centralized authority and hierarchy of leadership, procedures for dispute resolution, and shared goals and objectives. Above all, the Cosa Nostra once had, and to a lesser extent still has, the capacity to monopolize criminal ventures and even beyond that to exercise monopoly control over the underworld in general.

Monopoly

Just as a desire for market monopoly exists in the licit marketplace, so it exists in the illicit marketplace as well, and for the same reason—to optimize profits. Monopoly control is attained by forcing out and discouraging competition. In legitimate markets, this is usually done by having a superior product, better advertising, and lower prices than your competition, but it may also include bid rigging and predatory pricing. Criminal organizations monopolize markets through the threat and use of force and violence and the corruption of legal and political systems. The latter can involve payoffs to the police to allow a particular criminal enterprise to operate while driving its competitors out of business. This monopoly of a criminal market, and its functional corruption, permit an accumulation of wealth, power, and influence that solidifies the position of the criminal organization and protects its interests through a symbiotic relationship with the political system.

Generally, the only time monopolization is not a priority is when the demand for the product or service and the continued growth of consumers is so high that everybody can profit from a satisfactory market share. This has recently been true of some of the drug markets but is the exception rather than the rule.

Violence

The organized and systematic use of violence by sophisticated criminal organizations has a number of functions. It is directed internally as a means of enforcing discipline. It is used to protect or expand market share in a criminal activity or to keep recalcitrant customers in line. And it is used to establish reputation and deter would-be competitors and clients from failing to pay or otherwise comply. As already indicated, one of the major methods for establishing monopoly control is the use or threat of force and violence, which represent a form of harm in and of themselves. A more subtle harm flows from the fear and intimidation that are created when a willingness to use violence is demonstrated and that can extend beyond the direct parties to criminal activities to include innocent bystanders or residents of the community where criminal activities take place. An additional harm is then spun off when the affected persons are unwilling to report crimes to the police or to come forward as witnesses.

Corruption

The greatest harm to society caused by criminal organizations is corruption. Like violence, corruption serves the purposes of criminal organizations in several ways. Corruption provides the insurance against arrest, prosecution, and conviction and helps establish monopoly control over a market by enlisting the authorities to assist in driving out or discouraging competitors. As illegal business ventures become bigger, they become more exposed, are therefore more at risk—and thus have a greater need for insurance. As more capital is invested in a venture, criminals have more to lose—and thus a greater need for insurance. The longer a particular venture lasts, the more risky it becomes, which also creates a greater need for insurance.

Similarly, the amount of corruption is related to the scale of the criminal venture. Relatively low-level crimes or one-shot crimes may require no or only low levels of insurance (corruption): payoffs to local police or to street agents from various federal agencies may suffice to protect the small operation. Bigger operations, however, require bigger payoffs to higher-ranked people, especially in transnational and international criminal ventures.

The harm that emanates from corruption goes to the very integrity of the legal and political systems. Law enforcement becomes distorted, its legitimacy is undermined, and citizens lose respect for the integrity of the system and fail to support what they come to see as a corrupted process. People who live in communities where they believe the legal system has been corrupted do not report crimes or otherwise cooperate with the police, thus facilitating the activities of the criminal elements. Their cynicism may also become a rationalization for their own involvement in crime.

Mafia and the Russian Mafia

Mafia is a universally recognized term that has become synonymous with organized crime and at times is casually applied to a wide range of agents and activities that have nothing to do with the original, such as the *real estate mafia* and the *Soho mafia* mentioned by Servadio.[6] The word *mafia* is a handy, catchall label used by journalists, moviemakers, and popular fiction writers because it conjures up images that require no further elaboration in the minds of readers and viewers. Because the term *mafia* is used regularly to refer to different things, in unknown or dubious contexts, sometimes as a noun and sometimes as an adjective, it often ends up conveying more confusion than enlightenment.

Police and prosecutors use the *mafia* label on the grounds that anything warranting the characterization will be defined as a serious matter calling for strong enforcement efforts to counter and control it.[7] For law enforcement, labeling a criminal organization a mafia may have important consequences. For example, it may lead to a false assumption that criminal organizations possess characteristics they do not or that a criminal organization is not an organized crime problem because it does not look like the mafia stereotype.

Either of these erroneous assumptions has certain policy implications. Time and resources may be wasted spent looking for nonexistent "godfathers," capos, soldiers, secret codes, and initiation rites. Or the enormous pressure to nail mafia figures, especially godfathers, can lead law enforcement to create its own by grabbing some thug who may or may not be a crime kingpin and crowning him a godfather. Because catching mafiosi is exciting and high profile, it can be a seductive activity that leads law enforcement and the news media to feed each other misinformation and misinterpret or selectively interpret the available information. When this happens, the public is misinformed and misled, and the policy is misguided.

What does this confusion mean, then, for a work titled *Russian Mafia*? We have to deal with the confusion head on. How else can we discover whether there is a Russian mafia? As a shorthand label, *mafia* has implications not only for understanding the activity to which it is attached but for determining policy as well. Only by exploring the idea of mafia can we deal with the question of whether there is a Russian mafia and whether this is an apt label for what we see when we look at Russian crime networks.

The best known of the mafias is still the original Sicilian version, which today competes (both literally and figuratively) with a Chinese mafia, a Nigerian mafia, and an Albanian mafia, as well as with its cousins the Camorra, the 'Ndrangheta, and La Cosa Nostra, among others. Each of these is a criminal organization, possessing many of the characteristics described earlier. But whether they are truly a mafia or just an example of labeling is another question. For our purposes, we return to the original model as the best route to understanding its current versions, and this requires us to make a short trip to Sicily, since it is there that the mafia origins lie.

The Sicilian Mafia

Experts disagree about whether there has ever been a single organization in Sicily that could properly be called *The Mafia*. There is no disagreement, however, that there is a phenomenon called *mafia* and that there definitely are Sicilian *mafiosi,* as the individual mafia members are called. The dominant traditional characteristic of this mafia has been the private use of unlicensed violence—that is, violence that operates outside of the government. Private violence is contrary to the principle that only the state has legitimate authority to employ force to accomplish its objectives—whether arresting criminals or making war.

Gambetta[8] argues that the Sicilian mafia is strictly in the protection business. Mafiosi provide protection, of both the interests and the person, to one or more of the parties in a transaction. They act as a kind of civil court or Better Business Bureau to protect unstable transactions, when trust is scarce and fragile. The mafioso is thus a vendor of trust. Honor for the mafioso comes from his reputation for supplying credible protection.

The mafiosi have historically been men who wielded power through the systematic use of private violence as a means of control in the public arena. The mafia maintains a symbiotic relationship with the formal authorities. At the same time that mafias disregard the law and the legal and governmental apparatus in seeking their own ends, they also act in connivance with formal authority toward achieving those same ends.[9] Thus the mafia is peculiarly both outside and inside the government at the same time. The Sicilian mafia has also been said to be a form of behavior, a way of thinking, and a kind of power rather than a formal organization or (as it has been most popularly portrayed) a secret organized society. It is said to be a way of life that is peculiarly Sicilian, with a code based on Sicilian traditions and customs. "What does it mean to 'behave in the manner of the mafia'?" mafia expert Pino Arlacchi asked. "It means," he answered, "'to make oneself respected,' 'to be a man of honour' capable of revenging by his own force any sort of offense done to his own personality and capable equally of dealing out offense to an enemy."[10]

The notions of honor and respect are critical to defining the mafia. According to Catanzaro,[11] the best definition of a mafioso is that he is a "man of respect" and a "man of honor." These honorific titles mean being a man of his word and a man of action—being able to settle disputes with a few words, being able to quickly get to the heart of things in a dispute, fearing no one, not tolerating insults, reacting violently if insulted. Being quick-witted and tough—and, above all, being able to resort to violence so as to dominate through physical force—are, in this view, the foundations for being a man of respect. This respect and honor are then translated into authority so that "the status of the mafioso [rises] from criminal to respected member of the local elite, recognized and legitimated by the representatives of legal power."[12] Their position as men of honor, their broad base of social support in the community, their legitimacy, and their relationship to political institutions clearly distinguish the mafiosi from other criminals, including criminal entrepreneurs and those involved in more generic forms of organized crime.

The adherence of the mafia to certain fundamental beliefs that grew out of the feudal Sicilian culture—respect, honor, and *omertà* (the "code of silence")—are constants that would not appear to be readily transferable outside of Sicilian society. It appears that other criminals and criminal organizations can appropriately be called *mafia* only if one considerably broadens and redefines the term so as to lift it from its uniquely Sicilian origins and character. Perhaps, then, the Sicilian mafia could simply be seen as "the mother of all the Mafias."[13]

Anderson has tried to move the meaning of *mafia* into this broader perspective, starting with the premise that *mafia* means more than just "criminal activity that happens to be organized."[14] She argues that mafias exist where governmental functions are being performed by nongovernmental persons, particularly where the legal system refuses (or is unable) to exercise power. Mafiosi then act in lieu of the government and enforce contractual arrangements: "the essential characteristic of a mafia that differentiates it from other groups engaged in violent or criminal activity is corruption or substantial influence in at least some agencies or bureaus of the legitimate government."[15] This means the state does not have a monopoly on the use of violence, a situation that occurs either when the government is weak or when it is totally corrupted. It is the symbiosis between mafiosi and the governmental apparatus that distinguishes them from outlaws and bandits.[16]

Three conditions have to be present to facilitate the development of mafias[17]—a weak or corrupted government that is unwilling or unable to protect everyday transactions, lucrative criminal opportunities, and both excessive bureaucratic power and discretion among government authorities and governmental decisions that are unclear and difficult to monitor. In this latter instance, despite its failure to police transactions, government is otherwise broadly intrusive in controlling and regulating people's lives. This could be typified by excessive forms and paperwork. In addition, the government bureaucrats who exercise this control have considerable unsupervised discretion. If, on top of that, the functionaries are badly underpaid, we have the ingredients for an open door to corruption.

These defining characteristics and conditions that are ripe for mafia growth give us a framework to apply as we look for a Russian mafia. It is possible that we may find the conditions but not find a mafia or mafias because conditions are not sufficient to ensure that they develop. Nevertheless, this framework will set our parameters in our search for Russian mafias in both the United States and Russia.

Ethnicity

Now that we have some sense of the related but distinct concepts of organized crime and of mafia, we turn to the criminals who are involved in these sorts of activities. Organized crime has as one of its essential elements criminal collaborations—that is, people committing crimes together. In law, these are called *conspiracies*. Criminal conspiracies are not necessarily organized crime, but the reverse is not true. The legal definition of *conspiracy* implies that several persons come together, discuss, plan, and ultimately carry out criminal acts. If these conspirators are part of a criminal organization with a great capacity for harm, seek to create or maintain a monopoly, and are willing to engage in violence, they probably are conspiring to engage in some form of organized crime.

Not surprisingly, conspiracy requires trust—that all involved will keep their mouths shut; that if anyone is caught, he or she will not give up the others; and that the conspirators will do what they say they will do. In the licit world of business, education, and politics, trust among colleagues and collaborators is also essential, and it is often derived from checking references, sharing old school ties, making formal background investigations, and sharing past experiences.

How do co-conspirators ensure trust in a criminal world where trust is hard to establish? Although criminals are unlikely to be particularly reliable, trustworthy, or cooperative, the absence of legal and officially enforced guarantees forces criminal organizations to rely on trust to a far greater extent than is necessary in the ordinary business world.[18]

Criminals also use their networks to determine the trustworthiness of potential partners. As in the licit world, they look to shared upbringings, extended family connections, and common ethnicity to ensure trustworthiness. But ties also come from crime-related experiences, such as doing time in prison together. In neighborhoods of immigrants, important ties are established by shared ethnicity, kinship, and language. Because criminal conspirators often turn to others like themselves, immigrants turn to people from the same old country. In this rather simple way, ethnicity is associated with criminal organization and thus with organized crime.

Beyond this basic connection that exists anywhere that immigrants are found, organized crime in the United States has historically had a continuous ethnic dimension that shifts as immigration patterns shift. This dimension is controversial because it can be associated with stereotyping, stigmatizing, and scapegoating. No reasonable persons, ourselves included, argue that criminal behavior can be explained by ethnicity; if it could, all members of an ethnic group would be criminals. But ignoring ethnicity means ignoring important characteristics of the context from which organized crime emerges. For example, immigration at different times has been dominated by specific ethnic groups, and new immigrants often settle in neighborhoods where people of the same ethnicity live.

The ethnic character of U.S. organized crime was remarked on in a recent U.N. paper on migration and crime:[19]

> The role of migrants in organized crime is substantial in the United States. . . . If we look back into the history of migration into the United States at the beginning of this century, we see that various waves of migrants—the Irish, the Italians—brought specific crime problems with them. In some cases these disappeared, while in others (e.g., in the case of the Italian Cosa Nostra) they remained for decades, despite the successful integration of most newcomers into American society. The ethnic membership of the migrants makes the formation of gangs of the same origin easier because the language can be a natural barrier against intrusive investigations by the police. At the same time the ethnic factor can also remain an instrument to maintain the dependency of immigrants upon the criminal organization. . . . The bonds resulting from a common place of origin and its cultural and social rituals and values are exploited by organized crime to reproduce the same struc-

tures of hierarchy, complicity, conspiracy of silence and the same social cohesion which the migrants were used to . . . in their country of
origin.[20]

The first waves of immigration brought the Irish and the Jews,
the next wave brought the Italians and Sicilians, and now the Chinese,
Cubans, Dominicans, Jamaicans, Nigerians, Japanese, Vietnamese,
and Russians have arrived. Each group has brought specific crime
problems with it. And it is not only in the United States that this
connection exists. For example, Xhudo,[21] writing about criminal
gangs in the Balkans, notes that ethnic requirements are important in
the makeup of gangs in those countries, as well.

Those who already have criminal backgrounds in their countries of origin would be obvious prospects for organized crime in their
host country. For example, one form of the current global problem of
smuggling illegal aliens includes exporting known criminals—
prostitutes, hitmen, and others—whose refugee status is used as a
cover for criminal activity. The U.S. Immigration and Naturalization
Service reports that leaders of organized crime in the former Soviet
Union "piggyback" onto legal immigrants to allow criminals to gain
entry into the United States. Some are fugitives from justice, and
others are hired assassins. In Israel, it is estimated that approximately
2,500 Russian prostitutes, as well as a variety of other criminals, have
been smuggled into that country.[22]

It is reasonable to suppose that some immigrants import previously established criminal practices—or at least the kinds of values
and worldview that support criminality—into the host society. This
may well have been the case with those Sicilians who were mafiosi
before they came to the United States in the early 1900s, and it also
may be true of some recent Russian immigrants.

Ethnicity is not a cause of organized crime, but to deny or ig-
nore a connection between the two is misguided. It seems much more
plausible to view it as a factor that works in combination with others

in a variety of ways that are not readily apparent. One popular theory of the U.S. experience is that crime has been an alternative route to material success for ethnic immigrants who start on the bottom of the American social ladder.

Ethnic Succession up the Crooked Ladder

The best-known argument for associating ethnic identity with organized crime in the American experience claims that there has been an ongoing pattern of criminal activity by newly arrived ethnic groups. Various groups succeed each other in conducting their criminal business, and each, in turn, uses crime as a means of "making it."[23] Those who make this point cite crime in general—and organized crime in particular—as one path of upward mobility for immigrants.

Writing about ethnicity and organized crime nearly fifty years ago, Daniel Bell coined the phrase that seemed to capture the historical relationship quite succinctly. He said that "the urban rackets—illicit activity organized for continuing profit rather than individual illegal acts—is one of the queer ladders of social mobility in American life."[24] Further, he said that "the whole question of organized crime in America cannot be understood unless one appreciates [among other factors] the specific role of various immigrant groups as they one after another became involved in marginal business and crime."[25]

Ianni took up Bell's idea of ethnic succession. He concludes that one ethnic group succeeds another on the queer ladder of mobility and that the preceding groups then move on to social respectability.[26] This explains how the Irish were replaced by the Jews, who were in turn replaced by the Italians, and so on. More recently, O'Kane updated and elaborated on the Bell and Ianni thesis.[27] Calling it "the crooked ladder," O'Kane concurs that organized crime has been used by various ethnic groups but notes that organized crime is only one of the routes up the ladder of social mobility. O'Kane points to other routes—unskilled or semiskilled labor, retail small business, the professions, the clergy, entertainment, and urban politics—that can take immigrants from the lower class to the middle class.

The ethnic neighborhoods where new immigrants tend to settle when they first arrive in the United States are ripe with criminal opportunities and criminal role models because of the transient and unstable nature of the population, the relative absence of both formal and informal social controls, and the large numbers of young people (who tend to be more crime-prone than their elders). Moreover, just being an immigrant means that one is a risk taker: those who leave their homeland are more adventuresome and perhaps more entrepreneurial than those who choose to stay at home.

Within any immigrant population, some want to make a quick buck, and others are vulnerable to victimization. Almost every pool of immigrants also seems to contain the necessary supply of criminal labor to carry out crimes. Consistent with the crooked-ladder notion, Arlacchi says that this supply is spawned by the sort of general pathology that is associated with the socioeconomic hardships inherent in immigration.[28] Whatever their status at home, immigrants usually find themselves on the bottom of the socioeconomic ladder when they first arrive here. In particular, young male members among recent ethnic immigrants are "more likely to find other avenues of economic progress blocked" and consequently provide a ready-made base for recruitment into organized crime.[29]

This crooked-ladder thesis, however, does not tell us much about why members of some ethnic groups, more than others, seem to select crime as a means of upward mobility. Why doesn't the pathology of socioeconomic hardship affect all immigrant groups in the same way? And why is it that even among the seemingly more crime-prone groups only a relatively few individuals become criminals? The general crooked-ladder explanation fails because Bell and his successors fail to address these issues. They argue that the causes of organized crime are social forces independent of individual personalities and motives. We reject this notion. Instead, we believe that ethnicity interacts with personality and motive in a variety of ways to influence whether particular immigrants in particular ethnic groups become associated with organized crime. This connection is much more complex than the ethnic-succession and crooked-ladder explanations have made it out to be.

The combination of sparse legitimate opportunities with an abundance of illegitimate ones that characterizes the immigrant experience is, it seems to us, just one factor in choosing crime over noncrime. Other factors are illustrated in this description of the limitations and the hazards facing America's southern Italian and Sicilian immigrant children at the end of the nineteenth century:

> Whether born in a Southern Italian hovel or in an American tenement, the children grew to maturity in a period when education began to emerge as an increasingly important qualification for both public and private employment. And yet, lacking the social graces and often unable to speak or understand standard middle-class English, many of these children found school, with its regimentation and its middle-class teachers and traditions, a strange and often frightening experience. . . . school discipline emphasized the sublimation of desires and ambitions for long-term, deferred goals—an attitude that seemed unreal in the tenement world of immigrant children, where one seized material gratification whenever it was available. . . . To slum area youngsters like Salvatore Lucania (Charles "Lucky" Luciano), John Torrio, and Alphonse Caponi (Al Capone), excitement and economic opportunity seemed to be out in the streets rather than in the classroom.[30]

For Luciano, Capone, and others, immediate economic opportunity, in the form of criminal opportunity, was available on the streets; legitimate opportunities, even delayed opportunities, were limited. Both opportunity and socialization patterns were determined by ethnicity in neighborhoods of newly arrived Italian immigrants who were at the bottom of the ladder.

When Luciano et al. dropped out of school at their first chance at age fourteen, they formed street gangs of young toughs that acted as a sort of farm team for the big leagues of adult organized crime. Those youth who were especially street smart, ambitious, willing to take risks, and willing to do what they were told eventually were recruited into the big time. In this manner, the streets, gangs, and crime shaped by ethnicity formed a crooked ladder up for those youth.

There were other young Italians and Sicilians who had the same talents as Luciano and Capone but who didn't drop out of school, didn't join street gangs, and didn't eventually go into organized crime. They made different choices. Accounting for this has been the stumbling block for the crooked-ladder idea. For example, O'Kane avoided examining the issue of why one person chooses a legitimate career and another a criminal career by saying it was beyond the scope of his analysis. Further, he added that it is "beyond the realm of current social science explanation." We wholeheartedly agree that the choice is difficult to explain, especially with organized criminals, but not that an explanation is entirely beyond the realm of possibility. Instead, we believe that the profiles of the new Russian immigrants will give us a much clearer picture of organized crime.

Only Saps Work

Peter Lupsha disagrees with the theories of Bell and Ianni about the manner in which organized crime develops in American society.[31] He says that those who choose the queer or crooked ladder do not do so because they are frustrated by the few legitimate routes to wealth (or at least middle-class status) that are open to them. Instead, they see crime as an easy, exciting, and romantic route up the ladder. Those immigrants who turn to crime do so "not from frustration, or any long struggle of being excluded from the political ladder, or blocked from avenues for advancement. They [turn] to crime because they [feel] the legitimate opportunity structure [is] for suckers."[32] Some young immigrants, says Lupsha, decide that they are not going to be trapped in the nickel-and-dime world of ordinary work. This attitude, of course, is not restricted to either the young or immigrants.[33] In their study of white-collar criminals, Waring and her colleagues identify a group they call "opportunity seekers."[34] These offenders were perfectly able to do legitimate work—and in fact, occasionally did it when it suited them. They were, however, "always willing to use illegal behavior" and rejected legitimate means when those did not serve their purposes.

Even organized crime experts who otherwise focus on economic and social conditions give credence to this idea. Arlacchi says that the mafia "represented an excellent instrument of social ascent in a system of commercial capitalism, where risk, fraud, and the absence of scruples were indispensable qualities for success."[35] Similarly, Ianni calls organized crime "the result of an individualistic, predatory philosophy of success."[36] Unfortunately, no one has offered much hard evidence that gangsters or other criminals actually think this way.

Many years ago, in their textbook on criminology, Barnes and Teeters described what they called "the acquisitive urge."[37] They said a "something for nothing" psychology especially motivated organized crime, racketeering, corruption, and white-collar crime. With specific reference to immigrants, Barnes and Teeters concluded that some believed that their fortunes could be made by shortcut methods. Success accrued to those who developed "shrewdness, sagacity, and sophistication rather than by hard work."[38] This resulted in an emphasis "not on self-control but rather on greed, comfort, and even cupidity."[39] An "acquisitive urge" doesn't seem to be strange or atypical: we all like to have money and the things that money can buy. But all of us are not greedy. We all don't turn to crime, corruption, and racketeering to satisfy the urge. Certain factors must constrain it, and certain factors must encourage and facilitate it.[40]

One belief that would encourage illegal behavior is that "one is a sucker if one who is outside the dominant value system, or social strata, lives by the values of that dominant system."[41] Among those on the outside, at least initially, are newly arrived immigrants. If these immigrants share a belief in the value of hard work and saving, as many do, they are likely to adopt the straight and narrow route that they hope will lead upward. If, on the other hand, they reject that value or perhaps never believed it in the first place, they may instead seek shortcuts to "get rich quick" any way they can. The rejection or neutralization of mainstream values is not a new idea in explanations of criminal behavior.[42] Part of this rejection requires a cynical view of the straight world and a rationalization that, in Lupsha's words, "suckers and straights [are] inherently corrupt, dishonest, and hypo-critical."[43]

Working at a job, taking job training, or studying a new lan-guage are difficult and often boring. These are mundane activities that require self-discipline and sacrifice. One has to be some place, on time, perhaps early every morning, and all day—and not keep late hours. Doing crime, on the other hand, has flexible hours. It is excit-ing and dangerous. It is an adventure. It can also be immediately rewarding, both financially and in terms of peer acceptance. As long as one is willing to run the risk, and that is part of the adventure, crime can pay. It would presumably be an attractive route for new immigrants who think the straight world is for suckers.

A number of points must be clarified before we build on these ideas and frame an argument with respect to the Russians. For one thing, assuming that some Russians actually think this way (and that remains to be demonstrated), what might be the basis for such an outlook? Given that we are all a product of our experiences, what have Russians in particular experienced that might produce this col-lection of attitudes and rationalizations? If all Russians have shared this common experience, but only a smaller number actually become criminals, there must be some additional sorting mechanism. What is it?

Choosing crime is an individual decision, albeit one that is reinforced by peers, experience, and a talent for victimization. Those who opt for this route are not more frustrated by their inability to get a real job or more deprived (relatively or absolutely) than their immigrant peers who choose to play it straight and follow the legitimate path.[44] Lupsha more recently reiterates this idea with respect to organized crime:

> career organized criminals possess a culture, a world view, a mind set, that enhances the edge [the competitive advantage of organized crime]. They view the legitimate upper-world capitalists as "working stiffs," "straights" and "suckers." Only they the "wiseguys" see the world clearly. It is a dog-eat-dog Darwinian universe, shrouded in lies, corruption and hypocrisy, where only the killers, the strong, survive.[45]

This theory suggests that among those similarly situated at the bottom of the socioeconomic ladder, some are ready to opt for crime because they have or develop a cynical view of a world that is a jungle of liars, cheats, and thieves. According to them, you have to get while the getting is good, and you have to get others before they get you. Everybody is doing it, they rationalize. Those who are not are suckers who deserve to be taken advantage of.

Stephen Fox arrived at a somewhat similar conclusion with respect to this kind of thinking and its relationship to ethnicity in American organized crime:

> Over the course of the twentieth century, ethnicity functioned in conservative ways to help protect the stability of the underworld and stave off the ambitions of new gangsters from upstart ethnic groups. At the outset, in the 1920s, a combination of ethnic and economic factors

brought Irish, Jewish, and Italian criminals into the underworld. The relatively low status of these groups at that historical moment made crime seem a reasonable, even inevitable way up and out. . . .

Yet to stress ethnicity may obscure the individual gangsters and the options available to them. This point cannot be overemphasized: only a tiny, slimy portion of these ethnic groups became gangsters. Most newly arrived Americans played the game straight, committed no crimes, and rose by their own legitimate efforts. Gangsters decided to kill and steal for their living not because they were Irish, Jewish, or Italian but because they were bad people. Organized crime finally derived less from social conditions or difficult childhoods or there-but-for-fortune bad luck than from a durable human condition: the dark, strong pull of selfish, greedy, impatient, unscrupulous ambition. The history of the underworld demands such moral judgments. Criminals—human beings—created organized crime. As human beings, they must be held accountable for the choices they made and the harm they wreaked.[46]

This outlook may have its origins in the experiences of certain ethnic groups even before they migrated. It may be a product of the culture and the modes of survival that they have learned. Homer, for example, concludes that immigrants from some ethnic groups have a greater proclivity or aptitude for organized crime than others.[47] He says this might be associated with feelings of distrust, fear, and a lack of respect for American customs and the American legal system among those immigrating to the United States. Peoples who bring feelings of hostility toward government in general, based on their previous experiences, may be more susceptible to involvement in organized crime. If, in addition to negative feelings of this sort, such persons were to have an affinity for shady business deals, for gray- or black-market practices, and for corruption, then the potential would seem to be enhanced.

We use both the connection between ethnicity and organized

crime and the influence of individual attitudes and experiences in our analysis of Russian immigrant crime. This combination has not been used before. In fact, in commenting on Lupsha's ideas, Rupert Wilkinson observes: "The main defect of Lupsha's [1992] essay is that he does not talk about ethnicity. He says nothing of the fact that most of the modern criminals he mentions have Italian names." Criticizing Lupsha for "playing down the ethnic factor," he continues: "Whatever his position on the ethnic factor, Lupsha should have discussed it more openly—he might also have said more about contemporary criminals of other ethnic origins."[48] We take up this challenge.

A small, but very noticeable, minority of Russians—former citizens of the Soviet Union—are especially subject to an extreme form of cynicism and to a philosophy that you have to "get over" to get ahead. At the same time, we believe that in any group of ethnic immigrants, mired in a pool from which recruits to criminal organizations are drawn, those likely to be attracted to organized crime will be those who think in this fashion. To test the latter belief, we need to find out whether this characteristic is indeed associated with organized criminals. For this, we can look to mafia memoirs in which exmobsters detail their careers in organized crime.

Thomas Firestone examined thirteen books—mostly of the "as told to" type of autobiography—by former members of the Italian mob. The criminals include both major figures ("bosses") and small-time hoods. There is nothing scientific about this sample. Its value rests purely and simply in the first-person accounts of how and why these particular gangsters entered organized crime. Firestone concludes from these thirteen cases that "none of the mobsters claims to have chosen crime because he was denied the opportunity to pursue a legitimate career. In fact, quite to the contrary, most of the authors indicate that they could have had legitimate careers, but simply preferred to be criminals."[49] An example is Nick Caramandi, who was born and raised in the Italian American neighborhood of South Philadelphia:

[Caramandi] came of age surrounded by people like himself. . . . They were men and women of modest ambition who believed in hard work and in minding their own business. . . . [They were] nurtured by family ties and Old World values. . . .

Nick Caramandi had no chance to be a doctor, lawyer, or teacher. That, he says, is not an excuse, simply a fact. He was, by his own admission, a born hustler and a natural con man. And the mob was the only institution that put any stock in those talents. It was a distortion of the value system of his community. . . .

. . . Caramandi, a fifteen-year-old high school dropout, hung out with a group of older teenagers. Their talk was of drugs and money and girls. Their heroes were the guys from the neighborhood with connections and juice—the bookmakers, gamblers, and loan sharks who worked with or for the Angelo Bruno organization.

Caramandi listened and learned.[50]

Then there is Vincent Teresa, a long-time member of the New England mob. He describes a fellow gangster who grew up with him in Medford, Massachusetts. Teresa uses the common term *wiseguy* to refer to the young thugs who were trying to make their way in the world of organized crime:

Butch and I grew up in the same neighborhood in Medford. . . . For as long as I can remember, he was a smart-aleck kid. He always wanted to hang around with the wiseguys. Not that he had to. His family wasn't poor or anything like that. . . . He didn't have to go bad. He was like me in many ways. I had the same breaks. But both Butch and me was crazy about mob people, about the way they lived and dressed, about the broads, about the excitement of being a wiseguy—even the danger.

When he was a kid all he did was dress up and gamble just like the wiseguys. As he got older, he got to fingering crap games and card games for people who'd heist them.[51]

The third example is perhaps the best illustration of the attitude that seems to characterize these mobsters. Henry Hill, the focus of the book *Wiseguy,* is described by Firestone as having a point of view that is typical. Although not a made member, because he was not Italian, Hill for many years was heavily involved with the Lucchese crime family in New York City. Hill and his fellow wiseguys "considered legitimate careers depressing and viewed those who pursued them as 'suckers' ":[52]

> For Henry and his wiseguy friends the world was golden. Everything was covered. They lived in an environment awash in crime, and those who did not partake were simply viewed as prey. To live otherwise was foolish. Anyone who stood waiting his turn on the American pay line was beneath contempt. Those who did—who followed the rules, were stuck in low-paying jobs, worried about their bills, put tiny amounts away for rainy days, kept their place, and crossed off workdays on their kitchen calendars like prisoners awaiting their release—could only be considered fools. They were timid, law-abiding, pension-plan creatures neutered by compliance and awaiting their turn to die. To wiseguys, "working guys" were already dead. Henry and his pals had long ago dismissed the idea of security and the relative tranquillity that went with obeying the law. They exulted in the pleasures that came from breaking it. Life was lived without a safety net. They wanted money, they wanted power, and they were willing to do anything necessary to achieve their ends.[53]

As a whole, the thirteen memoirs are replete with schemes and scams of every variety, as well as with violence, booze, drugs, gambling, and every crime imaginable—from petty theft to murder. All the players are school dropouts. All hang on the streets with others like themselves from an early age. All are looking for adventure and excitement—for easy money and power. They show no compassion or empathy for their victims. These are the necessary requirements, it seems, for individuals who when brought together will make up a criminal organization.

Firestone concludes that these memoirs indicate that the causes of Italian American organized crime are more cultural than socioeconomic: "most of them became criminals not because they lacked other opportunities or had deprived upbringings but, rather, because they were raised in communities in which becoming a gangster was seen as a legitimate and even desirable career path."[54]

One makes a conscious decision to step on the first rung of the crooked ladder. Like many other choices, however, this decision is shaped and constrained by a number of factors. Among them, we suggest, is having an outlook that other people are suckers to be taken advantage of and that you are a sucker if you think you can get ahead by playing by the rules.

This attitude, for Russians and immigrants from some other ethnic groups, has at least some of its roots in the attitudes developed and patterns of behavior learned in their country of origin. Growing up in the Soviet Union, Russians were socialized into an environment that rewarded scheming and scamming and penalized playing it straight. They were taught to do whatever they had to do to survive. Such an atmosphere could be expected to produce at least some people who would be especially likely to view the straight world as made up of suckers ripe for the picking. When persons with this mindset immigrate and then find themselves at the bottom of the ladder and in an environment rich with criminal opportunities, their choice between crime and its alternatives is shaped by this combination of factors.

From all of this, we propose a model that serves as a template against which we can compare Russian émigrés to the United States. This comparison requires us to examine just who these Russians are, and we do that in the next several chapters.

CHAPTER 3

EARLY WAVES OF RUSSIAN IMMIGRATION TO THE UNITED STATES

There have been immigrants to the United States from Mother Russia since the earliest days of European settlement in North America. The peoples known as *Russians* came first from the Russian empire, then from the Soviet Union, and now from the various independent countries that replaced the USSR. Because the Russian state has dominated much of the Eurasian continent for hundreds of years, *Russian* became the generic label for all peoples from that part of the world, although they actually represent hundreds of different ethnic groups. The large-scale movement of "Russians" to our shores did not begin until the late nineteenth and early twentieth centuries, with by far the largest numbers of such immigrants arriving between 1900 and 1920. Although this book is concerned mostly with the nature and impact of Russian immigrant crime beginning in the late 1970s, it is enlightening to examine earlier migration to identify both parallels and contrasts.

Recent years have seen increasing levels of U.S. immigration in general and immigration from Russia in particular. Although the level of Russian immigration have varied considerably across the decades, recent numbers are actually lower than those from the early part of this century (Figure 3.1). This variation reflects a number of factors, including political and social conditions in the former Soviet Union, U.S. regulation of immigration, U.S. political and economic conditions, and global circumstances such as the two world wars and the

Figure 3.1 Russian Immigrants to the United States, 1820 to 1994. Sources: *Historical Statistics of the United States,* pp. 106–107; *Statistical Abstract of the United States,* vols. 1972–1996.

depression of the 1930s. It is not possible to attribute rises in the level of migration to single events, although such events certainly affected immigration rates. There was substantial Russian immigration as early as the 1880s, but the changes wrought by the Russian revolutions of 1905 and 1917, and the civil war that followed the latter, played significant roles in increasing the levels of migration during and immediately after these periods.

At the turn of the century, the prospect of fighting in the Russo-Japanese war, combined with the required conscription of Jewish young men for twenty-five years of military service to the czar, led many of these potential soldiers to flee west and eventually settle in the United States.[1] Immigration from Russia consistently totaled over 100,000 people per year between 1902 and 1914. It is possible that the same underlying social processes caused both the migration and the revolution. Similarly, some authors have argued that increasing anti-Semitism during these periods was responsible for the flight of many Jews from Russia.[2] The growth of the United States' economy during this period may also have encouraged the movement of many to a place that seemed to offer opportunities for a better life. As with peoples from other parts of the world, there were factors pushing people out of Russia and factors pulling them to the United States.[3]

At the same time that factors encouraged immigration, certain forces tended to discourage it. Perhaps the most important of these were the legal structures that limited the movement of people. The tremendous growth of immigration from all countries to the United States from the late 1880s until 1920 was followed by the imposition of major restrictions on immigration.[4] The Johnson Act of 1921 and the Reed-Johnson Act of 1924 brought immigration from Eastern Europe to a near standstill almost immediately and reduced overall immigration substantially.[5] Since the 1920s, immigration laws, especially those specifying quotas of immigrants allowed from individual countries, have been changed a number of times. By the late 1970s, for example, the cause of the "refuseniks"—Jews who applied for permission to emigrate from the Soviet Union but were not permitted to do so—had become a major cause and a political issue in the United States. Russian Jews eventually were allowed almost unlimited immigration because of the discriminatory treatment they received in the Soviet Union, and other Russians were likewise permitted to emigrate from the USSR to the United States as political refugees.

While U.S. policy on immigration shifted back and forth between permissive and restrictive, changing regimes in Russia also imposed or lifted restrictions on the ability of individuals to leave the country. By the time of the consolidation of the Communist regime in the 1920s, however, borders had closed.

A combination of factors, therefore, worked to create a high level of immigration from greater Russia to the United States during the period from roughly 1890 to 1920. The experiences of Russian immigrants of that period and responses to them were, in some ways, strikingly parallel to those of today. Although today the Brooklyn neighborhood of Brighton Beach is perhaps the best-known Russian area in the United States, at the turn of the century new immigrants were most famously concentrated in the Lower East Side neighborhood of Manhattan. Most of those Russians were also Jewish, and as is the case today, the response of American citizens to immigrants involved not only attitudes toward immigration in general but also attitudes toward Jews in particular. Finally, then as now, some of the mainstream journalists, public figures, and social scientists believed that this group of immigrants was particularly crime prone.

The Situation in Russia

Even at the turn of the century, the terms *Russia* and *Russian* were often used (as they are today) in a general way to describe people with a range of ethnic and cultural identities. Many so-called Russians did not even speak the Russian language. Instead, the term *Russia* referred to the specific territory that was the core of the Russian empire and to the general region of Eastern Europe where Slavic—rather than Germanic—cultural, economic, and political practices dominated. Politically, *Russia* meant the Russian empire, including much of what is now called *Eastern Europe.*

Few Jews resided within Russia itself, but a large Jewish population was incorporated into the empire's western territories. Most Jews were barred from living in Russia itself, and almost all were required to live in the area called the *Pale of Settlement,* which included the territories of eastern Poland, Lithuania, Latvia, Ukraine, and Belarus and the cities of Odessa, Warsaw, Vilnius, Kovno, and Minsk, among others. Even within the Pale, Jews were largely restricted to the villages known as shtetls and to the cities. The period prior to the mid-1880s, during the reign of Czar Alexander II, saw some movement toward the emancipation of Russian Jews and even some freedom to settle in other areas. In 1891, however, the so-called May Laws expelled Jews from Moscow and other major Russian cities.

Although serfs throughout the Russian empire had officially been emancipated in 1861, agricultural production remained rooted in serf-based practices. Because Jews were forced to live outside this economy and were severely restricted in their choice of occupations, most became artisans, peddlers, and tradesmen. Only a very few were permitted to attend Russian institutions of education, which further restricted their occupational options. Although the population in these restricted areas was growing rapidly, the lack of industrial development and restrictions on migration within the Russian empire made it very difficult for the Jewish population to support itself. Poverty was widespread.

Jews in the Pale of Settlement were also subjected to violent anti-Semitic attacks—pogroms—often with the tacit consent of the czarist authorities.[5] *The American Jewish Year Book 5667* reports that 254 pogroms that took place between April 1903 and June 1905 were almost all bracketed by the attacks at Kishineff and Bialystok, which created an international outcry.[6] Although scholars have debated the importance of these attacks as "push" factors in migration, there is no doubt that they contributed to the misery of life for Jews in the region. The act of official anti-Semitism with the largest long-term impact was a forged document known as *The Protocols of the Elders of Zion*, which deflected popular dissatisfaction from the czar to the Jewish population. This fabrication was created by the czar's secret police, known as Okhrana, in 1905 and was used to justify many anti-Semitic acts but by itself it cannot be said to have led individual Jews to leave Russia.

Because of its border location, the Pale was the scene of much fighting during the 1917 to 1920 civil war. This was a stimulus to migration. But even after the "official" end of anti-Semitism as promised by the Bolsheviks, migration continued to be an attractive option for Russian Jews. For a combination of reasons, migration thus remained high throughout this period. Internal economic, religious, and political factors all played a role, as did the favorable economic situation in the United States and other points of destination (including Australia, South Africa, Canada, and Latin America). Strong similarities can be found between the conditions creating the desire for emigration in the Russian empire of a century ago and conditions that have stimulated a similar desire in today's former Soviet Union.

The Jews leaving Russia were mainly artisans and peasants, not intellectuals, although they probably had a relatively high literacy rate compared to other immigrant groups. The overwhelming majority was religiously observant, but they were not the most religious nor were they of the rabbinical classes. Those groups remained behind, following the teachings of their religious leaders, many of whom argued strongly against migration to America.[7] A few well-known writers and other intellectuals—Sholom Aleichem, creator of the stories that were the basis for *Fiddler on the Roof,* is perhaps the best known—did immigrate. But they were a very small part of a massive stream.

Life for Russian Immigrants in New York

The millions of new Russian immigrants were a small part of the much larger wave of immigrants arriving in the United States from across Europe. Many arrived in New York City, usually through Ellis Island, and tended to settle there in much higher numbers than other immigrant groups. For example, in 1899 to 1900 some 72 percent of those Jews arriving in the United States named New York as their destination. This compared with 54.5 percent of Italian immigrants and considerably lower rates for members of other groups.[8] New York City had a large immigrant population. In 1890 about 42 percent of the population of the city were foreign-born whites, and another 38 percent were the children of immigrants.[9] Immigrants dominated some neighborhoods, with almost 90 percent of the population of the area south of Fourteenth Street made up of immigrants or first-generation natives.[10] Here Russian Jews steadily displaced the German immigrants of earlier years. This population continued to grow throughout the period, living in overcrowded tenements and many working in sweatshops for long hours.

Reformer Jacob Riis's 1890 work, *How the Other Half Lives,* deals with immigrants and the immigrant experience. He devotes two chapters to aspects of life in what he called "Jewtown." Although many of his descriptions and characterizations negatively depict Jews and Judaism, he nonetheless spent considerable time observing conditions in Jewish immigrant neighborhoods:

> It is said that nowhere in the world are so many people crowded together on a square mile as here. The average five-story tenement adds a story or two to its stature in Ludlow Street and an extra building on the rear lot, and yet the sign "To Let" is the rarest of all there. Here is one seven stories high. The sanitary policeman whose beat this is will tell you that it contains thirty-six families, but the term has a widely different meaning here and on the avenues. In this house, where a case of small pox was reported, there were fifty-eight babies and thirty-eight children that were over five years of age. In Essex Street two small rooms in a six-story tenement were made to hold a "family" of father and mother, twelve children, and six boarders.[11]

Home was the workshop for many, with sewing machines operated by adults and children and even the youngest assisting in various tasks "from the day he is old enough to pull a thread."[12]

Immigrants had other defenders, including the existing Jewish community in the United States. Although this group was at times embarrassed by the Russian Jews, their response to the threat that the new group posed to the gains they had made in American society was to encourage rapid "Americanization" of the Russians through a variety of social and charitable agencies such as the Educational Alliance. In 1910 the major article in *The American Jewish Year Book 5671* was titled "In Defense of the Immigrant" and consisted mainly of responses to the proposed restrictions on immigration that had been put forth by the Dillingham Commission on Immigration.[13]

The Lower East Side had long been an immigrant district, with the Russians and Italians simply displacing the neighborhood's previous Irish and German inhabitants. This area had also long been known for criminal activity ranging from petty theft to prostitution, gambling, and fencing. In her defense of the immigrants, Claghorn blamed this criminal activity on conditions in the neighborhoods in which they settled:

> The moral surroundings, too, are bad. Not only are there, first, the evil moral influences of overcrowding in general, but also the contact with elements of the population already deteriorated by a generation of tenement-house life. . . .
>
> The new immigrant, an unsophisticated Italian peasant or a poor Hebrew of quiet family and moral traditions, is brought into a district where vice has been developed through years of a sifting process which has taken elsewhere the successful of the former generation of immigrants and left the failures where violence and intemperance, especial faults of that earlier generation, are prevalent. . . .
>
> The Bowery, running up through the quarters where the newer immigrants—the Italians to the left, the Hebrews to the right—settled in greatest numbers, is the focal line of these evil influences, and the peculiar system of government which allows the conditions prevailing there to continue is to a great extent responsible for the evils seen to be growing in the foreign quarters.[14]

Within one square mile, 200 so-called disorderly houses, 336 gang hangouts, and 200 pool halls (which generally also provided opportunities for betting) could be found. There were also numerous dance halls (known as places where pimps, prostitutes, procurers, and their customers congregated) and gambling establishments.[15]

Some praised the arrivals, often with a somewhat patronizing air. For example, Claghorn writes:

> The poorest among them will make all possible sacrifices to keep his children in school; and one of the most striking social phenomena in New York City today is the way in which Jews have taken possession of the public schools, in the highest as well as the lowest grades.
>
> The city college is practically filled with Jewish pupils, a considerable proportion of them children of Russian or Polish immigrants on the East Side.
>
> In the lower schools Jewish children are the delight of their teachers for cleverness at their books, obedience and generally good conduct; and the vacation schools, night schools, social settlements, libraries, bathing place, parks, and playgrounds of the East Side are fairly besieged with Jewish children eager to take advantage of the opportunities they offer. Jewish boys are especially ambitious to enter the professions or go into business, and the complaint is made that they overcrowd such callings, refusing to enter occupations involving handwork as well as head work. . . . And, furthermore, the Hebrew usually shows such excellence in these special lines that the community probably gains materially rather than loses by having its services offered in this way.[16]

Although this description evokes stereotypes, it is sincere in its effort to portray the immigrants in a positive light, counterbalancing negative statements made by those agitating against immigration. Similarly, Ida Van Etten's essay "Russian Jews as Desirable Immigrants" praises their commitment to education, their organization of strikes, their temperance, and their lack of dependence on charity. She quotes statistics indicating that in 1892 Jews numbered only eleven of 2,170 paupers in the almshouse on Blackwell's Island and usually only between twelve and fifteen of what were typically about 1,000 patients at Charity Hospital.[17] Other reformers and muckrakers also defended the immigrants and pointed to the difficulty of the circumstances in which they lived.

A Jewish community was well established in the United States when this wave of immigrants began to arrive, but earlier Jews were defined mainly as Germans and thought of themselves as fairly well assimilated into life in the United States. This was similar to the situation in Germany and other western European countries where Jews thought of themselves as assimilated in ways that Jews in Russia were not. Many were not religiously observant, and some had adopted newer philosophies such as Ethical Culture.[18] The new wave—often Orthodox, speaking Yiddish rather than German, lower class, and less well educated—was seen to threaten the success of German Jews who were building a place for themselves within American society. This was especially clear in New York City, where an elite group of wealthy Jews—including the Goldmans, Sachs, Kahns, and others—had established themselves.[19]

For these well-established Jews, the arrival of the Russians was a distasteful embarrassment and threatened to undo all that they had accomplished in seeking to make Jews an accepted part of American society. Indeed, this group is often credited with coining the derogatory term *kike* for the new immigrants. The founding of the Hawthorne School—a reformatory for Jewish boys—by this German Jewish elite in 1907 was an effort to address the issue of crime in the Jewish community. Although many establishment Jews felt uncomfortable with acknowledging that Jews were criminals, circumstances soon forced them to face reality and address the issue.

In 1908 Theodore Bingham, the New York City police commissioner, accused the Russian immigrants of being serious criminals. In an article titled "Foreign Criminals in New York," he declares that half of all criminals in New York were Jews. He further concludes that Jews—along with Italians—had a criminal nature.[20] He writes, "They are burglars, firebugs. Pickpockets and highway robbers—when they have the courage; but, though all crime is their province, pocket-picking is the one to which they seem to take most naturally."[21] An earlier commissioner, William McAdoo, comments in his 1906 memoirs that Jews are "not apt, unless under great pressure, to resort to force or to commit crimes of violence."[22] Several years before that, *The American Metropolis* argued that the Lower East Side was completely dominated by crime and corruption and that Russian and Polish Jews were "the worst element in the entire make-up of New York life."[23] Although these assertions, especially those by Bingham, were undoubtedly driven in part by anti-Semitism, they also reflected a significant crime problem among the immigrant population. Various leaders of the Jewish community argued that with the exception of a small number of committed offenders—some who were involved in "white slavery" and some who were professional pickpockets in Russia—the overwhelming majority of immigrant Jews who were arrested had no criminal history in their countries of origin. This was, however, not a very palatable argument.[24]

Based on their own observation and the scrutiny of outsiders, "East Side leaders and institutions were steadily worried, more than they allowed themselves to say in public or admit to gentiles, about the spread of prostitution among Jewish girls and thievery among the Jewish boys. . . . Crime was a source of shame, a sign that much was distraught and some diseased on the East Side; but it was never at the center of Jewish immigrant life."[25] Many did not want to acknowledge or discuss the issue publicly, which Howe attributes to a general cultural pattern that avoided the discussion of difficult topics in public. On the whole, law-abiding Jews, both German and Russian, did not pay much attention to the criminal activities engaged in by other Jews until forced to do so by outsiders.

One strategy that the community adopted in response to assertions of criminality was to cite statistics that showed that the immigrants were, if anything, underrepresented in the criminal population. For example, some argued that the courts that were filled with Russian Jewish criminals were located in the neighborhoods that were overwhelmingly populated by this group and therefore their representation was not disproportionate to their population. Further, most offenses were against corporate ordinances (such as playing handball on the sidewalk) and sanitation regulations, such as misplacement of garbage.[26] It was frequently asserted that the majority of other offenses were prostitution, pickpocketing, and other nonviolent crimes.

The vast majority of adult immigrants were not serious or violent criminals. Their most common offenses involved violation of laws governing the operation of small peddling businesses. Then, as now, many of those summoned to court probably argued that operation of these businesses without violating some rules was impossible.[27] Riis, for example, describes an incident in which peddlers try to flee as the health officer, accompanied by a number of police officers, seizes the food sold at the stands and pushcarts and takes it to the dump. Riis writes that such business fights often came to the attention of the police and the courts:

> [The neighborhood's] troubles with the police are the characteristic crop of its intense business rivalries. . . . The police at the Eldridge Street station are in a constant turmoil over these everlasting fights. Somebody is always denouncing somebody else, and getting his enemy or himself locked up; frequently both, for the prisoner, when brought in generally has as plausible a story to tell as his accuser, and as hot a charge to make. The day closes on a wild conflict of rival interests. Another dawns with the prisoner in court, but no complainant. Over night the case has been settled on a business basis, and the police dismiss their prisoner in deep disgust.[28]

The seeming innocence of these kinds of disputes is subsequently undermined by Riis's description of many of them as involving "dancing schools" that often operated as fronts for illegal activity, including prostitution.

Conflicts between religious practices and civil authorities were another source of interaction with the law. Howe cites the kosher slaughtering of chickens in tenements as an example of the types of practices that inevitably brought the immigrants into conflict with the law, specifically the sanitary code.[29] Riis refers to "more than ten years of persistent effort on the part of sanitary authorities to drive the trade in live fowl from the streets to the fowl-market on Gouverneur Slip."[30] Another issue of cultural conflict that played itself out in the legal domain was that of divorce, where immigrants would obtain a religious divorce from a rabbi but not from secular authorities. If a remarriage occurred, the matter could result in a charge of bigamy.

In 1893 there were only 360 Jewish prisoners in New York State, and most of them had been convicted for nonviolent crimes, often related to gambling.[31] Overall, those classified as white immigrants were underrepresented in the prison population compared to their numbers in the general population, and this was true in both the high immigration states and elsewhere.[32] Joselit found that from 1900 to 1915 the proportion of those defendants charged with felonies who were Jews increased from 15.9 percent to 25.4 percent. Despite this dramatic increase, the number of serious Jewish criminals was never disproportionate to the size of the Jewish population.[33] In addition, of the felonies charged, only about 12 percent involved the commission of a violent crime. The remaining charges were for property crime, with a small percentage of violations of gambling and similar laws. Burglaries were common and often involved fences from the Lower East Side underworld, including a number of women, such as Annie Kahn and "Marm" Mandelbaum, the "queen of fences."[34]

Some adult immigrants who were not directly involved in crime nevertheless benefited from it—for example, by receiving money from rents paid by illegal businesses[35] or by benefiting from profitable relationships with Tammany Hall politicians. Some, such as Martin Engel, were politicians themselves. Then they too received bribes to protect the operation of illegal activities ranging from gambling to prostitution.

Juvenile Crime

Many of the children of immigrants on the Lower East Side, whether first or second generation, were involved in the crimes typical of urban delinquent children. These included not only thefts but also criminal activities that were organized by the adults of the underworld. As Joselit puts it, their parents were "unaware that their children learned the Torah of fighting rather than the Torah of Moses, that they returned home bearing scars instead of textbooks."[36]

The introduction of a Jewish boy named Meyer Lansky to this underworld as a youngster was probably not an uncommon story. Watching the crap games played on the street, he became fascinated and sought to bet. Losing his money on his first attempt, he soon realized that the way to make money was to be on the inside of the game and to understand how the crooked game was really played.[37] Later, but still only a teenager, he was allegedly involved in strong-arming scabs and attempting to become a pimp.[38] Even as he spent increasing amounts of time mastering the system, Lansky continued to attend school and earn excellent grades. He also celebrated his bar mitzvah, read extensively from the public library, and apprenticed to a tool and die maker. Because Meyer Lansky was one of those who seemingly could travel easily between the licit and illicit worlds, his experience tells us something about crime and opportunity. Like Lansky, some immigrants forsook their legitimate opportunities and chose to go on to become professional criminals—in his case, to become one of the most powerful mobsters in America. Others were delinquents as youngsters but instead chose to become law-abiding adults. Different choices can be made out of the same experience.

In what was ostensibly a defense of "The Jews of New York," Riis in 1896 praises the immigrants in many respects. But he also issues this warning: "the fact appears to be that crime is cropping out to a dangerous degree among the Jewish children of the East Side."[39] In a similar vein, a 1905 article indicates that more than one-third of the inmates at the House of Refuge and the New York Juvenile Asylum were Jewish.[40] These concerns provided strong motivation for the construction of what became the Hawthorne School, which was designed to address the problem of delinquency. Shortly after the school was opened, there were already too many Jewish delinquents to be accommodated.

By the end of the 1920s, however, predictions were being made that juvenile delinquency would soon almost completely disappear as a problem in the Jewish community. This prediction turned out to be correct. By the beginning of World War II, Jewish children citywide made up just 8 percent of all juvenile arraignments in New York City courts.[41] The Hawthorne School went from an enrollment of over 400 to only 127 by 1930. This rapid decline in delinquency was the result of a combination of factors, but immigration restrictions meant that the Jewish population was aging and was thus moving beyond the most delinquency-prone years.

A smaller number of young immigrants, when combined with the movement of many Jewish families into the middle class, meant that the recruitment pool of young immigrants to fill underworld positions was also shrinking. Further, the movement into the middle class meant that children were less likely to end up in the juvenile justice system. For those youngsters who did get into trouble, the emergence of delinquency prevention meant that more delinquents were diverted away from juvenile justice. Placement at the Hawthorne School came to be viewed as a last resort by the social workers of the agencies that sponsored it.[42]

Prostitution

Many of those living on the Lower East Side were probably able to avoid acknowledging the widespread practice of prostitution by either choosing to look the other way or avoiding the areas in which it was most blatantly practiced. A widely quoted warning in the *Jewish Daily Forward* said "it is better to stay away from Allen, Chrystie and Forsyth Streets, if you go walking with your wife, daughter or fiancee for there's an official flesh trade there."[43] Contemporary descriptions include stories of children being shooed off of the stoops of their buildings so that prostitutes could ply their trades and of synagogue members being disturbed as they went to and from their services.[44] Women were recruited for prostitution, often at the dance halls they visited for recreation, by young men known as cadets who had connections to pimps and gangs.

The involvement of any particular ethnic group in a criminal activity such as prostitution is difficult to determine objectively because different measurement methods yield widely varying results. The highest estimates were presented by the anti-Tammany muckraker George Kibbe Turner in an article in *McClure's* that is filled with anti-Semitic stereotypes and claims that two-thirds of those involved in prostitution were Jewish, mostly immigrants from Eastern Europe. Other estimates placed the numbers at or near their proportions in the population.[45] Deportation figures for prostitution or procuring were 3.5 per 10,000 for Jews compared to 19 for French, 11.7 for English, and 6.3 for Dutch and Flemish. Even in absolute terms, the number of Jews so deported—fifteen—was lower than any group but the Dutch and Flemish.[46]

Nevertheless, reviews of court records and newspaper coverage reveal many Jewish names listed among those arrested for acting as both pimps and prostitutes. Most of the prostitutes involved were Jewish, contrary to contemporary speculation about a world-wide conspiracy of Jews that engaged in kidnapping and victimizing innocent gentile girls. The evidence suggests that most of these women were recruited in New York, sometimes through the trickery described by the anti–white slavery activists but sometimes because of economic necessity or simply because the pay was better than that earned from toiling in a sweat shop.[47] Indeed, much of the uproar over prostitution was overlaid with the concern that the women involved had made themselves unmarriageable and that they were economically independent. Similarly, a story of seduction and kidnapping could also provide a way for young women who had willingly engaged in sexual activity to escape blame for it.

Some prostitution had always been practiced among Jews in the Pale, but rapid growth in prostitution among Jewish women seems to be associated with the period of the great migration. Related to this was the emergence of an international movement against "white slavery," a concept whose meaning changed substantially over the years. In the mid-nineteenth century, it referred mainly to the system of state-licensed prostitution in Europe but by the 1880s expanded to mean kidnapping girls and women and forcing them into prostitution. In the early twentieth century, it came to mean the coercion of women, through force or fraud, into prostitution.[48] The anti–white slavery movement generated a tremendous number of books, films, plays, and other materials. Frequently, these materials identified organizers of white slavery rings as Jewish, and the logic of the stories fit well with other anti-Semitic canards. Bristow describes this process as the "sexualization of the blood libel."[49]

In 1910 there was a Jewish-sponsored international congress on "The Suppression of the Traffic in Girls and Women," and in the same period several other international reports were issued and conferences held on the topic. One of the bodies that investigated the issue was the Dillingham Commission. It concluded, "There has been much talk in the newspapers of a great monopolistic corporation whose business it is to import and exploit these unfortunate women. The commission has been unable to learn of any such a corporation and does not believe in its existence."[50]

The International Benevolent Association (IBA)—a trade organization of about 200 panderers, pimps, and others involved in the prostitution business—was the closest thing to a broad organization of prostitution that seems to have existed in New York. Although seen as representative of a massive world-wide organization by some, the IBA was actually much like other benevolent associations, providing pensions and, perhaps most important, access to its own cemetery.[51] The latter was important because one of the few strategies that the Jewish community could use to punish those who engaged in pandering was to refuse to allow them to be buried in the community's plots, although this strategy was difficult to enforce in New York City.[52]

By 1914 Jewish prostitutes and cadets had faded from the Lower East Side scene. This was probably due equally to the efforts of reformers and to growing economic opportunities provided by the war, the organization of the workforce, the upward mobility offered by education, the aging of the population, and the decline in immigration from Russia. As Bristow puts it, "the golden era of Jewish vice was over" in New York as well as in other locations.[53]

Protection

Throughout the period of the early twentieth century, gangs and some individuals made money through the sale of protection to others. For example, starting in about 1906, a common threat made to force the payment of money was that of horse poisoning. This was extensive enough that merchants formed a fund and then an insurance scheme to deal with the expense incurred. They subsequently, and for several reasons, adopted a strategy of collectively paying off the principal gang—known as the Yiddish Camorra ("Black Hand")—that was victimizing them. In 1912 merchants formed the East Side Horse Owners' Protective Association, which cooperated with the police and eventually was able to put an end to the scheme. Other forms of protection and extortion took the traditional form of a demand for money in exchange for avoiding violence to one's person or property. More lucrative was the emergence of a new form of protection known as labor racketeering.

Labor Corruption and Racketeering

Both union leaders and manufacturers hired toughs to attack their opposition, whether they were scabs, strikers, or union organizers, and this hiring was often done through the auspices of racketeers such as Monk Eastman.[54] Ultimately, this led to a situation in which Jewish racketeers—including, most famously, Arnold Rothstein—served as intermediaries between the two groups, profiting handsomely off of both.

At the turn of the century, unions relied mainly on their own members for the use of force. This was often exercised in response to the violence inflicted by the companies, which generally had the police, their own paid enforcers, and other support on their side. In the early 1900s specialists, such as Dopey Benny, could count on a steady stream of business from the various unions that sought to organize the industries of New York. Other groups, such as the Browne and Myers Detective Agency, counted on a demand for strike breakers and guards.[55] The most important labor racketeer of the 1930s was Louis "Lepke" Buchalter, who controlled unions concentrated in the garment and trucking industries. The investigation and prosecution of racketeering that focused on Lepke led to the widespread recognition of prosecutor Thomas E. Dewey, who parlayed that fame into the governorship of New York and the Republican nomination for president.

Arson

Arson was a crime that the popular press strongly associated with Jews.[56] It was often carried out for the purpose of getting an insurance payout. About arson, Riis writes: "A fire panic at night in a tenement, by no means among the rare experiences in New York, with the surging, half-smothered crowds on stairs and fire escapes, the frantic mothers and crying children, the wild struggle to save the little that is their all, is a horror that has few parallels in human experience."[57] During the 1890s several large arson rings, the larger of which involved the cooperation of fire adjusters, were tried and convicted. The number of cases of arson that involved Russian Jewish immigrants declined considerably afterward, although a new team was convicted in 1913.[58]

Political Corruption

During most of this time of heavy Russian immigration, Tammany Hall dominated government in New York City. Although widely regarded as corrupt, the Tammany organization nevertheless had the support of many immigrants—in part because Tammany leaders were better politicians than the wealthy Protestants who formed their major opposition and in part because they operated a well-oiled income- and vote-generating machine. In 1894 the Lexow Committee issued its report based on an investigation of city corruption and concluded that Tammany had allowed gambling and prostitution rings to operate in exchange for protection money paid to politicians and policemen. Witnesses testified before the committee about corruption involving lawyers and bail bondsmen in the court system.[59] Many of those both implicated and testifying were Russian immigrants. Two years later, the findings of the Mazet Commission again illustrated the existence and extensiveness of Jewish criminal activity in New York City and the relationship of that activity to Tammany.[60]

An article published in 1909 claimed that prostitution flourished on the Lower East Side because of the complicity of Tammany. In exchange for protection, the organizers of prostitution were accused of providing votes and money, with many brothel operators actually serving as district captains.[61] Martin Engel, a Tammany political leader, owned many buildings throughout the Lower East Side, some or all of which were used for prostitution.[62]

Reformers, often representatives of the city's wealthy Protestant families, frequently attacked Tammany and its various operations. The muckraking reformers periodically succeeded in generating enough outrage at the corrupt practices that they could elect a reform mayor, such as Seth Low. The reformers' use of anti-Semitic statements and images made it difficult, however, for Jews who opposed corruption to support reform. Jimmy Walker, the last strong Tammany mayor of New York City, was associated with the operation of speakeasies and gambling parlors. His 1932 downfall—combined with the end of Prohibition and the gradual decline in the numbers of Russian Jews involved in crimes—led to a sharp decline in the Tammany type of political corruption.

Bootlegging

In January 1920 the Volstead Act prohibiting the sale of alcoholic beverages went into effect, and its unintended effect was to create, in essence, an entirely new area of criminal activity—the production and distribution of illegal alcohol. For the enterprising criminal, this became a highly profitable area that, because it was new, did not require any displacement of preexisting criminal operations. Prohibition offered many opportunities for illegal gain, and immigrant gangsters took advantage of them. Fried concludes that Prohibition was a particular "disaster" for the Jewish community that was continuing to struggle for acceptance. Without it, he says, many of the low-level gangsters who were then just entering their early twenties would have faded from the underworld scene.[63] Instead, a candy store of criminal opportunity was opened to them. Nine of the seventeen leading rumrunners were Jews.[64]

Arnold Rothstein, perhaps the leading gangster of his day, had up until this time engaged mainly in gambling and labor racketeering operations. With Prohibition he developed a bootlegging enterprise that involved importing alcohol from England. Significantly, Rothstein was a mentor to many famous gangsters, including a number who were Jewish. His protégés included Charles "Lucky" Luciano, Jack "Legs" Diamond, Dutch Schultz, Waxey Gordon, Abner "Longy" Zwillman, Frank Costello, and Meyer Lansky.[65] This ethnically diverse group of young men were often drawn from the Russian and Italian sectors of the Lower East Side. Rothstein was reputed in the newspapers to be the head of a huge underworld organization, but actually he acted more like an investor in the enterprises that his protégés ran. His business headquarters dealt only with the legal ends of this operation. As Lacey puts it, "The secret of his organization was the lack of it."[66] Bootlegging was for him just part of a diversified operation.

Waxey Gordon had a similar experience. Born on the Lower East Side, he moved from pickpocketing and small crimes to being a "labor goon, strikebreaker, dope peddler, burglar, extortionist, etc."[67] Working with Max Greenberg and with an investment by Arnold Rothstein, he was able to set up a major bootlegging operation. He was able to move off the streets and into the back room running an organization that had a great deal in common with legitimate businesses. Eventually, he operated a set of breweries in New Jersey that were nominally producing only "near beer" but, in fact, also sold ordinary beer at great profit. He, and others like him, were able to take on the appearance of successful businessmen, investing their profits in legitimate enterprises and living at fancy addresses.

For Meyer Lansky, who was about eighteen years old when the Volstead Act went into effect, and for his generation of criminals, Prohibition was to provide the basis for the organization of criminal enterprises that would last long after the Act was repealed in 1933. Lansky's legitimate front operation was a van and truck rental business that, besides supplying a front, also provided the underworld, including his own liquor operation, with the transportation that it needed to distribute its illegal products. He also developed gambling houses that provided profit both from gaming and from selling liquor to the bettors.

As had the criminality of Russian immigrants before World War I, the new Jewish gangsters offered an excuse for the invocation of anti-Semitic stereotypes, not only in New York but also across the country.[68] But this was not only, or even mainly, a Jewish phenomenon. In fact, one of the most important developments of the period was the cooperation between members of different ethnic groups, albeit most significantly among Jews and Italians. Some see this experience as marking the emergence of a more rational and businesslike model for organizing crime based on skills rather than ethnicity.[69]

When the bootlegging industry came to an end in 1933 with the repeal of Prohibition, some bootleggers retired from crime and turned their businesses into legitimate operations. Others, such as Meyer Lansky and Bugsy Seigel, were able to refocus their efforts on other areas of illegal activity, most notably gambling.

Violence

Besides the violence involved in the labor rackets, Russian Jewish immigrants or their children were involved in organized violence in other arenas. Often this violence operated in conjunction with their illicit businesses, such as gambling and bootlegging. Its use reflected a willingness to employ violence to enforce order, remove competition, or increase power in the underworld rather than simply the random use of violence for its own sake.

In 1912 Herman Rosenthal, who operated a gambling enterprise, was killed by several Jewish youths apparently at the orders of a corrupt police officer who thought that Rosenthal was going to expose the officer's acceptance of payoffs. This incident was one of the major events—along with the 1908 publication of Police Commissioner Bingham's article—that forced the uptown Jewish community to take a more active role in dealing with the crime problem.

After World War I two gangs, one led by Kid Dropper and the other by Little Augie, fought for control of the Jewish sections of the

Lower East Side. The police attributed at least twenty-three deaths to their battles.[70] Dropper eventually was assassinated, and his assassin was defended by Jimmy Walker, who was already working for Tammany but was not yet mayor of New York. The level of violence was high, but its victims were limited to those involved in criminal activity.

When Arnold Rothstein was murdered in 1928, his killers were never identified, but the investigation of the murder brought about the resignation of Mayor Walker and exposed the corruption of the Tammany officials. It is interesting that the murder of Rothstein was not viewed by either the popular or Jewish press as reflecting badly on the Jewish community as a whole.

The gang known as Murder, Inc. was largely made up of second-generation Jews and Italians and was headquartered in Brownsville, Brooklyn. Besides murder, the gang engaged in a variety of illegal activities including loan sharking, bookmaking, and racketeering. It was not an organization that was particularly rooted in the neighborhood in which it was located.[71] When the Brooklyn District Attorney William O'Dwyer began his investigation into the murder of a small-time crook known as Red Alpert, his staff eventually uncovered evidence linking the gang to as many as eighty murders over a ten-year period, including many murders for hire.[72] Among those convicted as a result of the O'Dwyer investigation was Lepke Buchalter, the labor racketeer.

Despite heavy Jewish involvement, these particular acts of the most extreme violence were, curiously, seldom associated particularly with Jews or Russians. This was probably due to a combination of factors. Most important is the largely successful integration of Jews into American society. In addition, those involved in this violence were often second- or third-generation immigrants; they were more likely to be seen as Americans, even if sometimes of a hyphenated kind. And there is the simple fact that the persons involved were not from a single ethnic group. They represented a true melting pot of criminals. The fact that the public response to this later criminality—the murder of Rothstein and the killings by Murder, Inc.—has a diminished ethnic tone is a reflection of those factors.

Continuity and Change in Russian Immigration

Although some individual Russian Jewish immigrants remained long active in the criminal world, most others made a successful transition to legitimate activities. The bulk of second-generation immigrants moved on to relatively normal lives, usually outside of the old neighborhood and into middle-class areas in the Bronx, Brooklyn, and Queens and suburban areas.[73] Most of them climbed the straight ladder of upward social mobility. Their roles in American intellectual, business, and arts life grew as they became "at ease in America."[74] Overall, crime ceased to be identified with these immigrants and especially with their children and grandchildren. Although a few well-known Jews, such as Meyer Lansky and Bugsy Seigel, were involved in organized crime, their particular criminal organizations were not thought of as Jewish by the mainstream media and public. Instead, they were seen as being more like generic corporate-style organized crime operations. Lansky and Seigel, in fact, were regarded by many as members of the mafia.

The examination of this early and larger wave of immigrants from Russia provides a number of points that should be kept in mind as we examine the crimes that Russian immigrants are involved in today. For example, we can look for a pattern of relatively high levels of criminal activity by immigrants and first-generation children that then fades with upward mobility and assimilation. Or we can look for differences—both in Russia and in the United States—between the early and late twentieth century that led to different outcomes.

Among the important differences between the two periods are major economic, political, and social changes in the United States. Today there are many fewer sweatshops, especially in the areas where

Russian immigrants live. The current social welfare system is broader than the earlier one. But a service-based economy that demands high levels of education and of English proficiency for success has emerged to replace the manufacturing economy that earlier immigrants found easy to enter. Public statements of anti-Semitism are much rarer and, when made, are quickly denounced. Jews as a group are more integrated into American society, but the Holocaust experience had led to changes in attitudes toward assimilation among many Jews. American attitudes toward immigrants in general, however, may not be radically different from what they were then.

The globalization of the economy is an important difference in the two eras. The technology of communication means that people today, no matter where they live, are more exposed to other peoples and cultures. They are less confined to their ethnic neighborhoods, and thus the ties of ethnicity may be less binding when they immigrate. Changes in technology and transportation also certainly make international crime much easier to organize and carry out today than it was at the beginning of the century.

In the case of the Russians, there are both similarities and differences between the two groups of immigrants. Both the first and last waves came from authoritarian countries—one ruled by the Russian czar and the other by the Soviet Union's Communist Party—in which Jews faced discrimination and violence. But today they come speaking Russian instead of Yiddish. Many are better educated than those from earlier generations, although persistent anti-Semitism throughout the Soviet and post-Soviet eras limited their educational opportunities. Given Soviet policies on religion, many, especially those of the most recent waves, come without a tradition of orthodox religious practice. Perhaps most significantly, more recent Russian immigrants come from a culture in which corruption has been a way of life—the means of survival—for more than eighty years. By comparing the experiences of immigrants from the two periods, we can see what, if any, difference these changes have made.

Another important lesson that can be learned from this comparison is to avoid appealing to stereotypes and relying on the popular press as a source of reliable information about foreign groups. Just as earlier conspiracy theories were disproved when it was shown that a few individuals, such as Rothstein, were able to organize and coordinate a number of enterprises, the conspiracy theories about today's menace of Russian organized crime may be overwrought. Most crime committed by immigrants in earlier decades was fairly minor. A few individual Russian immigrant Jews cooperated with people of other ethnic groups to create a mafia-style structure, but to the extent that this structure could be characterized in terms of ethnicity it would not be described as being Russian or Jewish. It is important not to generalize from the actions of individuals of a given ethnicity to all individuals sharing that ethnicity.

The organized crime of that bygone era was organized in the United States and not in Russia. In few if any instances (with the major exception of the smuggling of alcohol) was there indication of transnational organization. We should not be surprised to find that history repeats itself.

CHAPTER 4

"NEW" RUSSIANS
COME TO AMERICA

As described in the last chapter, during the late 1800s and early 1900s more than two and a half million Russians, the vast majority of them Jews, entered the United States to seek a new life in the New World. Since then, the east-west tide has waxed and waned, depending on the prevailing political exigencies in Russia, the immigration laws in the United States, and the relationship between Russia and the United States. The number of Russian émigrés coming to America remained at fairly low levels, with occasional peaks, until the late 1970s, when the numbers of Russian Jews permitted to emigrate was increased as a result of American demands and the Soviet government's desire for greater trade with the United States.[1]

Being Jewish had never been a helpful status in Russia, but this suddenly changed with the increased possibilities for Jewish emigration in the late 1970s. Although the trade-emigration link was intended to allow Jews to emigrate, some non-Jews passed as Jews by switching nationalities or assuming false identities, and others who had one Jewish parent and one non-Jewish parent switched their official nationality identification to Jew.

The fourth wave of émigrés escalated through the 1980s under Soviet President Gorbachev during the second half of the decade. John F. Kennedy International Airport in New York City was the single most important Western destination for these newcomers. It is not surprising, perhaps, that the surrounding region, stretching as far south and west as Philadelphia, became one of the top areas in the country for the relocation of émigrés from the former Soviet Union.

In New York City, Russians settled most visibly in Brighton Beach, the oldest and most prominent Russian community in the United States. This working-class, mostly Jewish community is located near Coney Island in the southern part of Brooklyn. Brighton Beach is currently home to up to 30,000 Russian émigrés, and another 40,000 to 50,000 émigrés are estimated to be living in the immediate New York metropolitan area in places like Rego Park, Queens, and Fort Lee, New Jersey.[2] All of these figures—which come mainly from the New York City Planning Commission and the United States Immigration and Naturalization Service—may be subject to underreporting because of the suspected large numbers of illegal aliens.

Many of the newly arrived Russian Jews have not been what their American sponsors expected. Not only do they not, for example, practice their religion, but they lack both a knowledge of and an interest in Judaism. Although some new arrivals may be pseudo-Jews, widespread anti-Semitism and official restrictions on religious practice of any kind meant that being a Jew in the USSR was a nationality and not a religious identity.

One of the new arrivals that we talked to was Sophia. In addition to being an émigré herself, she worked for many years to assist other ex-Soviets in coming to America. Sophia lived in the Russian neighborhood of Philadelphia. This community of some 20,000 to 25,000 people is located in the northeast section of the city near an area called Bustleton Avenue. Sophia was a music teacher in a special music school in Riga, Latvia (then a Soviet republic), until she came to the United States in 1982 following the emigration of her brother and mother. As with many Soviet émigrés at that time, she was able to come only at their invitation—what she calls a *grant*. This means that some individual or group was willing to assume financial responsibility for the newcomer. Sophia says that one reason that so many Russian émigrés live in Brighton Beach is that New York did not require such grants from either individuals or communities.[3]

Sophia described in some detail the process, and the problems, associated with emigration from the former USSR. Jobs and the language are the biggest problems. She could not find a job as a teacher, and her husband (an engineer) could not find a job in his profession. Most émigrés take whatever work they can get, study English, and look to advance themselves. When they first arrive, just about all of them are supported by sponsoring agencies or organizations, but many later had to depend on welfare. In part, this is because severe restrictions were placed on what they could take out of the USSR. At one time, each person was limited to $100, although this has now changed.

With help both from sponsors and from welfare, Sophia first studied bookkeeping and then located a job as a bookkeeper. Later she became a social worker for a Jewish agency working with Soviet émigrés, her husband became a machinist and advanced to doing computer work for a machine company, and both of their daughters graduated from college. This family seems to be one of the Russian émigré success stories that most Soviet émigrés envy. They successfully climbed the straight and narrow ladder of social mobility. She is dismayed, however, by the reputation of the latest wave of Russians arriving here—namely, that many are associated with organized crime and a Russian mafia.

According to Sophia, the only émigrés who go into business for themselves are those who cannot find other jobs. Jewelry stores—one popular self-owned business in the Philadelphia Russian community—often compete for business by buying and selling stolen goods, but Sophia does not believe that the practice is organized. Shoplifting is another problem that is particularly prevalent, she said, because taking goods from the old state stores in the Soviet Union—where the goods did not belong to anyone in particular but rather to everyone in general—was not regarded as theft.

Sophia said that most Russian émigrés that she has met are highly educated and highly skilled, especially those from the cities in Russia. Those from smaller cities and villages, on the other hand, have the most problems in adjusting and getting employment here because they are less knowledgeable about city life.

The Russian Criminals Are Coming

The Russians are far from being the only ethnic group that has immigrated to the United States during the last decade or the only group within which we find criminals and even criminal organization. One need only look at Chinese, Nigerian, Jamaican, Dominican, and, to a lesser extent, Vietnamese and Korean immigrants to find evidence of similar patterns. On the other hand, there are Indian, Pakistani, Guyanese, Afghan, and other groups that may contain individual criminals but that show no evidence of organized criminal networks. We want to find out what, if anything, is distinctive about the Russians and their experiences.

As the Russian neighborhoods in places like Brighton Beach and Bustleton Avenue became crowded in the mid-1980s, older émigrés started to move into the surrounding suburbs in New Jersey, Long Island, and suburban Philadelphia. Newspaper articles about this new phenomenon of crimes involving Russian émigrés—most often in Brighton Beach (which by that time had become a thriving enclave of mainly Russians and Ukrainians) and in Philadelphia— began to appear in the early 1980s. As is usually the case in such situations, the police or other law enforcement officials were the main sources of information for the media. This kind of information sharing creates a feedback process: reporters talk to law enforcement authorities in researching their stories, police intelligence agents routinely collect and analyze media stories for investigative leads and background information, police share information with other police, and the latter then talk to other media. The circle gets bigger and bigger, but at the center of the circle is often the same information and framework that governs the interpretation of that information. This is one of the ways the Mafia is born.

This feedback process becomes apparent when several major examples of media coverage from this period are examined. A May 1983 feature article in *Philadelphia Magazine* begins as follows:

> The Malina has come to Philadelphia, to Northeast Philadelphia.
>
> Imagine a completely new Mafia in this country. Every big city has its branch, and the organization's contacts in Europe are extensive. The Malina is such a Mafia.
>
> It is an international criminal conspiracy that will engage in any crime, from murder to espionage to drug trafficking to jewel theft, for the right price. Up till now, many of its members entered this country as Soviet Jews and most of its victims have been from the émigré community. But the Malina is growing. It numbers the KGB and the CIA among its contacts, and perhaps its clients.[4]

Among the sources for Mallewe's story were the Philadelphia Police Department (particularly the Intelligence Unit), the Federal Bureau of Investigation, and the United States Department of Justice Organized Crime Strike Force in Philadelphia. Apart from its promotion of the idea of the Russian Mafia, the story offers some interesting insights into the fledgling Russian crime. Among them is the description of the Russians as "highly educated survivors, skilled in all sorts of hi-tech gadgetry . . . already involved in sophisticated white-collar criminal stings."[5] White-collar fraud is predicted to be the benchmark for the growth of Russian émigré crime in the United States.

The *Baltimore Jewish Times* published an assessment of Russian crime on February 24, 1984, entitled "Is There a Soviet-Jewish Mafia in the United States?" Among the sources for this story were detectives in the Sixtieth and Sixty-first Precincts of the New York City Police Department. The latter has jurisdiction over Brighton Beach. One NYPD detective offers this description of the Russians: "They have a form of their own mafia here. What it took the Italians 300 years to perfect, the Russians have accomplished in a couple of years."[6] The article is well researched and comprehensive in its coverage, including the presentation of dissenting views concerning the mafia characterization. Nevertheless, the idea of a mafia association was clearly already established, not the least by the fact that the most prominent word in the article's title was *Mafia*.

In 1986, *New York* magazine ran a piece called "The 'Russian Mafia': A New Crime Menace Grows in Brooklyn." Among the major sources were again police from the NYPD's Sixtieth and Sixty-first Precincts and the FBI. The story acknowledges that the Russians were only "loosely called the Russian Mafia" and that "parallels with the traditional Mafia are somewhat tenuous."[7] But in spite of these disclaimers, the story mostly lives up to its title.

Putting aside the mafia labeling, the kinds of crimes attributed to Soviet émigrés, particularly in the latter two stories, are distinctive. They were mostly scams and confidence games of one kind or another. For example, one variation of the bait-and-switch maneuver (that can be pulled with a variety of objects) involved a real diamond and a phony diamond in identical settings. The Russian scam artists would take the prospective victim to a jewelry store where the real diamond was appraised. The real diamond and the fake diamond were then switched, and the victim was offered the latter diamond at a price less than the appraisal. Thinking he had gotten a real bargain, the customer would take the money and, of course, end up with nothing of value.

Daniel Burstein, in the *New York* magazine article, describes what was called the "white plastic" scam.[8] This involved counterfeit credit cards and store merchants who were willing to ring up phony purchases. A small cadre of Russians, and a few outsiders, had the cooperating merchants (some of whom were also Russian) ring up fraudulent charges based on pieces of plastic that were embossed with a legitimate cardholder's name, number, and expiration date. No merchandise actually changed hands, since the goal was simply to get telephone approval for a charge and for the merchant then to receive payment for the purchase from the credit card company. Over a several-week period in 1985, the group racked up several hundred thousand dollars in fake purchases that they split with the collusive merchants. The cardholders and credit card companies were left holding the bag.

Two themes stand out from these early stories. One is the characterization of the Russian criminals as a Russian Mafia. The other is the distinctive nature of most Russian émigré crime. Here we saw some of the first examples of the multiple versions of crimes of deception with which Russians were to become associated.

Despite the impression created by articles such as these, relatively little police attention, in general, was being paid to Russian émigré crime. Other crime problems were considered higher priority and were assigned limited resources. Police officers who spoke Russian were scarce, which isolated the police and the Russian communities. No information was provided by Soviet authorities about the previous backgrounds of suspected Russian émigré criminals, and American police saw little chance of getting any. Because American and Russian law enforcement simply did not cooperate on such matters, little was known about the specific nature and seriousness of Russian émigré crime, much less about how and how well it might be organized.

Despite the scanty and questionable information available, various federal agencies soon reported that approximately a dozen alleged Russian organized crime groups were based in New York City alone with an estimated membership of between 400 and 500 persons. At the same time, the New York City Police Department identified about 500 persons from the former USSR who were suspected of criminal activities. The Philadelphia Police Department likewise noted that a handful of émigrés who were linked to crimes were moving regularly between Philadelphia and New York City.

In the last generation, there was only one serious, in-depth piece of research on Russian crime in the United States, and that was done before the first rumblings about immigrant crime were heard. Between 1976 and 1980, Lydia Rosner studied crime in Brighton Beach and concluded that networks of interconnected criminals were based in Brighton Beach and committed crimes together. There was, she said, a "vast amount of at least informally organized crime" in Brighton Beach.[9] Rosner could only speculate about the commonly discussed conspiratorial ideas—for example, that Russian immigrant crime might be part of a structured network of national or international major criminal activities or that it might be controlled from within the USSR. These issues were of a wholly different magnitude than neighborhood-based informal crimes.

A few U.S. law enforcement agencies were paying attention to the issue and offered several explanations for the emergence of United States–based Russian crime. As reported by the media in articles such as those just cited, these explanations focus on the movement of people who were already involved in criminal activities in the Soviet Union to the United States. For example, one theory was that Soviet authorities (particularly the KGB, the Soviet intelligence agency) had released inmates from its prisons, rounded up other violent and troublesome offenders off the streets, and commingled them with Jewish émigrés permitted to leave the USSR in the mid-1970s. This might be called the *getting-rid-of-the-undesirables theory.* One version of this thesis held that the KGB fomented the emigration of criminals to undermine and discredit Russian communities in other countries, including the United States, and thereby make emigration unattractive to Soviet citizens.[10]

Other officials concluded that Soviet mobsters may have simply slipped into the United States among Russian and other Eastern European immigrants during the 1970s and 1980s. A related idea held by U.S. law enforcement was that members of organized crime groups from the Ukrainian city of Odessa, in particular, smuggled themselves out of the USSR, again with legitimate émigrés, assuming the identities of dead or jailed Jews in the Soviet Union. This we can call the *pseudo-Jew theory.* However, of the more than 100,000 immigrants from the USSR during the 1980s, U.S. authorities believed that only a few hundred were possibly members of criminal networks. Stephen Handelman, a journalist who spent five years in Moscow and is an expert on organized crime in Russia, offers another theory about how Russian criminals came to be here.[11] He says that when Russian Jews arrived in the late 1970s and 1980s, many had connections to the U.S. Central Intelligence Agency (or to the Israeli intelligence agency, the Moussad), which helped them relocate to the United States. These were not, he says, "big-time" criminals.

Whatever explanation was adopted—and all now appear to have some elements of truth—American authorities firmly believed that Russians who had been career criminals in the Soviet Union simply continued their criminal ways after arriving in the United States. The common assessment is that criminals there become criminals here. This assumes that Russian crime in the United States is largely a product of a professional criminal class that imported its criminal ways onto our shores. A number of the known crime figures who operated in Brighton Beach in the late 1970s and the 1980s fit this general pattern. Evsei Agron, Marat Balagula, Emil Puzyretski, and Boris Nayfeld, among the more prominent Russian gangsters, were part of an assortment of thieves, extortionists, and con men—some of whom were products of the Soviet prison system—and who had by some route managed to end up in New York.

The crime-there, crime-here model has echoes of what has been called the *alien conspiracy theory,* popular several generations back, that was supposed to explain American organized crime.[12] The alien conspiracy theory argued that organized crime in America could be mostly accounted for by the importation of the mafia from Italy in the 1920s. This has since been recognized to be a simplistic and very limited explanation of our organized crime problem. Other, more complex theories, such as the crooked-ladder thesis, replaced it. The idea of a conspiracy of Jews is especially dangerous because it appeals to a strain of anti-Semitism that itself is Russian in origin, but it is hardly surprising to see it repeated in this cultural context.[13] Nevertheless, the rather different idea that criminals and criminal ways can be transported like other goods has some merit and may be useful for understanding Russian criminals in the United States.

Imported Versus Indigenous Criminality

When immigrants move to a new land, they take some of their culture with them. This culture has many dimensions. It includes obvious things such as language, dress, habits, and social customs, as well as values, ways of thinking, and a way of looking at the world. After the newcomers arrive, they begin to take on aspects of whatever new culture they have moved into. They learn a new language and new customs. They eat new foods and enjoy new forms of recreation and entertainment. Besides these more concrete adoptions, they are also exposed to new values and new ways of looking at the world that may lead them to modify old values and beliefs. The overall process is called *acculturation.* Acculturation does not mean that the newcomers forget their old language and customs or their old values. Rather, the old is adapted to the new. Some things are added, others are dropped, and the final product is different from the original. The older the immigrants are, the less dropping and adding occurs, and the less complete is their assimilation into the new setting.

The two theories of organized crime that we juxtaposed in Chapter 2 are linked to this process. One, the crooked-ladder idea, concludes that some immigrants enter organized crime because crime is inherent in the immigration experience. Immigrants are blocked from legitimate social mobility because they don't speak English, lack job skills, and don't know how to maneuver through the various bureaucracies. They are discriminated against because they are foreigners. The crooked-ladder theory pays little or no attention to whether the new arrivals were criminals before they ever arrived at their new location or whether their attitudes toward law and crime are corrupted before or after arrival. Accounting for these variables requires an examination of where immigrants come from and who they are before they get here.

The crooked-ladder theory's emphasis on organized crime as a simple and universal pattern might be challenged if hostile attitudes toward law, law enforcement, and the state are widespread among a particular wave of immigrants and these immigrants have a higher than usual involvement in crime or, conversely, if a wave of immigrants has particularly positive attitudes and low involvement in crime. Such a situation would lend support to the idea that those with a particular aptitude for crime in one place are likely to continue their criminal activities in another.

Russian Mobsters Hit New York

Evsei Agron was one of some 5,000 refugees from the Soviet Union who entered the United States in 1975. Born in Leningrad, Agron, forty-three years old, was allegedly an extortionist, a killer, and a black marketeer who had spent a decade in Soviet prisons. Agron is also said to have been a *vor v zakone* in the USSR.[14] The *vory v zakone* ("thieves-in-law") are an elite class of professional criminals who have roots in the Russian prison system and whose history dates back to the czars. Journalist Nathan Adams argues that Agron was one of those career criminals dumped into the United States when the KGB weeded the Soviet prisons in the 1970s.[15] When asked his profession by immigration officials, Agron said he was a jeweler. Once in the United States, Agron settled in Brighton Beach. According to Uvanudze, Agron was never able to adapt to American life but instead "kept all his Soviet customs."[16]

In the decade after his arrival, Agron built a rudimentary criminal organization, estimated to include some twenty persons, whose main form of moneymaking was extortion but eventually expanded into prostitution and illegal gambling. Agron was a colorful character whose cruelty is said to have been legendary: "By 1980, Agron's enforcers were wrestling more than $50,000 a week from Brighton Beach businessmen. Those who resisted were beaten or tortured with electric cattle prods, at times by Agron himself."[17]

After several attempts on his life, Agron was finally murdered in 1985, a crime that has never been solved. Some believe that his overuse of his cattle prod was responsible, and others believe that he was killed because he wanted his piece of the enormously lucrative bootleg gasoline scam that had been engineered by several Russians and the Colombo organized crime family. According to Uvanudze: "Evsei continued to consider himself the boss and wanted to receive his profit from this affair, but the money was already too great. He had become unnecessary, he interfered in everything. In the end, the Colombo family agreed [with their Russian partners] that he must be killed."[18]

Some have called Agron the "first boss of the Russian Mafia in the USA." Kleinknecht calls him "a pioneer of a new organized-crime threat . . . a loose-knit assortment of thieves, extortionists, confidence men and white-collar swindlers."[19] Adams calls him "the 'Godfather' of a thriving émigré underworld. Increasingly, his life-style mimicked that of a Mafia don, holding court in neighborhood restaurants and chauffeured in limousines as he made his collection rounds, pausing on street corners to dispense favors to supplicants."[20] Others remember Agron's role as godfather to be more self-styled than real. "Agron was a low-life thug" who "specialized in extortion and blackmail," according to one profile shared with us. Cronwell reports these dismissive comments from one of Agron's fellow Soviet émigrés: "One Brighton Beach resident scathingly dismissed Agron as a fake. 'He was the one that pretended to be a Godfather. He would go round in a car with two big guys, they would open the door for him. Everything was staged.' "[21]

Agron was undoubtedly the first major figure in Russian émigré crime in Brighton Beach for a decade. However, he was not a mafioso, much less a godfather, in the traditional understanding of these terms. Agron established no tradition of honor and respect, except for respect that could be coerced with a cattle prod, and exercised no sense of legitimate authority that emanates from the people's support for and willingness to abide by the resolution of disputes, the mediation of contractual arrangements, and the solution of problems. Instead, Agron was "a thuggish neighborhood extortionist who presided over a loose-knit gang that terrorized the small émigré community."[22] He was, in other words, a common criminal. His successor, however—Marat Balagula—was not.

Marat Balagula was born in Orenberg, Russia, in 1943 and lived mainly in Odessa. He served in the Soviet army and managed a food cooperative in his home city. He also earned a degree as a teacher of mathematics and did further study in economics and mathematics. But Balagula did not pursue these professions and, instead, made his fortune in the black market. According to Robert Friedman, who interviewed and studied Balagula extensively, the young entrepreneur sold currency, gold, Russian artifacts, and stolen artwork to foreign tourists sailing on a cruise ship, of which Balagula was the bursar.[23] He also brought back valuables to sell on the black market from his trips to Australia and Western Europe.

Balagula and his family then emigrated to the United States, moving to Manhattan's Washington Heights in 1977. He told Robert Friedman that he saw how people live in the West, read about capitalism, and knew he could do well here. According to Friedman, Balagula studied English and worked for six months as a textile cutter for $3.50 an hour when he first arrived. Then he connected with Evsei Agron. In three years, Balagula did well enough to purchase the Odessa, a restaurant and cabaret on Brighton Beach Avenue. He also became Agron's financial advisor. In contrast to Agron, Balagula wanted to lead the Agron organization "into the upscale world of white-collar crime. His knowledge of global markets allowed him to make millions in the arcane world of commodities trading."[24] Balagula's greatest financial success was the gasoline-bootlegging scheme, where he reportedly made hundreds of millions of dollars. It is also alleged that it was Balagula who ordered the killing of Agron (his former mentor) in the dispute over Agron's role in the lucrative gas tax fraud.[25] He then became—along with other Russians, a Merrill Lynch employee, and colluding store owners—a party to the counterfeit credit-card scam described earlier. Balagula was caught and convicted of credit-card fraud in 1986. After his conviction, however, he managed to flee the United States, only to be returned two years later and given an eight-year sentence. In November 1992 and again in October 1994, he was convicted and sentenced to further prison time for evading federal taxes on gasoline.

As with Agron, Marat Balagula arrived in the United States already a thief and a black marketeer. Unlike Agron, however, Balagula, with his degrees and his experience, seemingly could have climbed high on the straight and narrow ladder of success. He chose not to do so. Instead, he used his skills to develop increasingly sophisticated schemes.

David Shuster is a smaller fry than either Agron or Balagula. A Ukrainian Jew, his profile is instructive and perhaps more typical of the run-of-the-mill scam artist who emigrates from Russia to the United States. Shuster was a witness for the government in the case of *United States v. Anthony Morelli et al.,* one of several federal court cases involving gasoline tax fraud. In direct examination by the prosecution, Shuster was asked about his life both before and after he immigrated to the United States. Forty-seven years old, and a graduate of a four-year technical college with a degree in construction engineering, Shuster said he became a pickpocket at age seventeen.[26] He had served two sentences totaling five years for criminal convictions in the USSR before immigrating. He came to the United States in 1980, settling in Ocean Park, Brooklyn. Asked by the prosecutor what he did for a living when he first arrived, he answered that he was a pickpocket specializing in stealing wallets. He concentrated his efforts in the wealthy areas of Manhattan and at JFK Airport.

Shuster also made a living by playing cards professionally at private clubs in Brooklyn. Asked whether these were legal card games, Shuster said: "For me it was legal. I understand by the law it's unlegal."[27] In addition, he played a middleman role in an international heroin transaction from which he made $40,000 and faced a gun charge. Ultimately, through connections with fellow immigrants from Ukraine, he got into the motor-fuel business, as he said, "by accident." Here again, however, his pursuit of the trucking and oil business consisted of tax evasion and smuggling. It was for this that he went to prison and became a cooperating witness.

As with both Agron and Balagula, David Shuster came from an urban environment; like Balagula he was well educated, and was seemingly well qualified to seek legitimate work in the United States. He could have operated his trucking and oil business legally but simply chose not to pursue these options. In short, Shuster may be the quintessential Russian immigrant who involves himself in crime in the United States—by disdaining the straight and narrow path and by exploiting his contacts and criminal experience to the fullest.

The Russian Imports

There was not much of a reason for concern about Russian immigrant crime in the 1980s. After all, the number of those involved (Agron, Balagula, Shuster, and others) was relatively small, and their crimes were localized. A handful of Russian gangsters—no matter how vicious or proficient they might be individually—would not have the critical mass and criminal sophistication to be even a major local threat in a place like New York City, much less a national or international one. The collapse of the Soviet Union at the end of 1991 changed this scenario dramatically, however. In the late 1980s and early 1990s, the flood gates were opened for people from all the former republics of the USSR to emigrate to the United States. For example, in 1992, 129,000 nonimmigrant (visitor) visas were issued to persons from Russia, Belarus, and Ukraine, compared to only 3,000 visitor visas issued to people from those areas in 1988.[28] Many of these visitors became the guests who never left—a fact that is supported by recent estimates that 30,000 illegal immigrants, many of whom entered as visitors, reside in Brighton Beach alone. Because of the suspected large number of illegal immigrants and the blurring of the distinction between Russians and those from other regions within the former Soviet Union, it is impossible to know the precise number of Russian-born people now living in the United States. Estimates of those coming here from any place in the Soviet Union put that figure at approximately 350,000, as compared to roughly 75,000 ten years earlier.[29]

The Russian population in the United States today is clearly many times larger than it was when the concerns about their crimes were first expressed in the news media. In addition, that growing population is concentrated in places like New York, Miami, and Philadelphia, and such concentrations provide the recruitment pool for criminal organizations. Historical patterns indicate that the growth of ethnic-based organized crime in any community is linked to the extent of recent migration into that community by ethnic groups having weak ties to the dominant political culture.[30]

Concluding that the Russian émigré crime problem was mainly caused by ex-Soviet gangsters who entered the country illegally ignored the possibility that other immigrants who were not criminals in the past could become involved in crime after they moved to the United States. Participation in criminal activities could, of course, occur as part of the crooked-ladder approach to upward mobility. It is also possible that law-breaking behavior that is taken seriously in the United States may be not serious in other countries. To some extent, some nominally illegal activities may even be thought of as normal behavior. In the Soviet Union, with its endemic corruption and frequent shortages in legal markets, manipulating the system through bribery and purchases in illegal markets was not considered outrageous behavior as long as it stayed within limits. To some extent, regardless of their own activities, everyone growing up in the Soviet Union had been affected by this. As a rabbi in Queens, New York, in the early 1980s said of Soviet émigrés:

> These émigrés are all—Jews and non-Jews—products of the Soviet system. They lie, they cheat, anything to get what they want, what they think they automatically deserve.[31]

Not all Soviet citizens or all émigrés fell into this category or engaged in these behaviors, but a substantial number did.

In *Homo Sovieticus,* Alexander Zinoviev (former Communist Party member, KGB collaborator, and member of the Soviet Academy of Sciences) offers a cynical and satirical portrait of this type of operator. *Homo sovieticus,* in his view, had to be flexible and behave as the situation demanded, without the restraints of personal conviction or moral principles:

> [Specimens of *Homo sovieticus*] are born, are educated and live in such conditions that it is . . . ridiculous to accuse them of immorality or to attribute moral virtues to them. . . .
> [*Homo sovieticus*] . . . is psychologically and intellectually plastic, supple and adaptive. Behaviour that is bad in itself is not experienced . . . as bad, inasmuch as it is experienced not on its own but merely as an element in a more complex whole . . . which doesn't appear bad as a complete entity.[32]

Some may dismiss this argument as little more than a rationalization of illicit behavior. Whatever the justifications and their merits, to become sovietized meant, as Zinoviev observes, to be "plastic, supple and adaptive." It meant having the ability to simultaneously say one thing, do another, and think a third.

The attributes and patterns of behavior Zinoviev associated with *Homo sovieticus* did not disappear with the disappearance of the USSR. "[The] Soviet Union is destroyed, but *Homo sovieticus* is alive" was the conclusion of Danguole Gaileviciute, who had first-hand experience of life in the former Soviet Union.[33] Born and raised in Lithuania, Gaileviciute worked there as a teacher and a journalist, ultimately going into business for herself. She describes these years as a time when cheating and betraying other people were the means of gaining a better life in Soviet Lithuania. To lie and to steal, she says, were "normal phenomena" for Soviet citizens because people stole from a government that was cheating them.

These patterns continued following the independence of Lithuania in 1991. Crime skyrocketed, but violence and theft were not the only threats. According to Gaileviciute, the crime that truly "demolished democracy and human rights and created depression among the people" was corruption. Contrary to the dreams and perhaps idealistic expectations of the vast majority of the people, she says, government in Lithuania became principally a means of gaining personal profit and legalizing crime. Bribery, she argues, "is like daily bread in the country. If you need something, you have to bribe." Those in power think only of their own needs, and "when they have a chance to get something, they take it." This atmosphere, she concludes, is continuing to foster a society where the strong exploit the weak and where each person "lives in fear and depression."

Similarly, Simis concludes that corruption was a "national phenomenon" in the Soviet Union. "But," he says—and this is the critically important distinction and implication we want to draw about this phenomenon—"this does not mean that the average Soviet citizen is immoral and inclines toward deceit. . . . The Soviet people are no better and no worse than others. *Homo sovieticus* is not immoral; he simply has two separate systems of morality."[34] One system was employed in private relations; the other in the public sphere in dealings with the government. This double standard, according to Simis, resulted from the alienation of the Soviet people from the Soviet government.

As is true within every country, the particular moral, social, and economic circumstances that characterized the USSR helped form all who grew up there. Because everyone lived under conditions where many moral compromises were made, distinctions between right and wrong were obscured—but also rationalized—by the need to do whatever was necessary to feed and clothe one's family. To counteract the unpredictability of the Soviet economy, Russians resorted to informal practices, such as bartering and deal making, to obtain what they needed and to do what they wanted. Their definitions of what is illegal, immoral, and corrupt thereby came to differ from Western definitions of these concepts.

Soviet children grew up steeped in black-market and gray-market or shadow-economy practices. Their parents bribed school administrators and teachers to gain their entrance into good schools and to win them high grades. These practices were seen to be normal and regular. As children and later as adults, they saw that their government was unable to provide people with the basic necessities but nevertheless lavishly rewarded high-ranking and loyal members of the ruling Communist Party.

The lesson they learned was that things could not be left to chance or to merit because meritorious claims usually were not recognized. You had to manipulate the system, or you and your family would suffer. Many commentators have discussed the general issue of Soviet citizens' tolerant attitudes toward illegal activity. A 1989 *World Affairs* article on crime in the Soviet Union concludes that there was "a broad and deeply engraved belief [in the Soviet Union], upon which a whole generation of young people has grown up—the belief that you cannot survive by honest labor."[35] A Russian journalist writing in the same issue despondently describes his fellow citizens:

"Virtually all of us steal. . . . In what other country do people steal automobile windshield wipers? . . . The concepts of honesty, nobility, and decency were no longer valued; they disappeared . . . from the society."[36] In his book *Public and Private Life of the Soviet People: Changing Values in Post-Stalin Russia,* Vladimir Shlapentokh also points to the low state of lawfulness among Soviet citizens: "In one way or another probably the majority of Soviet people end up as givers and takers of bribes each year. . . . Not surprisingly, when one feels forced to resort to illegal means to get the necessities of life, it breeds both cynicism and the conviction that a system that promises much, but delivers little—except for itself—is hypocritical."[37]

Russian economist Nikolai Shmelev describes a Soviet Union that in the 1980s was plagued by "massive apathy, indifference, theft, and disrespect for honest labor, together with aggressive envy toward those who earn more—even by honest methods." This outlook had, he believes, "led to the virtual physical degradation of a significant part of the people as a result of alcoholism and idleness. There is a lack of belief in the officially announced objectives and purposes, in the very possibility of a more rational organization of social and economic life."[38] Again, this observation emphasizes a disrespect for labor—sometimes combined with what Hedrick Smith called "the culture of envy—[a] corrosive animosity that took root under the czars in the deep-seated collectivism in Russian life and then was accentuated by Leninist ideology."[39]

Another important factor was a belief, reinforced by the Soviet system, that the "theft of state property, or its use for private profit, was not amoral or contrary to generally accepted norms."[40] This belief helped to blur the distinction between right and wrong and to furnish a rationalization for wrongdoing and was not purely a product of the Soviet experience. Among its roots was the centuries-old distinction between the personal property of peasants (the taking of which would be regarded as theft) and property belonging to the czar and the nobility (which was not so regarded). The latter property was considered to be fair game for the taking.[41] This belief simply carried over into the Soviet period with the state taking the role formerly occupied by the aristocracy.

Portraying in painful detail what he calls "the corrupted people," Simis says that the atmosphere of corruption bred in Russian minds the conviction that "everything can be attained by bribery."[42] The gap between the haves (the privileged few) and the have-nots (everyone else) "led to a pervasive determination to get hold of money by any means, whether legal and moral . . . or illegal and immoral."[43] *Homo sovieticus,* he argues, "instinctively responds to material deprivations, to lack of freedom, to the complete corruption of those who rule him, to the immorality of the regime by excluding everything connected with the state and the economics of the state from the sphere of moral values."[44] It is not hard to imagine that this double standard might be so ingrained in the consciousness of some who subsequently left the Soviet Union for a new life that they simply continued their old ways and saw anything having to do with the government as "fit for the taking." This may mean that we could expect some, and perhaps even many, Soviet émigrés to have few reservations about defrauding the government and government programs and mounting various scams and schemes against bureaucracies.

Corruption was "pervasive at all levels of the Soviet system."[45] However, it is important to understand that activities outside the legal economy took a variety of forms and involved different levels of involvement in illegal activities. For example, in Soviet Central Asia a second economy employing some 20 million people actively engaged in providing illegal services such as auto repair, apartment renovation, and minor construction jobs.[46] Such normal services were illegal because the state had monopoly control, and private entrepreneurship of this kind was prohibited. But these kinds of services were chronically unavailable (or available only on the payment of bribes) in the state-owned economy and thus were in great demand outside of it. The other side of the economic equation came from workers who could supplement their meager incomes by doing this work "off the books." Officially, they and those who hired them were all criminals.

Smith breaks down the "colored markets" in the USSR. The black market involved the distribution of illegal goods or services, such as prostitution; the distribution of items through illegal methods, such as stolen property; and the sale of items through illegal methods, such as selling items at higher than mandated prices.[47] The white market was the legal or state economy. Between these two extremes was a gray market in which Soviet citizens often felt it necessary to participate. This market was made up of the shadow economy and the second economy. The shadow economy was comprised of those activities deemed necessary by factory managers, farm directors, and others in similar positions to meet their production quotas. It operated outside official channels and contrary to the master plan. A farm manager, for example, might barter a portion of his crop production to a plant manager of a fertilizer factory for an unauthorized supply of fertilizer. The shadow economy included only activities done to cope with the demands of the planned economy.[48] The second economy, on the other hand, was made up of activities carried out by individuals for private gain. Carpenters, plumbers, electricians, and others doing work that was officially unauthorized operated this illegal economy.

These distinctions between markets are important for assessing the level of criminal involvement of the actors involved. It is also important to draw a distinction between the criminal involvement of the operators of the gray and black markets and that of the customers of these markets. The black marketeers were those most clearly and knowingly committing crimes. They either dealt in goods and services that were illegal, or offered legal commodities illegally. The black-market customers were akin to people who buy stolen goods from a fence, who buy drugs or sex, or who gamble. They know they are dealing with criminals but generally do not see themselves as doing anything wrong. The skilled workers and the teachers, lawyers, and other professionals who provided their services in the second economy either did not see themselves as criminals or rationalized what they were doing. They were, however, explicitly violating the law for the purpose of private gain. And the shadow-economy operators had to connive and scheme to meet their production quotas and their plan goals. The customers on the gray market—the second economy and the shadow economy—were not commonly regarded as criminals by themselves or anybody else.

The above distinctions suggest that it might be possible to rank the risk of criminal activity by émigrés based on which, if any, of these categories they fall into. At the top would be the professional criminals, including the *vory* (such as Agron). They would be followed by the black-market operators. Next would come practitioners in the second economy and then those in the shadow economy. At the bottom would be all the customers of these various markets.

Soviet citizens found ways to beat the system without getting caught. Actions such as bribing an official to do a favor, paying a premium to obtain desired goods, or buying from black marketeers were common practices accepted by the general population as necessary for survival. Clearly distinct from the crimes of the professional criminals, these crimes were regarded as necessary for survival and were a way of life for all Soviet citizens. Thus, as Rosner observes, "The immigration from the Soviet Union brought to America's shores many people for whom crime was but ordinary behavior."[49] This fact means that the pool of potential immigrant criminals is much, much larger than it might have first appeared.

Rosner distinguishes between "survivors" and "connivers." The former were "necessary" criminals who manipulated the system in order to survive. They did not consider themselves to be criminals, even though they regularly broke the law. The latter, on the other hand, were "real" criminals. It is the connivers who have been most frequently blamed as the originators of Russian crime in the United States, but it is critically important to understand that both types of immigrants know very well how to skirt bureaucracy and to adapt governmental services for private gain. Not all Russian immigrants came to the United States to commit crimes or became criminals after they arrived. Most did not and have not. But the possible crime problem cannot be considered to be limited to just exconvicts. Potential criminals are not readily identifiable by checking fingerprints to look up criminal records. While most immigrants may have indeed sought to shed what they learned in the USSR, others have seen even greater opportunities to put their skills at deception to work.

New Russians in America

Established Russian immigrants seem to feel that the "new" post-Soviet Russian immigrants are different. The newcomers are called everything from rude to morally bankrupt. They are said to have been lured to the United States only by VCRs, fancy cars, and the opportunity to make fast money.[50] One such person was a young entrepreneur named Andrei Kuznetsov.[51] While he was a student at Leningrad (now St. Petersburg) State University in the mid-1980s, Kuznetsov became involved in the black market. He traded rubles for dollars around the tourist hotels in Leningrad at a rate that was more favorable than the official exchange rate. In 1986 he was arrested for currency speculation with foreigners and was sent to prison for three years. After getting out of jail, Kuznetsov engineered an invitation to come to the United States in 1989. Using his contacts, he was given a job selling art at a plush gallery on Rodeo Drive in Beverly Hills.

According to Robert Cullen, who researched the case in both Russia and California, Kuznetsov then proceeded to "reinvent himself." Andrei Kuznetsov was neither a major career criminal like Evsei Agron nor even a small-time one like David Shuster. He was, instead, more like Marat Balagula—ambitious, educated, and talented. Like Balagula, his prospects for making it legitimately in America were excellent, and that, in fact, is what occurred—at least in the beginning.

Kuznetsov quickly began earning $5,000 to $15,000 a month in commissions at the art gallery. He was a good salesman with a rich clientele, and he himself had rich tastes. His lifestyle—flashy cars, glamorous women, extravagant flowers—soon outstripped his income. He began using customers' credit cards to make purchases and to pimp for expensive call girls. Eventually, he was caught and fired from the art gallery, but no criminal charges were filed against him.

Kuznetsov moved on to a new racket, devising a plan to take advantage of weaknesses in the system of personal check verification. When a customer presents a personal check to make a purchase at a store, a merchant or salesperson calls the bank to ensure that funds are sufficient to cover the check. Because the check can take several days to arrive at the bank and the bank may delay processing the check, a window of opportunity is available during which the same money can be used to write many checks for many purchases. And this is what Andrei Kuznetsov did.

He recruited shoppers—Russians from St. Petersburg—to visit California for a week or so and do the actual leg work for a share of the profits. According to Cullen's description:

> Once Andrei's operation was up and running, it worked simply. He usually had a couple of shoppers working for him in Los Angeles and two more in training. . . . promptly at 10 A.M., he, the shoppers and a driver would hit the streets in the Mercedes. Andrei would stay in the car and tell the shoppers precisely where to go and what to buy. They shopped steadily, all over Los Angeles, from the time the stores opened until they closed. . . . His shoppers' checking accounts had fake addresses and names, but they had money in them while the checks were being written. And Andrei never let them spend more in a single store visit than the account held. So, if a store manager telephoned the bank

to verify that the funds were on deposit, he would be told that they were. But by the time the checks were presented for payment, . . . he had withdrawn the money. And by the time the police started looking for the shoppers, they were back in Russia.[52]

Kuznetsov allegedly made some $50,000 a month from this scam and used the money to live life in the fast lane. He cruised the bar scene, entertained, and dated movie stars: "He spent his money as fast as he made it, living what a Leningrad boy might imagine to be the exotic and glamorous life of a Hollywood man-about-town."[53] But it all came to a crashing end in January 1992. This is how Detective William Pollard of the Los Angeles Police Department outlined that end in testimony at a U.S. Senate hearing:

In 1992, Los Angeles County Sheriff's Office deputies responded to a citizen's call concerning a car left running in a private driveway. When the deputies knocked on the door of the house in question, they were met by Sergei Ivanov, a Russian immigrant who was covered in blood. Upon checking the house for the source of the blood, they found two other Russian immigrants, Andrei Kuznetsov and Vladimir Litvinenko, murdered, execution-style. They also found a second Russian suspect, Alexander Nikolayev, pretending to be dead. The suspects were in the process of severing the tips of the victims' fingers in an effort to mask the identities of the victims. The suspects had also "gutted" the victims to recover the bullets which could be used against them as evidence.

When questioned, the suspects admitted to the murders but claimed they were victims themselves. They explained that the business of the two murder victims was to import Russian immigrants illegally and have them commit frauds with checks and credit cards. The two victims, according to Nikolayev and Ivanov, planned to hold their passports until sufficient merchandise accumulated through the frauds to repay the cost of their illegal immigration. The arrestees became tired of working for the deceased and committed the murder.[54]

Andrei Kuznetsov personifies the young criminal entrepreneurs who are now operating in both the former Soviet Union and the United States. They have the ability and the educational background to be successful in legitimate ways and to do so relatively quickly. But they also have the experience and, most important, an outlook on life that make it easy to bypass what is to them the hard and slow route to financial success. They want to run on the fast track instead.

Because of the nature of the society in which they were born, it is clear that today's Russians differ considerably from most other immigrants (both from other time periods and from other countries) in their ability to take advantage of either the legitimate or the crooked routes up the ladder of social mobility. Unlike the unskilled laborers and farmers who made up the bulk of earlier generations of Irish and Italian immigrants and their contemporaries, especially Chinese and Nigerians, the Russians are especially urban, well educated, and industrially and technologically capable. The Russians also have the distinct advantage of being less ethnically identifiable than the Asian, Nigerian, and Jamaican gangs. They can benefit from whatever ethnic and racial discrimination might govern the availability of criminal opportunities.

The Russians have not been closed off from the legitimate ladders of upward mobility the way other immigrants sometimes were. Despite their language barriers, they have marketable skills, and, indeed, most Russians have gone to work in the legal economy. In contrast to members of other immigrant groups who may have turned to crime partly out of frustration at being blocked from other avenues for advancement, it seems that for some Russians crime is a chosen career path. For some others, involvement in illegal activities, perhaps even while involved in legitimate work, may represent the continuation of types of behavior that were considered routine in their home country.

CHAPTER 5

THE RUSSIAN

CRIMINAL TRADITION

The Russian criminal tradition is the foundation for contemporary organized crime in Russia and has certain implications for Russian crime in the United States. Its principal components are what has been called the *Soviet mafia* and the crime bosses called the *vory v zakone,* variously translated as "thieves-in-law" or "thieves professing the code." Understanding the history and characteristics of this tradition, especially those aspects that are distinctive to Russia, will allow us to better explain current developments in Russia and Russian criminal émigrés in the United States. Because the transnational nature of current Russian organized crime has global implications, it is possible that some émigrés who are involved in crime in the United States may have previously been a part of the giant Soviet bureaucracy that included the Soviet mafia, and there is evidence that some have been *vory v zakone.* It therefore is important to understand both the historical and current traditions of Russian crime and how they relate to each other.

The state bureaucracy and the Communist Party of the Soviet Union employed millions of people, and what is referred to as the Soviet mafia existed within them. None of the numerous *nomenklatura* ("government officials"), *apparatchiks* ("party functionaries"), or officials of the KGB could have been untouched by the endemic crime and corruption involving the Soviet mafia. The Soviet mafia included the *avtoritety* ("thieves-in-authority"). Besides the official functionaries already mentioned, the *avtoritety* included the army of directors, managers, and supervisors of the far-flung Soviet command economy who ran the economic enterprises, such as collective farms, factories, and state stores. The entire conglomerate is sometimes referred to as gangster bureaucrats; Stephen Handelman calls these bureaucrats *comrade criminals.*[1] Some of those involved in the Soviet mafia became major actors in the current organized crime scene in post-Soviet Russia.

The *vory v zakone* and the class of professional criminals who made their living from crime and were often affiliated with *vory* make up the other criminal tradition continuing from the Soviet era. Soviet criminals such as Evsei Agron, described earlier, and, more recently, Vyacheslav Ivankov, profiled later in this chapter, are examples of the possible influence exercised by these crime bosses in the United States.

The criminal activities of the Soviet mafia developed into a familiar institutionalized crime pattern that was one of the main antecedents for Russians' acceptance of crime as a way of life. The *vory v zakone,* on the other hand, preceded the establishment of the Soviet Union and deliberately remained separate from it. As has been true for at least the last 100 years of Russian history, a symbiotic relationship existed between the underworld and the upperworld in Soviet Russia: the Soviet mafia engaged in a multitude of white-collar crimes, the *vorovskoy mir* ("thieves' world") was involved in all sorts of crimes of the non–white-collar variety, and the black market and the shadow economy intersected the two.

The Soviet Mafia

It is important to draw a distinction between the meaning of the term *mafia* as it is commonly understood in the West and as the term was employed in the Soviet Union (and is still used today in Russia). The Soviets used *mafia* to refer indiscriminately to (1) organized criminal groups, (2) clans that controlled politics and the economy in particular regions, (3) corrupt government employees, and (4) the Communist Party. All but the organized crime groups overlap with the *avtoritety.* Soviet citizens blamed an ambiguous mafia for the half-empty shelves and long lines at state stores, and for the lack of bed space in hospitals. They also used it to refer to diplomats who profited from their work abroad, to prostitutes, and even to butchers and chess players.[2] In the old Soviet Union, *mafia* referred not primarily to broad criminal conspiracies encompassing a variety of rackets but mostly to occupationally specific corruption. Thus, there was a fishing mafia, a fruit and vegetable mafia, a hotel mafia, a transportation mafia, and so on.[3] As a result, according to Sergei Avdienko, "such a meaning of the word MAFIA [sic] did not necessarily have to include in its meaning participation in criminal activities or persons or entities described by the word, and definitely differed entirely from the meaning of this word in the West."[4]

The term *mafia* was well known in the Soviet Union from movies and books. It was associated with organized criminality and included all sorts of organized violations, or perceived violations, of the law. *Mafia* became the catchall characterization for persons who controlled various goods and services of all kinds—when that control was exercised to the detriment of the consumer of those goods or services and to the personal or political benefit of those doing the controlling. Because there was so much of this kind of activity in so many areas, a multitude of mafias prospered. These were strictly self-interested kinds of mafias: groups of individuals, driven by the desire for economic advantage, manipulated the Soviet system to gain that advantage. These mafias were not like those in Sicily, which also were motivated by money and power but which controlled membership and rules and traditions. Because the Sicilian mafiosi provided quasi-governmental functions—such as protection, contract enforcement, and dispute mediation—they were viewed by many as being a positive force in the community. The Soviet mafia, however, was not associated with honor and respect and should not be confused with the real thing. Nevertheless, as Naylor points out, "It is astonishing how much confusion uncritical transplantation of a word or phrase from one context to another, alien one, can cause."[5]

History

In the early 1900s, at least some professional criminals in Russia plied their trade in close collaboration with the revolutionaries who comprised the fledgling Bolshevik movement. In fact, it was difficult at times to distinguish one from the other. The Bolsheviks encouraged and participated in pillaging and mob violence as means of destroying the regime of the czar,[6] and, like many revolutionary movements throughout history, they committed what the state defines as criminal (or terrorist) acts, including assassination and murder, and stealing, damaging, and destroying the property of the power they were seeking to overthrow. To finance their revolutionary movement, the Bolsheviks also organized armed robberies that were euphemistically called *expropriations.* After toppling the czar in 1917, the Bolsheviks opened the gates of the prisons, releasing political prisoners and criminals alike.

Perhaps even more important than the cooperation between revolutionaries and criminals was that the "historical legacy of bureaucratization and rampant official corruption was one of the most salient features of a system inherited by the Bolsheviks with their seizure and consolidation of power between 1917 and 1920."[7] While the Soviet regimes added their own peculiar character to this legacy and vastly increased both the bureaucratization and the corruption, "the roots of official corruption [extended] back into Russian history."

The Communist Party of the Soviet Union

The Soviet mafia also was the product of the powerful Communist Party of the Soviet Union, which exemplified especially well Lord Acton's maxim that power tends to corrupt and that absolute power corrupts absolutely.[8] Its power over Soviet society corrupted the Party so completely that the highest levels of organized crime in the USSR were actually white-collar occupational crimes committed by the *apparatchiki* and the *nomenklatura* throughout the ranks of the Party. Officials abused and exploited their positions for personal and political gain.

As a result of this abuse and exploitation, the real organized crime figures in the USSR were officials occupying key positions in the state bureaucracy.[9] The positions of these high-level (and sometimes not very high-level) bureaucrats enabled them to successfully conceal large-scale thefts and bribes by bribing others, by sharing their profits with those who otherwise might have blown the whistle, and by tampering with documents at their disposal. These functionaries could be accurately called "white collar gangsters."[10] Those crimes identified by the criminologists Barnes and Teeters as most motivated by that acquisitive urge—traditional organized crime, white-collar crime, and corruption—were all very much a part of the Communist Party's day-to-day operation.

An important basis for this bureaucratic crime was the state's dual system of administration in which Party figures supervised industrial managers, collective farm chairmen, educators, scientists, writers, and others. This duality was the origin of the *apparat.* Not only did it give the *nomenklatura* a right of appointment to all posts of importance in society,[11] but it also allowed the Communist Party to exist above the law. For example, Party members could have legal charges brought against them only with the permission of the relevant Party committee. People who were expelled from the Communist Party could have official charges brought against them, but no one could be simultaneously a Party member and a criminal defendant without Party approval.

Both Simis and Vaksberg have described how a system of tribute developed, especially in remote parts of the country. This system became a "characteristic and generally accepted form of corruption on the lower rungs of the ladder of the ruling class."[12] The tribute system had two features: district Communist Party leaders regularly received gifts from everyone dependent on them and also accepted bribes for performing particular actions: "And since all institutions and enterprises in the district [were] in such a position of dependence, the range of goods and services that might be offered [was] limited only by the possibilities of the district itself."[13]

This system of tribute produced the *avtoritety,* or comrade criminals. Only by committing theft, cheating the government and their customers, and falsifying accounts could officials and managers of state farms, collective farms, food stores, and restaurants bear the burden of the tribute system. This "permanent corruption of the ruling elite at the district level [gave] birth to a system of true organized crime."[14]

Because of the unique social, political, and economic characteristics of the Soviet Union, a distinctive form of organized crime thus evolved. Simis describes this form as follows:

> The criminal world of the districts include[d] store and restaurant managers and directors of state enterprises, institutions, and collective and state farms. They [were] all members of this ruling monopoly—the Communist party. . . .
>
> The second component in this system [was] also made up not of gangsters or mafia families but of members of the lowest ranks of the ruling party-*apparat,* and this [was] also highly typical of the system of organized crime in the Soviet Union.
>
> The final characteristic of the system [was] that the ruling district elite acted in the name of the party as racketeers and extortionists of tribute, and that it [was] the criminal world per se who must pay through the nose to the district *apparat.*[15]

The corruption and power of the Soviet mafia reached a zenith during the eighteen years of Leonid Brezhnev's reign as Soviet leader from 1964 to 1982. More than ever, those in power positions were "ignorant cynics" and "vulgarian self-seekers"[16] who had pushed out what remained of the pragmatists and functionaries who had at least attempted to make the bureaucracy work: "their places were taken exclusively by members of the new clan, namely the celebrants in the all-round and ongoing festival of plunder."[17] The best example of this was in the former Soviet Republic of Uzbekistan.

The Uzbek Mafia

Uzbekistan, in Soviet Central Asia, was the cotton-growing center of the Soviet Union. By means of a relatively simple bookkeeping device, the Uzbek version of the Soviet mafia reaped billions of rubles in embezzled profits. As with every product in the USSR, there were production quotas for cotton. Producers were paid for meeting their quotas and received bonuses for exceeding them. For years during the Brezhnev reign, the Uzbek mafia systematically inflated reports on cotton production by millions of tons. The profits from this nonexistent cotton went into the pockets of the cotton barons and their associates in the republic. These funds were "injected into shadowy black-market dealings, including the purchase and sale of official positions, which fostered universal corruption in the republic."[18] The profits amassed during this organized corruption were extraordinary. It began to unravel only when a relatively low-level criminal investigator was caught taking a bribe. When the KGB searched his home, they found diamonds, rubies, thousands of Swiss watches, a million rubles in cash, a mile-long length of gold brocade, and innumerable pairs of the ever-valuable blue jeans. And this was only a little fish!

It was not only in Uzbekistan itself that pockets were lined with cotton profits. Following the tribute system, shares were dutifully passed up the line all the way to Moscow. The Soviet leader's son-in-law, Yuri Churbanov, who was a deputy head of the Ministry of Internal Affairs, benefited, and ultimately Brezhnev himself benefited. Churbanov was convicted and sent to prison; Brezhnev died.

It is estimated that the Uzbek cotton affair involved altogether more than 30,000 people.[19] One of those people, Akhmadzhan Adylov—whom Vaksberg called the "Godfather" and the "very worst" and the absolutely most powerful figure in the Uzbek clan—is an excellent example of the power of the *avtoritety*. He was director of the Papskii cotton combine and one of Uzbekistan's top cotton barons.[20] He was also a deputy of the Supreme Soviet of the USSR, a member of the Central Committee of the Uzbek Communist Party, and a hero of socialist labor. Although he had no official administrative or political power, through the de facto power he assumed Adylov created his own small, sovereign state, over which he reigned:

> No one could enter his territory without permission; its borders were guarded by government militia, who were nominally under the jurisdiction of the Uzbek minister of interior [where Churbanov was deputy] . . . but who in fact were in the service—and pay—of Adylov. This miniature state had its own system of investigation, police control, and underground prison, which was used to confine and torture residents who demonstrated the slightest independence.[21]

He used the millions of rubles at his disposal to bribe the top officials in Uzbekistan and their superiors in Moscow. Adylov was arrested and sent to prison to await trial in 1984, when Moscow authorities (at the behest of former KGB chief Yuri Andropov, who had become Soviet leader) finally moved to investigate the Uzbek mafia.

When the Uzbek cotton scandal and political corruption were exposed in the mid-1980s, it was the biggest criminal case of its kind in the history of the Soviet Union. Because the case received enormous publicity, its repercussions reverberated far from its origins. The corruption at the core of the Communist Party of the Soviet Union was suddenly laid bare.

The Soviet Union has disappeared, but the Soviet mafia has not. As we show in the next chapter, many former Communist Party *apparatchiki,* KGB officials, *nomenklatura,* and *avtoritety* have adeptly changed hats. They have reinvented themselves as democrats, liberals, nationalists, and patriots. In Russia today, that old mafia is very much at the center of organized crime at the highest levels.

Vory v Zakone

The second major Russian criminal tradition is that of the *vory v zakone* or "thieves-in-law." The title *vor* or "thief" used in this context is potentially misleading to those not from the former Soviet Union. The persons to whom this label has been affixed are not petty thieves but are highly skilled specialists and craftsmen who make their living from crime and have their own subculture with strict rules for membership and elections, complex systems of tattoos, an extensive jargon, and customs of nicknames, gestures, songs, verses, and sayings. The *vory* are unique to the part of the world that was the Soviet Union and are most often from the former Soviet republics of Russia and Georgia. With less than 2 percent of the Soviet population, Georgia had more than 30 percent of the Soviet *vory* population.[22]

A *vor* is most simply defined as "a professional criminal and a repeat offender who is not engaged in any legal activity"[23]—a definition that could apply to numerous criminals in the United States as well. *Vor* is a title for which a criminal must be proposed and then elected by other *vory.* We were told by both Russian and Georgian experts that Georgians sometimes buy the title of *vory* and thus are not respected and treated as equals by the Russian *vory.* To be chosen, a criminal must have considerable leadership skills, personal power, intellect, and charisma. As one respondent told us, *vory* do not have much formal education, but they are smart and self-educated from all the reading they do in prison. Once a *vor* has undergone his coronation, as it is called, he must live according to a strict set of rules.

Violation of these rules can result in a trial by his fellow *vory* and even a death sentence.

History and Origins

Russian and other authorities who have studied the *vory v zakone* differ about when their history begins. During the seventeenth century and even earlier, Russia had large numbers of thieves and bandits, which were mostly of the common thief variety and had little organization and mutual cooperation. These thieves lacked the criminal sophistication, traditions, and organization that came to be associated with the later professional criminals and the criminal elite called *vory*.[24] Even at that time a symbiosis existed between politics and crime: "In a society where land and all who labored on it were the property of the czar, political resistance and criminal activity were nearly indistinguishable."[25] This trend of professional criminals being political revolutionaries and vice versa is one that has continued in Russian history.

During the eighteenth and nineteenth centuries, more organized and distinguishable criminal bands of thieves operated in droves across the expanse of Russia. But not until after the Bolshevik Revolution of 1917, especially beginning in the 1920s, did a professional underworld—a thieves' world (*vorovskoy mir*), including the *vory*—arise. This new professional criminal class was unknown in czarist Russia, and it was also unlike anything seen elsewhere in the world.[26] A multimillion-man army of thieves and armed gangs of bandits with their own laws, traditions, and slang ranged throughout the land. These professional criminals became responsible for the vast majority of crime in the Soviet Union, and their aristocracy were the *vory v zakone*.

According to Afanasyev and Gurov, well-organized criminal associations of *vory* really took shape in the 1930s. During that decade, when the Soviet dictator Joseph Stalin was in power, a vast prison camp system was constructed across the USSR and was the primary spawning ground for the *vory*. The criminal associations that developed were characterized by "complete submission to the laws of criminal life, including obligations to support the criminal ideal, and rejection of labor and political activities."[27]

In one of the few personal accounts of this underworld by a former member, Mikhail Dyomin describes how one was elevated to higher status in the thieves' world on the path to becoming a *vor*. The procedure of "elevation to the law" differs little from admission to the Communist Party:

> As a rule, it happens at a general meeting. The *patsan* [a young thief in a kind of probation status] being presented to the society gives a brief account of his life, listing every possible exploit, offering each accomplishment up to the collective judgment. If the thieves agree on a judgment and that judgment is good, one of the authoritative thieves—one of the members of the Central Committee, so to speak—rises and adjourns the convocation with the ritualistic phrase: "Look on him, thieves, and look well! Remember, the sentence isn't subject to appeal. We're all responsible for him now!"[28]

Tattoos are another important element of the subculture of the thieves' world. They serve both as a form of communication and as an element of bonding. In Russia, tattoos give material and psychological advantage to prison convicts—such that the inmate without tattoos is looked down on.[29] These tattoos are not, for example, generally worn by white-collar or political criminals, who in this as in other ways had low status in the gulag. Among the thieves, however, tattoos are a secret language, "understandable only to the initiated."[30] The *vory* usually have an eight-pointed star tattooed across their chests, just below the collarbone, indicating that they are a professional criminal. The same symbol tattooed on the kneecaps means they do not bow down to anyone or anything. This reflects their anarchical world-view.

The antigovernment philosophy is a critically important characteristic of the *vory*. According to Serio and Razinkin, the tradition began shortly after the Bolshevik Revolution when the enemies of the new Soviet state wanted to mount a political opposition to it and recruited into their ranks traditional professional criminals.[31] Among the laws adopted to govern this marriage of convenience were prohibitions on working or taking part in the work of society, on taking up arms on behalf of the state, and on cooperating with authorities as either a witness or victim.

That such rules may not have been first promulgated only after 1917, however, is hinted at in Solzhenitsyn's monumental expose of the Soviet gulag:

Their commune, more precisely their world, was a separate world within our world, and the strict laws which for centuries had existed in it for strengthening that world did not in any degree depend on our "suckers" legislation or even on the Party Congresses. They had their own laws of seniority, by which their ringleaders were not elected at all, yet when they entered a cell or a camp compound already wore their crown of power and were immediately recognized as chiefs. These ringleaders might have strong intellectual capacities, and always had a clear comprehension of the thieves' philosophy, as well as a sufficient number of murders and robberies behind them. The thieves had their own courts *(pravilki)*, founded on the code of thieves' "honor" and tradition. The sentences of the court were merciless and were executed implacably, even if the condemned person was quite out of reach and in a completely different camp compound. (The types of punishment inflicted were unusual; they might all jump in turn from the upper bunks onto a convicted person lying on the floor and thus break his rib cage.)

And what did their word *frayersky*—"of the suckers"—mean?

It meant what was universally human, what pertained to all normal people. And it was precisely this universally human world, our world, with morals, customs, and mutual relationships, which was most hateful to the thieves, most subject to their ridicule, counterpoised most sharply to their own antisocial, antipublic *kubla*—or clan.[32]

The term *frayer* is especially pertinent for us: it was used to refer to the straight world—all those honest, hard-working people who were viewed as victims to be taken advantage of.

Vory see themselves as very separate from ordinary criminals, whom they claim to despise. Asked what the relationship was between the *vory* and a thief who robs with a gun, one replied,

None whatsoever. Or rather, we despise them, and in jail, we make them clean our boots. Only juvenile delinquents and working stiffs on a drunk pull jobs like that. A regular thief is supposed to take money away by using his brains or the skill of his hands.[33]

This brief introduction to that criminal world demonstrates that, even before the Soviet mafia existed, there were already the beginnings of a unique brand of Russian organized crime—the thieves' world with the *vory* at its apex. A significant attribute of the *vory v zakone* is the *v zakone* part of their title, which is the transliteration of the Russian term for "in law." The *vory* are outlaws in the sense of the laws of the upperworld, but they are not without laws of their own.

The Law or Code

Because the thieves' world is isolated from the mainstream of society and rejects its obligations, it has developed its own laws to define the limits of that isolation and rejection.[34] As previously indicated, the thieves' code has provisions restricting cooperation in any way with the state:[35]

◆ The *vor* is expected to turn his back on his birth family and to have no family of his own except for the criminal community that is his family.[36]

◆ The *vor* is forbidden to work and must live only by criminal activity.

◆ The *vor* must give moral and material assistance to other thieves.

◆ The *vor* must recruit and teach his craft to the young.

◆ The *vor* must limit his drinking and gambling. Becoming drunk or being unable to pay gambling debts is prohibited.

◆ The *vor* must not become involved with the authorities, participate in social activities, or join social organizations.

◆ The *vor* must not take up weapons on behalf of the authorities or serve in the military.

◆ The *vor* must abide by and carry out punishments determined by the thieves' meeting (a combination dispute resolution and court forum).

◆ The *vor* must fulfill all promises made to other thieves.

One personal account of the importance of the *vory* comes from Yuri Brokhin's interview with a person he calls Zhora the Engineer, who, he says, is a celebrated professional pickpocket:

> But we do have a kind of organization in the sense that we help each other out and we have a certain code. . . .
>
> If we see a colleague getting caught or arrested, we try to stop it right there from getting any further. We'll use money, influence, whatever we can. Once somebody's on the inside, we'll try to spring him if we can. If there's a conflict between two of our people, one of them can call a meeting and we'll decide collectively who's right and who should be punished. In those cases, our decision is binding. But we have no "leaders."[37]

Zhora the Engineer explained that as early as the 1970s, the code's restrictions on working the black market, speculating, or becoming an underground businessman were outdated. Presciently, he said that regular thieves needed to revise the code because others were making millions in the shadow economy: "[W]e, the best organized and most respected class, we're left out in the cold. We keep the code religiously, instead of taking up some of these businesses ourselves and putting them under our control."[38] Two decades later, this is exactly what has taken place.

Fifteen years later, an interview whose subject was purported to be a "real lord of the thieves" appeared in the *Literary Gazette International* and stressed the importance of following the thieves' law and what would happen if he violated those laws:

> **A:** Get it on the ears, that's for sure.
> **Q:** What do you mean?
> **A:** It means what it says. A meeting of the brothers is convened, they take a deck of cards and hit you on the ears with it. Get out of here, they say. You ain't thief anymore.[39]

Kruzhilin, the interviewer, concluded that the thief's law is more illusory than real because it is widely violated, in part due to its dogmatic quality.

Activities

An important responsibility of a *vor* is maintaining a kind of insurance and benefits plan called the *obshchak*. Illegal funds from criminal activities, monies collected as fines for violating the thieves' code, and contributions that thieves are required to make to the *obshchak* are invested to protect the funds and help them to grow. A principal means for maintaining this fund is through investment in a variety of legal enterprises.

The *obshchak* is said to have several purposes.[40] The size of the fund lends authority and prestige to the *vor* and the thieves affiliated with him. In prison, the *obshchak* is used to bribe prison authorities and buy food, alcohol, and drugs for inmates from the *vor*'s criminal group. On the outside, it is used to bribe law enforcement and other public officials. The *vor* in the previous *Literary Gazette International* interview described the use of these funds:

Q: Whose money do you have, if it's not your own?
A: Community. It's like a pool. . . . I help people in labor camps—I buy them tea, butter, canned food, warm clothes, vodka, cannabis, pot. I have four camps to take care of, so I need plenty of dough.[41]

Funds also are used to plan and carry out new crimes and to provide financial assistance to the families of group members who are in prison. Monies from the *obshchak* that are used to help prisoners and their families are expected to be repaid. The main source of the repayment is, of course, further crime.

A second major activity of a *vor* is to recruit young new talent and teach them his criminal craft. The experts in Georgia and Russia whom we interviewed all agreed that this is an important activity. The *vory* are said to spend a lot of money and time on this recruitment, even sending representatives into the schools for this purpose. For now, the very high unemployment rate, the poor economic prospects, and the need for survival are believed to make this recruitment of the young very successful.

Georgian officials estimate that about 80 percent of the *vory* are no longer in Georgia but have moved to Moscow because that is where the most lucrative opportunities are. Despite this, Georgian youth—particularly those from the street culture—very much want to be or be like *vory*. The *vory* have a very romantic image, and they have money for cars, clothes, entertainment, and other desirable things.

The Georgian youth with whom we spoke ranged in age from fifteen to twenty-seven and included both young men and women. Most of them agreed that young boys in Georgia aspire to be *vory*, although some said that was more true during the Soviet period than it is now. It was then that more of the most powerful *vory* were still active in Tbilisi. They estimated that the proportion of those boys said to currently have such aspirations ranged from 20 to 60 percent. The main reason these boys are said to be attracted to the *vory* is because they have authority and command respect. A few young people believe that seeing American films has also stimulated a general attraction to become a mobster.

The Georgian young people described the current relationship between *vory* and youth in Tbilisi. There is, they said, a street culture of what are called "old boys" that operates on a neighborhood basis. Areas of the city are divided into territories that are controlled by groupings of these old boys. In each of these neighborhoods or territories, they operate a kind of black market. Among the old boys is a more criminally sophisticated group known as the "bad boys" who are said to be affiliated with *vory*. The bad boys victimize the other, weaker, street boys and run the black-market operations. The neighborhood *vor* (who may not be that much older than the boys and who may not be a true *vor* because he has merely bought the title) takes a cut off the top from all these operations. In return, he acts as a *krysha* or "roof" providing protection for the boys. The *vor* also acts to mediate disputes among the bad boys.

It is our impression that the important *vory* who were once active in Tbilisi have moved to Moscow. For several reasons—some of those who are left have bought the title, most are very young (only twenty or slightly older), and many have not paid their dues by going to prison (sometimes because they bought their way out)—we have concluded that the *vory* traditions are breaking down in Georgia.

Current Role in Russian Organized Crime

There is some disagreement in Moscow about how powerful the *vory v zakone* are on today's Russian organized crime scene. Some experts view them as the leaders of the criminal world sitting at the apex of a criminal pyramid. Others argue that the *vory* are the oldest and toughest of the various criminal associations now dominating Russian organized crime. After all, these experts point out, the *vory* survived in their seventy-five-year struggle with the KGB and, because they are the most criminally sophisticated, have monopoly control over the non–white-collar crime areas of criminal activity, especially extortion.

Other experts dismiss the *vory* as the smallest and most primitive part of Russian organized crime. According to this perspective, *vory* are mostly involved in street crimes, like robberies, thefts, and burglaries, and, because they have been unable to join those who commit more sophisticated crimes, are relatively rare at the top of organized crime in Russia. From this perspective, the highest level of organized crime is still dominated by the old *avtoritety* and Soviet mafia members.

Experts agree that Russian organized crime is controlled by many (one estimate is fifty) different criminal associations and that *vory* make up one or more of those associations. These criminal associations have divided the country into spheres of control and assigned various specialties to different associations. A criminal association not only commits crimes but provides social support for its membership, maintains criminal traditions, and arbitrates disputes. These are much like the functions of the *vory*. Each criminal association is made up of a variety of smaller criminal groups (of fifteen to thirty persons each) that have come together to increase their crime capacity and to gain security.

There are said to be approximately 400 *vory* currently operating in Russia, but as we have noted, not all of them are Russian, and they do not necessarily know one another. Rather than groupings of *vory* being defined by nationality, as was often the case in the past, they are now more likely to be organized by geographical area and crime specialty. This is part of a more general phenomenon in which business interests override ethnicity as a basis for membership and where some criminal groups and associations include people of different nationalities.

Those authorities who argue that the *vory* are major actors on the organized crime scene say they overcome any deficiencies they may have in formal education and business experience by hiring accountants, economists, lawyers, and others as consultants. By buying the talent they need, they become key players not just in Russia but also in global organized crime. According to this view, *vory* have bought factories, real estate, ships, publishing houses, and television stations in Russia. The *vory* have opposed investment by other countries in the rapidly expanding sphere of Russian business because they want to gain a major share of the privatization process.

The *vory* also have expanded their role in traditional crimes such as drug dealing and arms trafficking. A Russian journalist with extensive experience covering organized crime in the former Soviet Union told us that the world has been basically divided into spheres of influence and that different *vory* control different countries. One of the major domos among the *vory* is supposedly Vyacheslav Kirillovich Ivankov, who reportedly controlled criminal activities in ten countries. We conclude our look at the *vory v zakone* by profiling this man Ivankov, whose name and picture have been so prominent in media coverage of Russian organized crime in the United States.

Yaponchik

Vyacheslav Ivankov, nicknamed *Yaponchik* ("Little Japanese"), was, from shortly after his arrival in the United States in 1992 until his arrest by the FBI in 1995, a mysterious and even mythical figure. The speculations tossed around about him created an image of a man who was called "the father of extortion" and the Soviet Union's "most influential *vor.*"[42] He was the "leading crime boss of the Russian Far East" and was reported in the largest Russian language newspaper in New York City to be the "Red godfather" sent to New York by his fellow *vory* to organize and control Russian criminal activities there.[43] U.S. authorities, especially the Federal Bureau of Investigation, certainly seemed to believe and acted as if Ivankov were a major crime boss. Who is this man Ivankov, also known as Yaponchik? What was he doing here? And was he really the Russian crime boss? The Ivankov/Yaponchik case may be the quintessential illustration of how and why a mafia is created.

Background

Yaponchik was allegedly born in the Soviet Republic of Georgia and grew up in Moscow. He was a champion amateur wrestler in his youth who first went to jail after a bar fight in which (according to his Moscow lawyer) he was defending the honor of a woman.[44] After his release, he began his climb up the Soviet crime ladder—like so many others—by dealing stolen goods on the black market.

According to Russian law enforcement authorities, Yaponchik formed a criminal organization (called *Solntsevskaya*) in approximately 1980. Among its activities, this group used false police documents to search the homes of wealthy individuals and steal money and other valuables.[45] In 1982 Yaponchik was caught and convicted for robbery, possession of firearms, forgery, and drug trafficking. He was sentenced to fourteen years in prison and during his imprisonment (he served ten years) was supposedly initiated as a *vor v zakone.*

According to Yaponchik himself, his prison activities during this period antagonized the Russian Ministry of Internal Affairs, which subsequently conspired with the FBI against him.[46] In a 1995 interview with a Moscow correspondent, Yaponchik said that the

Ministry could not forgive his efforts to reform the Soviet prison system while he was locked up in Siberia—efforts that were in support of his lifelong resistance to communism. The FBI, he says, was taken in by the criminal authorities who run the criminal state that was Soviet Russia.

That Vyacheslav Ivankov might not be just any ordinary Russian criminal could be surmised from his supposed acquaintance with Yuri Churbanov, the Brezhnev son-in-law who was involved in the Uzbek cotton scandal.[47] His early release from prison in 1991 reportedly resulted from the intervention of a powerful politician and the bribery of a judge on the Russian Supreme Court.[48]

Activities in the United States

Yaponchik came to the United States in March 1992 with a regular business visa indicating he would be working in the movie industry. How was a man with a felony conviction, ten years in prison, and a reputation as one of the most powerful criminals in Russia able to so readily receive a visa to come to the United States? U.S. Immigration and Naturalization officials told us that immigration officials in Moscow were overwhelmed and had neither the time nor resources to investigate the criminal backgrounds of all visa applicants. U.S. officials had to depend on both inept and corrupt Russian authorities for this background information.

The real reason for Yaponchik's being here is open to some dispute. The Russian Ministry of Internal Affairs advised the FBI in January 1993 that Yaponchik had come to the United States to "manage and control ROC [Russian Organized Crime] activities in this country."[49] Handelman says, however, that his American police sources initially denied they had received any such warning.[50] Nonetheless, this advice was ultimately taken to heart by the FBI. Alexander Grant, news editor for *Novoye Russkoye Slovo,* told us in 1994 that Yaponchik was indeed the highest-ranking Russian criminal in the United States but that he was "not criminally active here."[51] Grant said that Yaponchik had to get out of Russia because "it became too dangerous for him there—dangerous because of the new criminal entrepreneurs who don't respect the likes of Yaponchik."

Whatever his original reason for coming, Yaponchik was indeed criminally active after he arrived in the United States, but, as with so much else about him, the scope of his criminal activity is open to controversy. One view is that "Ivankov's New York branch of the *Solntsevskaya* gang had about 100 members and was recognized on the street as the premier Russian crime group in Brooklyn" and, further, that Ivankov's was the strongest of the Russian organized crime groups in this country.[52] Similarly relying on FBI sources, Sterling concluded that "[m]uch as Lucky Luciano did with the American mafia sixty-odd years ago, Yaponchik is turning an assortment of unruly and loosely articulated Russian gangs on American soil into a modern, nationwide crime corporation."[53] If there is any evidence to support any such assessment, however, it is not apparent.

When he was arrested by the FBI in June 1995, Yaponchik was charged with supervising the extortion of several million dollars from an investment advisory firm run by two Russian businessmen. He and three codefendants were convicted of this extortion in July 1996. On the face of it, there was nothing particularly sophisticated about the crime. In fact, one is led to wonder why, if Yaponchik was indeed the boss of a large criminal organization and the most powerful Russian mobster in the United States, he was directly involved in arranging and negotiating with the extortion victims. Organized crime bosses are usually insulated from this sort of direct involvement. Further, it was alleged in the FBI's arrest complaint that the murder in Moscow of the father of one of the victims was part of the threat used to further the extortion. Yet in a telephone conversation dealing with this murder—a conversation that was a part of the arrest complaint—Ivankov, who was supposedly masterminding the scheme, seems ignorant of the murder. Finally, if Yaponchik were the new Lucky

Luciano, where were the other charges that one might expect could have been derived from his over two years of high-level criminal activity before the particular extortion began in November 1994?

Was Yaponchik a Russian Mafia Chieftain?

Ivankov is clearly a serious criminal. Information from Russian authorities, his prison experience, and even his tattoos all suggest that he is a *vor*. He probably is the toughest Russian criminal in the United States, but it is doubtful that he is or was the head of a major criminal organization or a mafia boss. There is no evidence that he attempted to gain monopoly control over any criminal activities or that he systematically used violence or corruption. On the basis of this single crime, it is difficult to assess the economic, physical, psychological, and societal harm caused by his offenses. The description of the crime itself, however, suggests that it was a rather blundering effort. Finally, returning to one of our mafia criteria of organizational capacity for harm, Yaponchik was said to have had only a loosely affiliated group of some ten people and not an extensive and sophisticated criminal organization.[54]

In the meantime, Yaponchik has been sentenced to U.S. federal prison for nine years and seven months. In a recent interview from prison, Yaponchik accuses the FBI of feeding the myth of a Russian Mafia to prove the usefulness of their Russian section.[55] They are, he says, "only tilting with windmills." According to Yaponchik, there is no myth about organized crime in Russia because everyone knows that "Russia is one uninterrupted criminal swamp." The criminals are in the Kremlin and the Duma (the legislature), and anyone who thinks that someone like him is the head of all these "bandits" is delirious.

CHAPTER 6
THE NEW RUSSIAN MOBS

I n this chapter we use the major themes developed earlier as a framework for examining the current state of organized crime in Russia itself. Guided by these themes, we look at the capacity for harm among today's Russian criminal groups and the types of harms they cause. We also look at their ethnic makeup and whether they are actually Russian. Then we consider whether it is appropriate to—as many do—call them a mafia. Beyond these more general concerns, we are also interested in the individual members of the new Russian mobs, but unfortunately, the information we have available tells us about groups and not about individuals. Nevertheless, we can look at the overall nature and harm of Russian organized crime with illustrative examples drawn from specific situations. One case example that we use to compare organized crime and crime that is organized is the crime of alien smuggling.

In the United States, little about organized crime can be learned by looking at the official statistics produced by the Department of Justice or other law enforcement agencies.[1] No figures on persons or criminal organizations arrested, prosecuted, or convicted of organized crime are published. At least at first glance, it appears that there are indeed official data about organized crime in Russia, but in reality, the situation is nearly the same as in the United States. For example, according to official reports of the Russian Ministry of Internal Affairs, 8,222 "criminal groups" or "organized criminal rings" having a total of 32,068 known members were uncovered by law enforcement agencies in Russia in 1995.[2] In 1991 (the first year of post-Soviet Russia) there were just 952 organized criminal rings and 14,997 members. Those rings with international connections—in Poland, Hungary, Germany, Italy, Israel, Canada, China, Japan, Afghanistan, and the United States—were said to have increased fivefold between 1991 and 1995. Beyond noting that the new figures are larger than the older ones, interpreting these data is more of a problem than it first appears. For example, the average size of the groups (approximately four persons) is relatively small, and the average group actually decreased in size substantially over the five years.

The official reports of a large number of quite small groups in Russia reflect in part the Russian penal code's broad definition of what constitutes an organized criminal group. As in the United States, there is no definition of organized crime in Russian law. The Russian penal code stipulates that an offense has been "committed by an organized group, if it has been committed by a stable group of persons who had previously united to commit one or more offenses."[3] This is a wide net and probably explains why nearly 40 percent of all persons convicted in Russia in 1995 were convicted of having committed crimes as group members.

The official Russian figures, and especially their use, have been widely criticized. Serio, for example, concludes that "the official number of organized crime groups operating in the Russian Federation as stated by the Ministry of Internal Affairs has been cited by both the mass media and researchers *ad nauseam,* shedding little light on the meaning of the figure."[4] Similarly, the Russian newspaper *Izvestia,* in one of a series of articles on crime in Russia, ponders the worth of this particular information:

> But how should we understand criminal groupings? There is an indicator—"the percentage of people who have committed group crimes." But what does this "percentage" tell us? Several youths rob a street stall and an armed gang robs a bank—both of these are "group crimes." . . . And can one really compare a criminal group from 1985 with the well-organized and well-equipped bandit formations of today?[5]

Of course, among the official figures some "real" organized crime groups may be hidden, but some criminal organizations probably do not appear in the data simply because they have not been exposed.

Groups of two, three, or four people are unlikely to be able to match large-scale criminal organizations in their ability to cause significant harm. Instead, these are often ad hoc groups that come together temporarily to commit particular crimes. In other cases, siblings or friends may decide to commit a crime together. Thus, it would be highly unlikely that such small groups would possess those characteristics—criminal sophistication, structure, self-identification, and reputation—associated with organized crime. In contrast, well-known organized crime networks such as those from Colombia, China, and Italy have memberships ranging from the hundreds to the thousands, and their size is one determinant of their ability to cause harm.

Another way to use official data is to look at statistics concerning offenses that are frequently associated with organized crime. These include banditry,[6] smuggling, firearms trafficking, prostitution, drug trafficking, and trafficking in pornography. As Table 6.1 shows, there have been enormous increases in such crimes between 1991 and 1995. The absence of details about these crimes does not permit us to judge their specific harmful effects nor whether and how well they might have been organized. Nor can we determine the involvement of known criminal groups in them.

In addition to the crimes enumerated in the table, Russian criminal organizations are also said to be heavily involved in extortion, kidnapping, bank fraud, counterfeiting, contract murders, and trafficking in strategic and dangerous materials.[7] Over 2 million economic crimes were reported in 1995, including a variety of credit and finance and currency schemes. One indicator of the growth of capitalism in this former communist state is that more than 500—300 in Moscow alone—pyramid schemes were being investigated in 1997.

Table 6.1 Number of Reported Offenses in Russia Characteristic of Organized
Criminal Activities, 1991 to 1995

	1991	1992	1993	1994	1995
Banditry	18	9	44	249	304
Smuggling	30	47	121	1,780	1,698
Violation of Russian Federation customs legislation (section adopted July 1, 1994)	N/A	N/A	N/A	577	1,700
Illegal bearing, acquisition, marketing, theft of firearms, munitions, and explosive materials	26,506	41,049	56,894	64,226	58,773
Keeping dens and promoting prostitution	268	248	527	1,580	1,756
Organization of or keeping dens to use drugs	181	270	494	703	733
Manufacturing or marketing of pornographic objects	62	108	147	450	845
Involving juveniles in criminal activities	935	13,221	17,962	20,794	24,823

Source: Adapted from Dolgova, "Organized Crime in Russia."

Pyramid schemes involve defrauding naive investors of their funds. Crimes associated with the vast privatization process have also been reported. As private interests take over more and more of what were previously state-owned industries and resources, enormous sums of money (estimates say upward of $100 billion) have disappeared or been diverted, allegedly into the pockets of organized crime figures and corrupt and criminal politicians. The oil, timber, iron, and coal industries, as well as the fur and precious metal and stone markets, have been especially lucrative targets. Many Russians, in fact, consider privatization to be little more than officially sanctioned robbery.

When we interviewed Professor Victor Luneev of the Russian Academy of Sciences in Moscow in May 1997, he argued that this latter type of economic crime is now the most highly developed form of organized crime in Russia. Russian treasure and capital goods—the natural resources and wealth of the country—are being stolen and exported abroad. He said that the thieves in authority—the old Soviet mafia—are the principal perpetrators of these crimes. During the Soviet era, these thieves used their positions of authority for illegal gain, and many of them remain well connected for continued illegal activity whether as state officials or as operators in the new private sector.

The Harm Capacity of Russian Organized Crime

One of the indicators of any criminal organization's capacity for causing harm is its degree of criminal sophistication. Criminal sophistication refers to the ability to carry out complex, high-stakes (high-risk and high-return) crimes. Marks of criminal sophistication include technical proficiency, political connections, crime duration, and geographical scope. Because of the vast unemployment and underemployment in their country, Russian criminal organizations now have access to a wide array of people with technical expertise. These include university-trained specialists such as chemists, managers, and economists, former KGB and police personnel, former members of the military, computer scientists, and a variety of other professionals. High-technology military weapons, state-of-the-art computers, automobiles, and communications equipment are also available to them.[8]

In 1995 the newspaper *Izvestia* reported a case that illustrates the sophistication of some of the economic crimes being committed by Russian criminal organizations that rely on technical experts. In this case, the arrangement was with a group of Moscow computer hackers:

The reported operation involved breaking into the computer system of an Austrian bank. Some $25,000 was invested over a six-month period during which the operation was being set up. Connections were established with personnel in the target banks both from which and to which the stolen money would be transferred. People in a Moscow telephone station were hired. A small apartment in Moscow was rented under a false name. This apartment housed the necessary computer equipment, including a small power generator that would ensure operation even in the event of a power failure. In addition to the main computer operator, there were 10 or 12 other operators engaged, since it was determined that one computer alone could not break into the target bank's computer system. Only the main operator, and a few others, knew the true objective of the operation. The actual break into the system was made not through the computer network, but via a telephone line, where detection was deemed to be much less likely. At a designated time, 13 computers simultaneously attempted the break into the bank's system, some going after the built-in detection systems and others flooding in fictitious bank transactions. The bank's computer was overwhelmed.

It was determined beforehand that if the break-in were to be detected, and the bank security officer contacted Moscow, the persons in the Moscow telephone station were to provide a wrong number and to warn the main operator to get out. Once in, the operator sent a money order (unfortunately the amount is not indicated) to the target bank, while the other computers jammed the system with numerous simultaneous transactions. The money was then transferred from one bank to another five or six times in order to cover their tracks, and then moved abroad for money laundering. A month later, the laundered money was transferred back to Russia.[9]

Banks have been a major target of Russian organized crime. These banks are an important cog in the privatization process that is itself the biggest target for exploitation by the more sophisticated of the Russian criminal organizations. Criminal groups invest their illicitly gained fortunes in the burgeoning private sector, especially in real estate and retail trade, as well as in commercial banking. It has been estimated that criminal organizations control some 50,000 companies and 40 percent of Russia's GNP.[10] As one Russian journalist pointed out: "In other countries, mafia activity is still limited to business that is either illegal or semi-legal, or that, in any case, does not affect the daily lives of the population. Our mafia penetrates all pores of business and trade."[11]

The larger and more successful criminal organizations also use their substantial resources to influence politics at the local, regional, and national levels. They may control deputies in the legislature who, in turn, influence or effectively block legislation that might be detrimental to their interests.[12] Vladimir Miljutenko, a Russian journalist, told us that representatives of criminal organizations lobby for their interests in the Duma (the Russian national legislature) and that some connected persons actually work in the Duma.[13] Besides conventional bribes and payoffs, the corruption of governmental officials includes making political donations, paying for expensive trips abroad, and providing loans on very favorable terms. According to American press accounts in November 1997, corruption may now also include the payment of book advances to highly placed officials in the Russian government. It is estimated that approximately half (roughly $7 billion) of the profits gained from the shadow economy by criminal organizations is being spent on corrupting officials and controlling economic and political institutions.[14]

The symbiotic relationship among business, crime, and politics in Russia means it is difficult to know where one begins and the others end. Many of the key players at the highest levels in the Russian hierarchy are involved in all three, and this is a central characteristic of Russian organized crime: it means that organized crime is much more sophisticated and powerful in Russia than it is almost anywhere else in the world.

How the important Russian criminal organizations are structured is subject to debate. Some observers describe what they call a mafia hierarchy with runners, lackeys, waiters, small-time speculators, and smugglers on the bottom; hooligans and hitmen who provide the muscle for the top-echelon criminals and businessmen in the middle; and chiefs who are either *vory v zakone* ("thieves-in-law") or *avtoritety* ("thieves in authority"), at the top.[15] Kreye says that the *avtoritety,* in particular, "combine the power of old-time party connections, government access to resources, and the strength of mafia enforcement."[16]

Azalia Dolgova, who has been one of the principal researchers of organized crime in Russia for many years, emphasizes the continuing dominance of the *vory v zakone.* She told us that they are one of the larger criminal associations in Russia that have the international links necessary to carry out the most complex and sophisticated crimes.[17] Sergei Advienko, a Russian investigator working for Interpol, offers a slightly different classification of these criminal groups.[18] He says there are local criminal groups essentially defined by their immediate districts or neighborhoods. Then there are other groups associated with particular leaders. The latter either disappear when something happens to that leader, or they too simply become associated with their particular neighborhoods. The third type is identified by ethnic origin, such as Azeri, Armenian, Georgian, Chechen, and Tatar. Because Russia (and even more so the Soviet Union before it) is made up of literally hundreds of ethnic groups, ethnic origin occupies a special place in defining organized crime in Russia.

Given this complex breakdown, there is clearly not one Russian organized crime monolith. Whether or not they use the label *mafia,* none of the experts we consulted believe there is only one Russian Mafia. What we see instead is a variety of criminal organizations that, in Phil Williams's words, are "highly diverse and fractured, with ethnic divisions, divisions based on territorial and sectoral control, and generational splits."[19] There is also general agreement among Russian and non-Russian specialists that there are actually only between thirty and fifty criminal organizations that are truly large and powerful, that have seriously penetrated the economic and business spheres, and that operate abroad as well as in Russia. Disagreement about whether they have overseas operations is the main reason for the difference of opinion about whether there are closer to thirty or closer to fifty such organizations.

Drawing on a variety of sources—local and international police, Interior Ministry officials, prosecutors, journalists, government officials, and businessmen—Guy Dunn examined the characteristics of what he believed were the thirty principal Russian criminal organizations.[20] Although concluding that there is no set structure among them, he found that there is commonly a leader who is well connected with government and business. Below him are various deputies, such as strategists, economic advisors, banking consultants, and counterintelligence specialists. Next in the hierarchy are the team leaders—for example, accountants, bankers, and extortionists—who generally are unemployed professionals who have been enticed into organized crime. At the bottom of Dunn's proposed hierarchy are the common criminals—smugglers, bodyguards, pimps, hitmen, and others.

Dunn says that there are really only six organizations or "gangs" in Moscow, and thirty in Russia as a whole, that wield power and satisfy all qualifications for being major criminal organizations.[21] Of the six based in Moscow, all three are comprised of ethnic groups from Chechnya. Dunn's sources estimated that the Chechen organizations have more than 1,500 members spread among their three different groups—the *Tsentralnaya,* the *Ostankinskaya,* and the *Avtomobilnaya.* These organizations have much of the character of the *vory v zakone* described in the previous chapter. For example, they share a single, very substantial *obshchak* ("pooled resources") that is used to pay lawyers, bribe officials, and support imprisoned members. They have links to the highest levels of the Moscow city and national governments. They are also connected with the former KGB and with other officials charged with investigating organized crime. Their international criminal operations include banking, trafficking in stolen cars, illegal oil deals, drug smuggling, and prostitution, and their scope extends into Germany, Austria, Britain, Poland, Turkey, Jordan, the Netherlands, the former Yugoslavia (especially Serbia), and Hungary. In Moscow, the Chechen criminal organizations control hotels, casinos, and restaurants and engage in counterfeiting, financial swindles, arms trafficking, kidnapping, smuggling and exporting raw materials, and extortion.

Their rivals for power are two major criminal organizations made up of ethnic Russians—*Solntsevskaya* and *Podolskaya*—which are in constant conflict with the Chechens. Both Russian groups allegedly have criminal operations in the United States. In fact, one of the leaders of *Solntsevskaya,* which has an estimated 4,000 members, is the Yaponchik mentioned in the previous chapter.[22]

The final major group described by Dunn is the Twenty-first Century Association, which is headed by a Georgian lawyer who was trained as a diplomat.[23] Besides extortion, kidnapping, prostitution, and other traditional organized crime activities, the Association is said to control some 100 companies (also including hotels, casinos, and restaurants) and to offer insurance, investment, banking, and pension services. The Association is also said to have criminal operations in the United States.

Besides these big six, the thirty or so other major organizations likewise have reputations for violence and intimidation and for controlling various spheres of criminal enterprise. Besides committing crimes, the organizations provide social support for their members, arbitrate disputes, and maintain their criminal traditions. As Williams points out, "conflict between different groups reflects the powerful bonding mechanisms within particular criminal organizations, bonding mechanisms that provide the basis for trust in a milieu without formal laws and rules. Ethnicity provides one such mechanism, as does territoriality, and the common experience found in . . . karate and sportsmen organizations."[24] We can readily see that all these groups share many characteristics with their American counterparts. That those characteristics are not peculiarly American suggests that they share a certain universality and transnational nature.

Harms

As we pointed out earlier, criminal organizations use violence and corruption to gain monopoly control over criminal markets. This violence, corruption, and monopoly control result in a variety of economic, physical, psychological, and societal harms. Each of the experts we interviewed in Moscow provided overwhelming evidence of the presence of such harms in Russia today. In addition to the massive political corruption that extends into the executive, legislative, and judicial branches and up and down the local, regional, and national governmental ladders, they described the interlocking nature of crime and business. Business decisions and contracts in many cases are made and enforced only with the intervention of criminal organizations.

The legal system and the judiciary appear to be unable to regulate contracts and are thus bypassed in favor of organized crime. This impotence results from a combination of corruption, coercion, and intimidation. The corruption undermines the struggling effort to build democratic institutions—institutions that require democratic foundations and values if they are to succeed—and is causing considerable harm to Russian society as a whole. One result is cynicism, a mockery of the rule of law, and calls from the average Russian, who is on the outside looking in, to get tough in enforcing law and order. Increased law and order is seen by many of the disillusioned as best achieved by a right-wing, authoritarian, military form of government. Much of the support for the rightist former General Alexander Lebed in the 1996 Russian presidential elections came from this source, and Lebed continues to be one of the more popular politicians in Russia today. Democracy itself is viewed by many as inappropriate or unworkable in Russia, at least under present conditions. Some of the most enlightened people we spoke with in Moscow believe that only a military government can govern under current circumstances.

The power of organized crime in the economic sphere is illustrated by the *avizo* ("letter of credit") scam run by one of the Chechen groups in the early 1990s.[25] Between 1992 and 1993, that particular group stole 36 billion rubles by forging letters of credit that were cashed in Moscow banks. Most of the money was transferred to banks in Switzerland, Austria, and Singapore. Among the people involved in the fraud were bank officials and at least one high-ranking law enforcement official. Ironically, when the Moscow banks that had been victimized were facing bankruptcy, they had to turn to the group that had victimized them to bail them out. In similar cases, such bail-outs have usually come at a high price. The bailed-out bank, or other business, must take on partners and surrender control to the criminal organization. Through arrangements such as these, as well as by outright extortion, criminal organizations have come to dominate much of the economy.

Criminal organizations have played a substantial role in creating the economic crisis in Russia. Dolgova gives us an inkling of this when she asks what it really means when the International Monetary Fund extends a badly needed $10.2 billion in credit to Russia on the condition that tariffs for the export of gas and oil will be abolished, when, according to the World Bank, about half of the $15 to $20 billion worth of gas and oil annually trafficked out of Russia is being smuggled by organized crime.[26] Given that $10 billion of the gas and oil money goes into the pockets of organized crime, the effect, she says, is the same as if the IMF simply gave the $10 billion directly to them.

Louise Shelley has argued that organized crime is replacing the former Soviet authoritarianism with its own brand of authoritarianism.[27] This new authoritarianism is clearly harmful in numerous ways. Russian criminal organizations intimidate journalists and scholars, acquire mass media outlets to circumscribe news coverage, undermine labor unions, and perpetuate violence that goes unprosecuted and unpunished. Shelley concludes that "post-Soviet organized crime groups intimidate individuals, promote violence, corrupt governmental structures, limit free markets, circumscribe expression and undermine the rule of law."[28]

Contract killings are perhaps the best example of the psychological and physical harm being caused by Russian organized crime. A lethal combination of readily available recruits (often unemployed former members of the military, security, or law enforcement) who are trained in killing, a plentiful supply of weapons (especially guns), lucrative targets, and a motive for murder have resulted in an explosion of murders for hire. The Russian news agency TASS reported in 1996 that the number of contract killings per year had reached 500. Hundreds of those murdered have been associated with organized crime. For example, the 289 contract killings that were reported by the Ministry of Internal Affairs in 1994 included seventy "gangster leaders" as victims.[29] Among the more notable in recent years was the murder of two of the most powerful personages in the Russian criminal world, the Georgian brothers Amiran and Otari Kvantrishvili. Their killings remain unsolved.

Killings have not been limited to gangsters, however. Public figures from a variety of fields—including politicians, legislators, law enforcement officials, entertainers, sports figures, journalists, entrepreneurs, and especially bankers—have all been murdered. Among the 289 murdered people cited above were thirty-five businessmen and ten government officials. The possible motives behind these killings vary. While conflicts over power and turf probably explain the hits on mobsters, some of the government and law enforcement officials may have become too threatening to organized crime interests. The same could be said for journalists, since often those exposing crime and corruption have been killed.

It is likely that the businessmen and celebrities were in most cases killed because they resisted being extorted. Professional hockey players who have left the former Soviet Union to play in Canada and the United States have (along with their families) been the special targets of extortion that threatens murder.

Last, but certainly not least, are the murders of ordinary citizens. One chilling example involved Yuri, one of the leaders of a Moscow criminal group specializing in the privatization of real estate:

> Yuri's people approach elderly apartment dwellers and offer them a kind of life insurance. They promise to take care of them, cook food, nurse them if they're ill, with the single condition that the insurance buyer leave them the rights to the apartment when they pass away. The elders sign up. The next day they are dead.[30]

Besides this killing of pensioners for their apartments, there have also been murders of elderly persons after they were observed receiving visitors from Europe or the United States—often in the belief that the visitors probably gave them valuable gifts or money.

Ethnicity in Russian Organized Crime

Some observers report that each ethnic criminal group in Russia has its own criminal specialties. "Chechens . . . are engaged in illegal export of petroleum and petroleum products and rare metals, banking operations, and car deals (stolen cars). Azerbaijani groups are involved in drugs, gambling, and trade; Armenians engage in robbery and auto theft, extortion, and bribery. Georgians specialize in apartment burglaries, hold-ups and robberies, and hostage-taking."[31] The journalist Miljutenko gave us a slightly different take on the specialties. He told us that Chechen groups control gasoline and that Armenian groups control gold and jewelry markets. These specializations appear to be subject to change as groups move in and out and first one and then another is ascendant. Miljutenko added, however, that ethnicity is now less important as a defining element than are business interests. He said many criminal groups have a mixture of members from different nationalities. Two vice ministers of the Georgian Ministry of State Security (formerly the KGB)—with whom we spoke in

Tbilisi in April 1997—also downplayed the role of ethnicity, saying that organized crime is now set up according to business interests and not nationality.

Other observers, however, continue to emphasize the ethnic dimensions of Russian organized crime.[32] According to Dolgova, ethnicity plays a clear role in defining the memberships of specific criminal organizations. Likewise, Miljutenko says there is still an advantage to ethnic exclusivity: criminal organizations can use their ethnic identity and separate language to protect themselves from infiltration by local law enforcement. In the *Izvestia* article referred to earlier, it was pointed out that among the officially reported criminal groups, there were some 600 constituted on an ethnic basis.[33] Since this figure and much of *Izvestia*'s other information about the ethnic character of Russian crime come from the Ministry of Internal Affairs, we must be cautious in interpreting it. Nevertheless, it is the best information now available.

Just as some Americans strongly associate crime and black people, Russians often link crime to people from the Transcauceses. As in the United States and in other countries with significant minority populations, it is difficult to sort out how much of the disproportionately high involvement in crime by these peoples is real and how much is a result of biased government and law enforcement policies and practices. *Izvestia* reported that more than half of the criminal groups identified in Russia were made up of peoples from the Transcaucasian and Caucasian regions in or bordering southwestern Russia. Besides Chechnya (home of the Chechens), this area includes Dagestan, Ingushetia, Azerbaijan, Armenia, and Georgia. Before 1991, the first three were part of the Russian Federation, as they are now; Armenia, Azerbaijan, and Georgia were separate Soviet republics that are now independent countries. Ironically for Americans, these peoples are all referred to as "black people" by ethnic Russians. They have historically been subjected to repressive measures, including deportation from one area to another, sometimes thousands of miles away. In the case of the Chechens, there was a massive relocation to Central Asia by Stalin during World War II.

The Chechen gangs have the most intimidating reputations of any of the criminal organizations in the former Soviet Union[34] and are believed to be very violent. Like La Cosa Nostra in the United States, they are viewed as the elite of the Russian criminal world. The Chechens, a Muslim people living in the Caucasus region of the Russian Federation (in Chechnya), entered into a military struggle for independence from Russia in the mid-1990s. The Russian military's invasion of Chechnya at that time was said to be necessary to subdue a "criminal state" that was dominated by organized criminal gangs and that was the source of organized crime being exported into Moscow and elsewhere. In similar fashion to the American stereotype of Italians as being part of La Cosa Nostra or the mafia, the well-established criminal reputation of the Chechens, which is believed by a broad spectrum of Russians, is exploited by the state for its own ends.

The ethnic dimension of organized crime in Russia seems to arise mostly from its importance as a basis for creating bonds among members and not from any link to organized crime as a crooked ladder of social mobility for migrants. Groups from the ethnic minorities mentioned above have always fiercely maintained their independence from Russia and the Russians, in words and ideas if not in fact. This may be especially so for the Chechens. As subjugated peoples, they have seen themselves as freedom fighters, as their military engagement with Russia indicates. This kind of sharing of the experience of victimization—along with family ties, language, customs, and roots, and the moral rationale of resisting against an unjust government—cements very strong ethnic ties. For some, this resistance may even provide a rationale for engaging in criminal activity inside enemy territory—Moscow—where, not incidentally, the best pickings also can be found. This type of ethnic identification is most obvious with respect to the Chechens, who usually explicitly limit network membership to ethnic Chechens. With their strict hierarchical arrangements and strong clanlike relationships, these groups most closely resemble the Sicilian mafia.

Is There a Russian Mafia?

The question of whether there is a Russian Mafia or mafias in the former Soviet Union is a thorny one because of disagreement about the applicability of the *mafia* label to accurately describe the present situation in Russia. Some (mostly Russians) challenge its accuracy and claim that its promiscuous use gives a misleading picture of events there. As has been the case in the United States, they argue that the mass media, usually with the collusion of law enforcement, has appropriated the term *mafia* as a catchall term for organized crime in Russia. For example, Avdienko called the *mafia* label a "popular bugbear, used [by sensation-seeking journalists] to inflame public opinion in Western countries."[35] A similar view was expressed by those we interviewed in Moscow. Dolgova said "the mafia term is applied by journalists and publicists, and it does not mean the same thing [in Russia] as in Sicily and Italy." Even though he is a journalist himself, Miljutenko agreed that the "mafia image" had been created by the mass media. It is, he said, only an artificial, journalistic term.

Going beyond the media hype issue, Patricia Rawlinson—who is one of the relatively few Western scholars to do a recent study of Russian organized crime—concluded that "the term 'mafia' is inappropriate for the activities of Russian criminal groups." She says that "organized crime in Russia does not have the strict codes observed in the more traditional forms of mafia groups."[36] She adds the further distinction that Russian organized crime has less structure than, for example, organized crime in Italy and has more turnover at the bottom of the crime pyramid.

Others who criticize the *mafia* label share the view that *Russian Mafia* is clearly a misnomer because, they say, organized crime in Russia is not even predominantly Russian. They ask how it can be considered Russian when it is mostly being committed by Armenians, Belorussians, Jews, Georgians, Ukrainians, and others who are not ethnic Russians. Miljutenko said it is called *Russian* because of its location in Russia and especially in Moscow. The more accurate term, he said, should be *Eurasian organized crime.*

The *Russian* label does seem to us to be inaccurate, since many of the people who engage in organized crime in the former Soviet Union are not ethnic Russians. They speak Russian and come from regions that have in many instances been dominated by Russia for generations, but they do not regard themselves nor do Russians regard them as Russians. We do not want to make too much of this point, however. Americans use *Russian* to refer generically to all peoples from the former Soviet Union, and Russians do not particularly object when this designation is used in a positive sense.

The accuracy of the term *mafia,* on the other hand, is more problematic. If we broaden and redefine the term to lift it from its uniquely Sicilian origins and character, as we proposed doing in Chapter 2, then it may indeed apply. Unlike Rawlinson, we think the presence of codes and structure by themselves is a too limited way of assessing either what is organized crime or what is mafia. Formal structure is only one of the dimensions for determining the harm capacity of a criminal organization. It makes far more sense to define organized crime in terms of what it does—its functions and its capacity for harm—than simply to focus on structure and structural accouterments. We take that approach to the question of whether there is a mafia in Russia.

The character of a criminal organization is governed by the social context in which it operates. That context, in turn, is fixed by the demand for goods and services, by the actions of law enforcement, by the availability of recruits (and the ability to attract them), and by the nature and extent of competition from other criminal organizations. Like us, Albini et al. conclude that the social conditions of a country either foster or stifle the development of a mafia. Starting from the premise that a mafia is not a monolithic secret crime society but rather "a method or modus operandi of a criminal endeavor" that "can exist anywhere," they conclude that current social conditions in Russia are indeed fostering such development.[37]

The Russian social context is marked by weak and corrupted government, in general, and law enforcement, in particular. The legal system, for example, is both unable and unwilling to enforce the contracts that business and commerce require to operate. In a vacuum of legal authority, contractors are forced to turn to outside parties to enforce contracts and resolve disputes. Those outside parties must have authority, credibility, and respect to carry out that task. Certain criminal organizations can fill this role well. That reality is one of the factors accounting for the intimate relationship among crime, business, and government in Russia. It is important to note, however, that not all criminal organizations in Russia are able to supply this protection for market transactions. In fact, Varese estimates less than one in five can exploit the opportunity to play this quasi-governmental role.[38] If his estimate is correct, that means roughly 1,600 of the estimated more than 8,000 criminal groups could possibly qualify as being mafias. Whatever else this large number means, it further suggests that Russia is not dominated by a single mafia—or single other criminal organization, for that matter.

The principal service that criminal organizations provide in Moscow and other Russian cities is protection. The mafias perform a necessary function in a fledgling market economy that lacks regulation and legal enforcement, and they do so in response to requests for assistance from businessmen. It is important to emphasize that the service of providing protection is a commodity. It is not extortion, although that is certainly also present and may involve some of the same criminal organizations. Extortion, in contrast, involves coercion and threats. And it is the commodity of protection that distinguishes mafias from other criminals and criminal organizations.[39]

One form this protection service takes in Russia is what is

known as a *krysha* or "roof." To get a sense of how this *krysha* system works, we have the following description from a Russian criminal who testified during U.S. Senate hearings on Russian organized crime in the United States on May 15, 1996:

> To understand Russian organized crime in this country [the United States], you must first appreciate the situation in Russia. . . . there are two things you must do to operate a business successfully in Moscow. First, you must pay the right government officials under the table. . . .
>
> The second thing you must do to run a successful business is purchase a *krisha,* literally "roof" in Russian, which has come to mean protection. The more important you are, the higher the roof must be. In Moscow, organized crime provides the roof.[40]

The *kryshas* are reputed to play major roles in economic crimes. They move into legitimate businesses in what one respondent described to us as a kind of complementary president of the firm they are protecting. In this role, they provide protection to keep the firm from being infiltrated by other criminals. There is often a thin line here between being invited into a business and forcing one's way in. Voronin offered this distinction: "[Russian] street thugs . . . are basically low-level muscle who extort payoffs for 'protection' to small businesses. The far more profitable level, known as the 'roof,' is peopled by traditional crime bosses, along with some of Russia's emerging entrepreneurs. . . . Businesses that deal with these groups are brought under the 'roof' . . . [and] protection is provided."[41] This protection, and sometimes other services, do not come cheap, costing between 30 and 70 percent of profits. Since an estimated 80 percent of commercial enterprises are buying protection from *kryshas,* the mafias have a lucrative business.

There is no single overarching entity that can be called the *Russian Mafia.* Most criminal organizations are not mafias, and they are neither exclusively nor even mainly Russian or monolithic. There are, however, in a very narrow sense, some mafias in Russia, and some of them are composed of Russians.

Attitudes Toward Legitimate Activities

Because it lacks detailed information from individuals, the empirical evidence on the influence of attitudes about legal economic activities and violations of the law in the new Russia and among the new Russian mobsters is thin. We need biographical sketches, memoirs, and in-depth interviews of people involved in crime. There is, however, some general evidence that at least aspects of a criminal worldview are prevalent in Russia. A survey of young people in Russia, conducted by Igor Ilynsky and his colleagues in 1992 to 1993, examined the attitudes of these youth toward work. Their finding is that work had, for most youth, "lost its meaning as a means of self-assertion and self-realisation."[42] Ilynsky concludes that Russian society

> has a younger generation which wants to live well and possess everything, but which has neither the desire, nor the ability, to work intensively, honestly and diligently. . . . Many young people do not associate material prosperity with work; what is more, they are prepared to break the law for the sake of money. For the absolute majority of the young, work is meaningless and does not represent a natural component of life. Work is mostly viewed as a necessary evil, a forced action.[43]

A 1993 survey of juvenile delinquents in a labor colony (a correctional facility) produced comparable results.[44] It found that a "large number of juveniles . . . think that any labor is burdensome and that one can make a living without working. In the case of most of the respondents, labor does not meet their vital interests, and it is not necessary if there is some other way to make a living."[45] The attitudes reflected in these surveys are neither unusual nor unique to Russia. Nor do we claim that they are representative of all Russian youth. We do, however, believe they show that the necessary conditions exist for the recruitment of some Russian youth into organized crime.

Less scientific, but also revealing, is an examination of scams in Russia reported in the *New York Times* for March 17, 1994. The conclusion of the investigation was that Russia had become a "breeding ground for flim-flam artists" and for "a new breed of hucksters" that had its origins in the shadow economy and the black market of the Soviet era.[46] Ranging from multimillion dollar deals to run-of-the-mill frauds, the Russian scams include fake lotteries, phony investment schemes, fake companies selling nonexistent services, and the "sale" of apartments that are not, in fact, for sale. While a talent for swindling is also not unique to Russian criminals, what seems to be a relatively high incidence of such schemes—all of which represent ways to get money fast without working very hard for both perpetrators and victims—may indicate that this view of the world is widespread among contemporary Russians and others from the former Soviet Union.

Organized Crime and the International Migration of Persons from the Former Soviet Union

People who live outside the territory of the former Soviet Union have a great concern that organized crime there will spread over their own borders. One type of international criminal activity in which organized crime in general has been engaged is alien smuggling. Alien smuggling entails moving people illegally across international borders. Because of its transnational nature and because it has become a profitable venture for a variety of organized criminal groups, we believe it is of interest to see whether there is a Russian connection.

Although most of the focus in this area has been on the smuggling of Mexicans and Chinese into the United States, the practice is actually prevalent across a range of ethnic groups. People from the former Soviet Union have been suspected of participating in several types of alien smuggling, although these suspicions have not always been supported by strong evidence. An example is trafficking in children for adoption or for body parts. The criminal investigator from Belarus who was assigned to the Tri-state Joint Soviet Émigré Organized Crime Project was asked by his superiors in Minsk to investigate allegations that Russian children were being adopted and brought to the United States to be used for body parts. Those allegations proved to be unfounded. For other forms of alien smuggling, however, the evidence is stronger.

Smuggling of Migrants from Other Countries

Since the demise of the USSR, Moscow has become a central distribution point for migrants from a variety of countries seeking to illegally enter Western Europe and the United States.[47] It is estimated that between 200,000 and 300,000 Africans, Afghans, Kurds, Somalis, Iraqis, Chinese, and other Asians are living in Moscow on any given day and waiting to be smuggled to other countries. Some Russian migrant smugglers act as middlemen in collaboration with smugglers from other countries, such as China. In other instances, however, smugglers from the different countries—most notably China—operate their Moscow pipelines themselves and use Russian criminals in only minor roles.

Illegal immigrants, from whatever country of origin, need forged paperwork (such as passports, birth certificates, visas, and airline tickets) of sufficiently high quality to successfully migrate. According to the International Organization for Migration, "the illicit trade in fraudulent documents feeds from organized migrant trafficking. Stealing, forging and altering travel documents and work and residence permits has become a major criminal activity as the ability to migrate largely depends on possessing the necessary documents."[48] The production of such documents is the specialty of many Russian criminals. Given the vast experience of Russian citizens with circumventing the old Soviet bureaucracy, many potential criminals are highly skilled in producing a variety of types of documentation. On the international scene, false documentation is created by using either stolen passports or blank passports provided by corrupt officials.[49] This problem is exemplified in Moscow, where according to the Immigration and Naturalization Service, 100,000 new Russian passports were "lost" in the early 1990s.

Smuggling Illegal Immigrants from the Former USSR

A second type of alien smuggling moves persons from the countries of the former Soviet Union to establish legal residence in Europe, Israel, or the United States. Israel reports an increase in the use of forged documents both to acquire immigrant rights and to carry out crimes.[50] According to Israeli authorities, the procedure for documenting potential migrants and issuing of visas and other permits in Moscow is poorly controlled, and an industry operates out of Moscow producing false documents certifying Jewishness. A major form of visa fraud involving Russians in the United States is the establishment of false companies that are then used as a basis for inviting "coworkers" into the country. Commonly, "Russians pay 'firms' to 'transfer' them to the United States. In a related scheme, bogus companies established in the United States sell 'business invitations' to migrants in Russia. Once in the United States, these companies may help the migrant regularize his or her status."[51]

In the United States, the Immigration and Naturalization Service told us that there are increasing indications of illegal migration from the former Soviet Union into the United States. So far, however, only twenty-seven illegal immigrants from what is officially called the Confederation of Independent States (the confederation of many of the former Soviet republics that was formed after the demise of the USSR in 1991) were processed by the INS in 1992 to 1993 and only thirty-six in 1995 to 1996. According to the INS, these migrants usually arrive by air, often through Seattle, Washington.

Migrants are often induced to leave home under false promises and are at times forced into crime to pay their debt. In the United States, female illegal immigrants from the former Soviet Union have been put to work as prostitutes, bar girls, go-go dancers in peep shows, and, in one known instance involving women from Estonia, as nannies. The situation in Israel is similar, where women are put to work in massage parlors, for example. Males are also exploited, often forced to act as drug couriers and small-time extortionists. In all these cases, the migrants are forced to pay back the costs incurred in bringing them into the country.

In each of these first two types of Russian participation in alien smuggling, the smuggling of people is simply another money-making venture for entrepreneurs who have turned to crime and for professional criminals. These are examples of the crimes of deception at which certain Russian criminals are so skilled. Smuggling people and smuggling consumer goods and raw materials are similar, and some of the same people are involved in smuggling both goods and people. The Russian traffickers are given money by would-be emigrants, and then, depending on their level of sophistication and the continuity of their organizational structure, they may use this money in other criminal ventures.

Smuggling Criminals

The last form of alien smuggling involves exporting known criminals, ranging from prostitutes to hitmen, out of the former Soviet Union by using refugee status as a cover for criminal activity. Some of these criminals are assassins, and others are fugitives from justice in Russia who are sent out of the country to "cool off." Others are so-called *Tyazhiki* or "shadow people," who are undocumented residents of former Soviet republics and are hired as enforcers to travel throughout the United States and Europe to commit violent acts, including murder.[52] The Immigration and Naturalization Service told us that leaders in Russian organized crime sometimes "piggyback" on aliens being smuggled in to insert criminals into the United States.

Historically, prostitution has been one of the illegal services provided by organized crime in the West, and alien smuggling from Russia has especially become linked to prostitution. In fact, prostitution of Russian women who are illegal immigrants has become one of the main criminal exports from Russia to the rest of the world: "Organized prostitution by post-Soviet criminals has become an export commodity to foreign countries mainly since 1990. It has reached epidemic proportions as post-Soviet and East European prostitution rings develop in far-flung areas of the globe. Russian, Polish and Ukrainian women, for example, have been turning up in many of the countries of Eastern Europe, Germany, Austria, the former Yugoslavia, Israel, Greece, the United States, China, Turkey, Belgium, the Netherlands, Finland, Sweden, Italy, South Africa, Thailand, Hong Kong, Korea and Cyprus."[53]

Prostitution from Russia figures into the issue of alien smuggling in a number of ways. For example, in 1995 Greek authorities arrested a number of Greek policemen who were masterminding foreign call-girl trafficking rings in their country. Scores of Russian and Eastern European women were enticed to come to Greece with promises of wealth and a better life. Once there, their passports were confiscated and sold to nightclub owners, and the women became virtual prisoners and were forced to prostitute themselves. In Israel, it is estimated that approximately 2,500 Russian prostitutes, along with a variety of other criminals, have been smuggled into that country. In the case of the prostitutes, some go willingly, and others are coerced.

Russian Organized Crime and Alien Smuggling

Clearly, some evidence is available of alien smuggling from Russia to other countries, including the United States. Although such activities need to be organized—because they require coordination of complex activities, cover long distances, and involve many people—they do not appear to be a form or activity of organized crime. In the extensive four-year investigation carried out in collaboration with the Tri-state Joint Soviet Émigré Organized Crime Project, not one case of alien smuggling in the New York, New Jersey, or Pennsylvania area was uncovered. Criminal investigators learned that Russian women worked as prostitutes in the mainly Russian community of Brighton Beach, New York, and as go-go dancers in New Jersey, but no evidence connected these women with either alien smuggling or organized crime.

Law enforcement does not seem to believe that alien smuggling is a significant activity of Russian organized crime in the United States. For example, in his 1996 testimony before the U.S. Senate's Permanent Subcommittee on Investigations investigation into Russian organized crime in the United States, the Commissioner of U.S. Customs reported that the main criminal threats to the United States posed by criminal groups from the former Soviet Union were narcotics smuggling, money laundering, commercial trade fraud, and the smuggling and sale of illicit munitions and strategic materials.[54] In the eighty-two Customs investigations conducted between 1991 and 1996, the crimes involved were those stipulated above. The Commissioner mentioned alien smuggling only to indicate concern about the increasing numbers of front companies that filed suspect employment-based nonimmigrant and immigrant visa petitions. Such companies are being established, he said, for the purpose of money laundering and other activities related to organized crime.

At these same hearings, then Deputy Assistant FBI Director James Moody reported that two types of Russian criminal enterprises were working in the United States.[55] The first, he said, are frauds and financial crimes that are crimes of opportunity designed to illegally obtain money. The second more closely resemble traditional organized crime that involve extortion, kidnapping, drugs, and other violent crimes.

In our interviews with representatives of the Immigration and Naturalization Service (perhaps the agency most closely associated with the alien smuggling issue), we were told that some organized alien smuggling involves Russians but that no evidence of organized crime activity had yet been found. According to one INS official, the known groups involved in these activities do not resemble La Cosa Nostra: they are believed to lack hierarchical structure and continuity, they are said to have overlapping memberships with networks committing other crimes, and they employ some individuals who participate only temporarily and others who are engaged on a more permanent basis. These patterns are consistent with what has been seen with other Russian émigré criminal activity. The INS conclusion is that the Russians are not major participants in alien smuggling activities but that their potential for possibly becoming more heavily involved is very great.

Based on the relatively little that is known about Russian alien smuggling, then, it appears that this crime is organized but that genuine organized crime in Russia is not trying to control alien smuggling. It may be that the Russian mobs' penetration into the Russian national economy and their degree of control of the vast privatization process are so great that they have no current need for "small potatoes" activities such as alien smuggling.

Although some joint criminal ventures involve persons still in Russia and Russians overseas, and some international criminal activity is directed from Russia, there are enormous differences between the nature and magnitude of organized crime in Russia itself and crime engaged in by Russians overseas. We should keep in mind Luneev's contention that the real problem of Russian organized crime now rests in the economic crime connections between Russia and America.

CHAPTER 7

AN OVERVIEW OF SOVIET ÉMIGRÉ CRIME IN THE UNITED STATES

Since the beginning of the Gorbachev regime in the USSR in 1986, but with increasing intensity since the collapse of the Soviet Union in 1991, magazines, newspapers, and law enforcement officials have warned of an "increasing threat" from Russian organized crime and the arrival of a Russian Mafia in the United States.[1] It was clear in the early 1990s that the *idea* of Soviet émigré organized crime as a threat to the United States had emerged and seemingly been accepted by large segments of the media and by some law enforcement agencies. For others in law enforcement and for some researchers, however, the Russian Mafia remained a potential problem to be investigated. The Tri-state Joint Project on Soviet Émigré Organized Crime (formed by the New York Organized Crime Task Force, the New York and New Jersey State Commissions of Investigation, and the Pennsylvania Crime Commission) was established to develop a more systematic and general understanding than was currently available to law enforcement, criminologists, and the general public.

Working with the Tri-state Project, we sought to move beyond the few high-profile cases that were defining Russian organized crime in the United States and the simplistic application of a mafia or La Cosa Nostra model to a new immigrant group and a society vastly different from the America in which that model had developed. To do this, we examined the broad range of criminal activities in which Soviet émigrés had been involved. Instead of focusing on the most notorious or violent incidents, we sought information from a wide range of law enforcement officials—especially prosecutors and organized crime intelligence specialists—some of whom had not identified themselves as Soviet émigré crime experts or been so identified by the media. In this we greatly benefited from the investigative approach of the Tri-state Project. Although the Project did seek to help its member agencies in the development of cases, it generally took a broader view of émigré crime. Its stated goals were to

◆ Determine the extent to which Russian émigré crime is organized,
◆ Ascertain whether any type of structure exists within the Russian émigré criminal community,
◆ Identify the methods and techniques Russian émigrés use to carry out their criminal activities, and
◆ Define the relationships maintained with other criminal groups operating in the United States and abroad.[2]

These aims made the cooperation of the Tri-state Project particularly useful for achieving our goal of taking a sober look at Soviet émigré crime in the United States.

Patterns of Soviet Émigré Crime in the United States

To assess whether the criminal activities in which Soviet émigrés have been involved can be accurately referred to as organized crime, we must examine both the nature of those crimes and how they are organized. That is, we need to determine whether there are criminal organizations—made up of Soviet émigrés—that have the structure, self-identification of membership, sophistication and planning of offenses, and reputation that allow them to obtain what they want through the threat rather than actual use of violence. We also examine whether these organizations, should they exist, establish monopolies in certain markets, use violence, or engage in corruption.

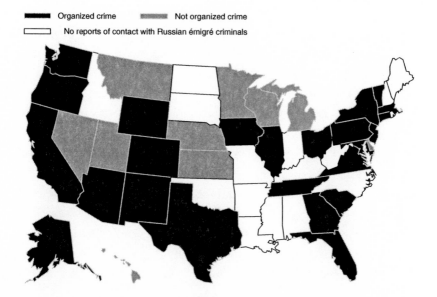

Figure 7.1 States That Reported Russian Émigré Crime and That Described It as Organized Crime

On the National Scene

The map in Figure 7.1 illustrates the extensive geographic spread of reported crime committed by people from the former Soviet Union, based on the results of our national law enforcement survey.[3] The map shows "some contact," not the amount or intensity of that contact. The concentration in coastal states, with a few inland exceptions, may reflect the traditional concentration of immigrants around ports of entry. Because existing immigrant populations facilitate the transition for newly arrived immigrants, crimes committed by émigrés are more likely to be reported in states that have higher émigré populations. The coastal concentration should not, however, overshadow the reports of Soviet contact in many noncoastal states (such as Utah, Wyoming, Montana, Colorado, Nebraska, and Illinois).

Agencies reporting contact were asked further questions about the extent and nature of their experiences with Soviet émigré criminals, including whether these offenses were considered to be organized crime and whether Soviet émigré crime was a serious law enforcement problem. We did not define *organized crime* or *law enforcement problem.* About 37 percent of respondents described what they saw as organized crime, and 60 percent said Soviet émigré crime was a law enforcement problem.

Respondents who reported contact with Soviet émigré criminals were asked what type of crimes were involved. By far the most common was fraud, reported by more than half of the respondents, and money laundering, drugs, and violent crime were each reported by about 30 percent of the respondents. The prevalence of these types of crimes—especially fraud—corresponds to what past research on Russian émigrés has found and what is known about the importance of these crimes in the former Soviet Union.

Much of the media attention that has been paid to crime by émigrés from the former Soviet Union has focused on the so-called Russian mafia and organized crime and on the extent to which this crime poses serious challenges for law enforcement agencies.[4] We suspected that in addition to the actual character of Soviet émigré crime in an area, other factors might play a role in determining whether an agency would report contact with Soviet émigré offenders and whether respondents would report the offenses as involving organized crime or as being a serious law enforcement problem.[5] We decided, therefore, to look at whether the nature of the agencies and their locations affected their reporting patterns.[6]

Federal agencies were more likely than state or local agencies to report contact with criminals from the former Soviet Union. This could be because federal agencies are concerned with issues such as tax fraud, customs violations, and the smuggling of nuclear substances, activities in which some Soviet émigré criminals have been known to be involved.[7] Local jurisdictions, on the other hand, concern themselves with the more mundane street and property crimes.

Agencies that were located in New York, New Jersey, or Pennsylvania were more likely to report contact with Soviet émigré offenders. This could be because of the concentration of Soviet émigré crime in this region, but it could also reflect the existence of the Tri-state Project and the litigating of several major cases involving Soviet émigrés in this area. The size of a state's population had no effect on the reporting of Soviet émigré crime, but states with a large Russian immigrant population were more likely to have agencies report contact with Soviet émigré offenders. This result was expected because a larger pool of potential offenders increases the chances that some will come to the attention of law enforcement.

The definitions of Soviet émigré crime either as a serious law enforcement problem, as organized crime, or as both are related but distinct. These characterizations can offer two very different views of Soviet crime. Although not perceived as being organized crime, Soviet émigré crime might still be considered to be a law enforcement problem. Conversely, the presence of Soviet organized crime does not necessarily make it a law enforcement problem, if the agencies believe they are dealing with it effectively.

Federal agencies were most likely to report both organized crime and law enforcement problems, followed in order by state, city, and county agencies. Other factors, such as population and being in the tristate region, were not important in shaping these perceptions.

Having specialists dealing with Soviet émigré crimes increased the chances of Soviet émigré crime being characterized as organized crime but did not increase its chances of being reported as a serious law enforcement problem. This could mean that agencies having such specialists are more likely to seek out (and to see) Soviet émigré organized crime or that they determine that Soviet émigré crime is organized crime simply because they have structural incentives to do so. Such incentives might include gaining additional resources for combating what is portrayed as a high-profile problem. If this is true, it would have important implications for the kind of mafia stereotyping described earlier. On the other hand, the presence of a specialist may simply reflect the existence of a problem.

Those agencies that reported that Soviet émigrés had been involved in fraud, extortion, and racketeering were more likely to report the presence of organized crime than were other agencies. With the exception of extortion, the same crimes were significant when it came to reporting law enforcement problems. Extortion and racketeering have, in particular, been associated with organized crime in the United States and elsewhere. Their presence may lead law enforcement officials to conclude that the label of organized crime is appropriate, independent of any knowledge about the nature of the structure of the organized crime groups and their other activities. The results of these investigations indicate to us that there seems to be widespread recognition of a "Soviet émigré crime problem" and that the problem is frequently understood as organized crime.

Soviet Émigré Crime in the Tri-state Region

We examined the records collected by the Tri-state Project to determine the types of crime that Soviet émigrés in the region were known or suspected to be involved in. Of course, other crimes of very different types may never have come to the attention of the Tri-state Project because they were not reported to law enforcement or the Project. In this sense, as in any attempt to characterize the behavior of a group of offenders, we must be cautious in drawing overly broad conclusions. Despite these limitations, we found the information in these records both broad and extremely useful. The survey was supplemented by interviews with law enforcement officials and by the growing academic and journalistic literature on Soviet émigré crime. Of course, some Soviet émigrés, like people from all ethnic backgrounds, are involved in various forms of crime. These range from shoplifting, sometimes of an organized kind, to automobile theft, drug selling, and murder. Although violent offending of the most extreme kinds occurs among Soviet émigrés, including numerous murders that remain unsolved, our examination of the materials created or collected by the Tri-state Project investigators indicates that most of the offending by Soviet émigrés is concentrated in the kinds of offenses that bureaucracy and the service economy most encourage—frauds, smuggling, money laundering, and similar activities. This supports our belief that Soviet émigrés who become involved in crime may have a higher propensity than criminals from other groups to choose crimes that involve swindles or huckstering.

The Bootleg Gas Schemes: The Emergence of Soviet Organized Crime in the United States?

Fuel tax-evasion cases are the largest and best-known cases of crime involving Soviet émigrés. These frauds take advantage of the ways in which taxes on motor fuel are collected by various states and by the federal government. The three most important forms of fuel tax evasion are substitution, sale of adulterated fuel, and daisy chaining. To understand how these frauds operate, it is necessary to know something about the fuel business and how it is taxed. There are many different types of fuel oil, but fuels that are used for motor vehicles are subject to special taxes, often designed to support highway construction and maintenance. These taxes are imposed at both the state and federal levels and generate substantial revenues. The collection of these taxes is complicated by a number of factors. First, diesel motor oil, which is taxed, is in every way identical to home heating oil, which is not subject to the same taxes. Second, there is little opportunity for consumers or anyone else to test the purity of the fuel sold at the pump. Third, fuel passes through many steps on its way from a refinery to a pump at a service station, and each of these steps provides opportunities for fraud, many of which have been taken advantage of by Soviet émigrés and others.

Some fuel tax-evasion schemes are relatively simple. In a substitution scheme, a wholesaler indicates on its official records that it sells only home heating oil and thus is not required to pay tax but then turns around and sells the fuel to service stations, indicating in its official records that only heating oil has been sold. In one instance, described at a public hearing in New Jersey, an investigator posing as a potential customer called a fuel distributor and was told that it did not deal in diesel fuel but sold only home heating oil. Later, a truck that had been filled at that company's facilities was stopped, and the driver had invoices indicating that he would deliver diesel and gas to a truck stop. The driver indicated that he had also made deliveries in other states.[8] A variation on this approach is to sell fuel that has been mixed with other substances to increase the profit margin on sales. A number of companies were accused of selling adulterated fuel.

Daisy-chain schemes are more complex than those involving substitution or adulteration of fuel. These schemes are designed to take advantage of how taxes are collected, and some were in operation long before Soviet émigrés became involved in them. According to investigators, four of the five traditional New York organized crime families were involved in the daisy-chain schemes at various times. The best-known figure from the daisy-chain prosecutions is Michael Franzese, a reputed member of the Colombo crime family. Daisy-chain schemes take advantage of the fact that in some states, including New York, New Jersey, and Pennsylvania, transfers between whole-salers are untaxed and the tax on motor fuel is supposed to be paid by the wholesaler at the time the fuel is sold to a retailer. These untaxed transfers can be used to provide cover for the nonpayment of the taxes. A licensed wholesaler sells fuel to another wholesaler, generally a fictitious company controlled by the licensed wholesaler. This second wholesaler is called a "burn" company and indicates on invoices for fuel leaving its possession that tax has been paid. Another wholesaler-to-wholesaler transfer may be made to further compli-cate the paper trail. Finally, the fuel is sold to a retailer, often con-trolled by related individuals, for a bargain price that is supposed to include tax.

The many transfers—which occur only on paper—from one

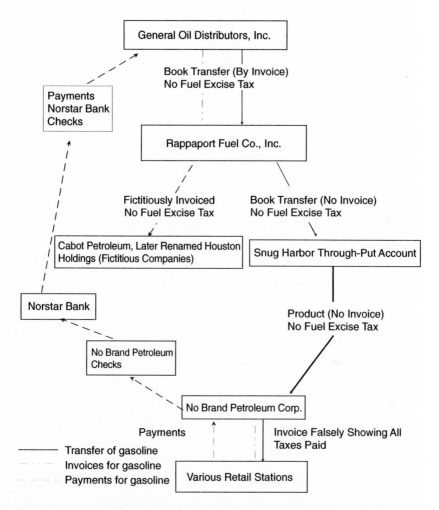

Figure 7.2 Conceptual Diagram of the No-Brand Petroleum Daisy-Chain Scheme (Designed After Exhibit 31 of the New Jersey State Commission of Investigation Public Hearings on Motor Fuel Tax Evasion)

company to another are the daisy chain to which the name of these schemes refers. Investigators describe the chain as having three separate strands representing the fuel, the paper trail, and the payments. Figure 7.2, based on an exhibit from the New Jersey public hearings, illustrates one such scheme. According to Raymond Jermyn, chief of the Rackets Bureau for the Suffolk County (New York) district attorney, the conspirators would also close one fictitious company and open a new one at the end of each tax quarter.[9] There were many such schemes, and they defrauded the state and federal governments of millions of dollars in uncollected tax revenues.

Soviet émigrés were involved in a number of the daisy-chain schemes in different jurisdictions, including New York, New Jersey, Pennsylvania, and California. The earliest Soviet émigré to become involved in the daisy-chain scheme seems to have been David Bogatin, who joined Michael Markowitz, an émigré from Romania, and Philip Moskowitz, who had a long history of involvement in illegal activities and some connections with organized crime, in the fuel business in 1982. The following year, Lev Persits became involved in their companies. Persits was already involved in other criminal activities in Brighton Beach.[10] Using the services of lawyers, accountants, and bankers, the collaborators set up a large scheme that covered its trail well.

Marat Balagula, described earlier, operated another fuel syndicate. In 1977, a year after arriving in the United States, Balagula owned fourteen gas stations. By 1983, he had formed two fuel dealerships. He bought fuel from a corporation owned by Boris and Benjamin Nayfeld, both of whom had been involved in a variety of criminal activities.

The tristate region ultimately had several simultaneous schemes. For example, in New Jersey, Vladimir Zilber, Monya Elson, Arkady Siefer, and Edward Dougherty operated one scheme, with Dougherty acting as the link between it and the Italian organized crime families. David Shuster and Joseph Reisch operated another scheme.

Although the motor-fuel schemes are often thought of as pure frauds, it is important to keep in mind that they also generated violence. For example, Ilya Zeltzer was killed in 1986 during a shootout inside a gas distribution office, allegedly in a dispute involving some aspect of the scheme. Lev Persits was paralyzed after being shot in the back. Philip Moskowitz, also allegedly involved in bootleg gas, was tortured and murdered in 1987. Michael Markowitz, a major figure in the schemes and a friend of Moskowitz, was shot to death in 1989, allegedly to prevent his cooperation with the authorities. David Shuster was shot but not killed in 1991. Emil Pyztretsky, allegedly a mob enforcer who was involved in the gas schemes, was killed a few months later in 1991. Vladimir Zilverstein was shot but not killed in 1992, reportedly as a result of a dispute with Italian organized criminals involved in the gas scam.

The fuel tax-evasion schemes were complex conspiracies and caused a great deal of harm in terms of both money stolen and violence involved. Economic harm to the fuel market occurred because unfairly low pricing undercut the legitimate retail fuel businesses. The collaboration of Soviet émigrés with traditional organized crime families was one reason for the growing fear that their crimes would ultimately be similar in nature and effect to existing organized crime structures. What is interesting about this collaboration is that the Russians operated under the umbrella of La Cosa Nostra families. In effect, through their cooperative arrangements, the Russians enjoyed the benefits of a sophisticated criminal organization without actually being one. To succeed the scams needed the reputation for intimidation and violence that La Cosa Nostra families could provide.

The possibility that Soviets could succeed other ethnic groups just as those ethnic groups succeeded those that had come before them seems a reasonable one on its face.[11] Despite these possibilities, however, there is no strong evidence that these conspiracies represent a new example of organized crime. Despite their importance in the marketplace, the Soviets involved did not establish an effective monopoly over the distribution of low-cost fuel oil; given the presence of the Italian organized crime, it is doubtful that they could have done so. Rather, a number of such schemes involving members of a variety of ethnic groups developed over time. There was also no evidence that those Soviets involved felt any sense of self-identification or membership in a group.

Other Frauds

Beyond the fuel tax-evasion schemes, fraud was the most common type of crime found in the Tri-state Project's records. Many of these frauds are similar to those found in other locations and committed by members of many ethnic groups. Such frauds exploit some legitimate sector of the economy by taking advantage of gaps in the bureaucratic operations or by corrupting the bureaucracy itself. A common characteristic of these frauds is that the schemes involve the appearance of a legitimate operation and often take the form of a formal organization—for example, the burn companies in the fuel tax-evasion schemes. This does not, however, mean that offenses are formally organized but, rather, that they are flexibly structured, which allows the charade to be better maintained.

In other instances, formal organizations that have legal operations may be used to carry out the offense, often with the active or passive assistance of some of their employees or owners. A number of such incidents involve Medicaid fraud. In these cases, bills for nonexistent or nonmedical services are submitted. The services not provided range from medical examinations to the purchase of medical equipment. In one scheme, several Soviet émigrés established relationships with medical receptionists at a company providing ambulette services. In exchange for a kickback, the receptionists gave clearances for $47 trips for "ghost" patients, which then were paid by Medicaid. In another instance, a home attendant service was actually used as a front for the operation of a prostitution ring. This arrangement allowed the services offered by the prostitutes to be billed as medical expenses.

Soviet émigrés in Pennsylvania operated an automobile insurance ring that staged accidents to receive insurance payments. Starting simple, it grew to involve attorneys, medical personnel, durable medical equipment companies (which supply items such as wheelchairs), and even a used-car dealer who supplied the vehicles used in the staged accidents. The ring submitted over $1 million in phony claims in the early 1990s. Here, again, the involvement of actors and companies in the legitimate economy was an essential part of the organization of the crimes. The organization of this scheme, however, is not fundamentally any different from that used by other accident insurance scam teams operating elsewhere or carried out by people from other ethnic groups.[12]

Other lower-level forms of fraud also appear to be common, and the range of types is quite broad.[13] Many are thefts that involve elements of deception, and, in those cases, the victims are generally members of the Soviet émigré community. For example, in several incidents of jewelry switching, an inexpensive piece is substituted for the real one while the offender pretends to inspect the piece. In another instance, a company offered the service of shipping packages to the former Soviet Union but, after collecting payments for the shipments, actually shipped them to their confederates.

Counterfeiting, like fraud, is an area of nonviolent criminal activity in which some Soviet émigrés have been active. Counterfeiting credit cards, checks, Immigration and Naturalization Service documents, passports, and other documents is another area of activity involving a number of separate individuals who organize the market and supply others with their products. A confidential informant reported that he knew someone who sold working visas and social security cards for $3,000 and green cards (required for noncitizens to be legally employed in the United States) for $6,000. This informant also described a money-laundering scheme in which counterfeit dollars were produced in the United States, taken to Russia, and exchanged for rubles, which in turn were exchanged for real dollars. Alexander Yegemenov and Mikhail Syroejine were indicted for or-

ganizing a large scheme involving the production and sale of counterfeit Immigration and Naturalization Service documents.

Numerous reported incidents involve the production and sale of
counterfeit credit cards, which are then used to make purchases that
are sold on the stolen goods market. In one instance, two Soviets were
arrested as they attempted to purchase a $12,000 photocopier with a
counterfeit card. The card number was apparently obtained from a
business where the card had been legitimately used in the past. One
émigré was arrested for a scheme that involved the removal and re-
placement of the magnetic strips on stolen credit cards. Many of the
fraudulent cards from this particular operation were carelessly done,
however, with such obvious errors as misspellings in the names of the
banks. The operation of this ongoing market indicates that this type
of offense requires a degree of organization, although individuals who
purchase the cards may operate on their own.

Soviet émigré involvement in a variety of money-laundering
schemes was also reported. At times these followed well-known patterns—such as laundering through casinos, purchasing of money orders that were quickly used to buy other merchandise, and making
large cash mortgage payments. A number of Soviets were associated
with David Sanders (Sendorovich), whom authorities consider to be
a known money launderer with ties to La Cosa Nostra. In other
schemes, émigrés' ties to locations in the former Soviet Union were
used. For example, some funds were laundered through a nonexistent
textile factory construction project. Large amounts of money were
transferred for the project, but no construction ever took place. A
number of cases of apparent money laundering involved large cash
transactions just below the $10,000 that would require the filing of a
Currency Transaction Report by the bank receiving the deposit. Law
enforcement authorities monitor these reports to detect the movement
of large amounts of cash that may be generated by illegal activity.

Soviet émigrés have also been active in the drug and drug para-
phernalia markets. These cases generally involve established net-

works of individuals and include both the importation and street-level sale of drugs. Sixteen individuals—including David Podlog, Alexander Moysif, and seven other Soviets—were indicted for the distribution and possession of controlled substances, including heroin and cocaine, in New York. Moysif pleaded guilty and testified against Podlog and others. The conspirators, in this instance dealing with an undercover law enforcement agent, took orders, prepared, and delivered the drugs using a route through Poland.

Boris Nayfeld (previously mentioned in the description of the fuel-tax schemes), Shalva Ukleba, Alexander Mikhailov, Simon Elishakov, and Valery Krutiy were indicted in New York for the smuggling, distribution, and sale of heroin during the period 1990 to 1993. The drugs they moved originated in Southeast Asia, were smuggled into Poland, passed through Belgium, and then were brought to New York. In one case, Mikhailov traveled from Thailand to Denmark with heroin secreted in a television picture tube. Not indicted in this case but mentioned several times as a customer of the group was the same David Podlog. There is evidence that areas within the former Soviet Union are being used as transshipment points for drug importation to the United States, especially for those drugs grown in the eastern Asian areas that were once part of the Soviet Union or its areas of influence.[14] Therefore, it is not surprising that individuals from those areas are involved in the sale and distribution of illegal drugs.

Two other groups of Soviet émigrés were indicted for the operation of factories producing crack vials in New Jersey and Pennsylvania. The vials were stamped "Made in Taiwan" and had a variety of brand names on their labels. When one of the participants in this crime was arrested, the car he was driving contained 1,520,000 vials and 1,480,000 vial caps. The vials were distributed to drug dealers and retail stores, often owned by Soviet émigrés, from New York to Atlanta.

Smuggling

Besides drugs, smuggling incidents involving Soviet émigrés range from aluminum to weapons to currency. In one instance, a resident alien was arrested when she was discovered by customs agents to have $78,400 strapped to her body as she came off a plane from Moscow. She claimed that the money came from the sale of a house in Russia, but the documentation for this transaction was found to be forged. In other instances, schemes to smuggle diamonds and weapons were reported. In one case, Soviet émigrés reportedly sought to purchase weapons that would then be smuggled to the Serbs fighting in the former Yugoslavia.

Drug marketing, smuggling, and money laundering are all activities frequently associated with traditional organized crime in the United States. These are areas in which crime networks composed of individuals from the former Soviet Union provide illegal goods and services through an organized market. It does not seem to be the case, however, that the Soviet émigrés have established monopoly control over any of these activities, even within particular geographic areas. Instead, they cooperate with older organized crime networks, specifically La Cosa Nostra. The Soviets, thus far, seem to pose little threat to the existing control of drug markets but rather are willing to provide services to those already involved.

Violence

We earlier identified the use or threat of violence as a crucial element in a criminal organization's capacity for inflicting harm. Violence is a major way by which criminal organizations establish their reputations. In particular, the use of violence in the course of extortion is strongly tied to organized crime. Soviet émigrés have shown both a willingness and a capacity to use violence, including murder, extortion, and assaults. Enforcers work in the extortion of businesses in

Brighton Beach, Brooklyn, but they work for whoever pays them. Fights sometimes occur over extortion victims, and victims who refuse to pay are beaten. There is little evidence of monopoly control of extortion by any clearly defined group.[15]

At least sixty-five murders and attempted murders in the United States have involved Soviets and Soviet émigrés since 1981 and, according to investigators, have indications of organized crime involvement.[16] Although this may seem to be a small number for a sixteen-year period, considering the number of Soviet émigrés who are involved in criminal activities it is actually quite large. If the killings involving La Cosa Nostra were isolated over some fixed period of time and contrasted with the total number of murders in the same period, that number also would appear to be quite small.

A number of the Soviet killings occurred in the tristate area, and many remain either unsolved or unprosecuted. Witnesses are seldom willing to cooperate with the investigation, which may be a sign of intimidation, either through direct threats or through a reputation for violence. The murders and attempts that have occurred so far seem to be neither systematic nor designed to protect a criminal enterprise, as is generally the case with traditional organized crime. Instead, they appear to have been motivated mainly by greed or personal vendetta. In some instances, one homicide seemed to trigger a long series of murders and attempted murders. In most cases, the offender apparently was paying back the victim for some offense. Soviet émigré violence is not random; care seems to be exercised in choosing victims and in avoiding harm to innocent bystanders. But the threat of violence is clearly used to intimidate others in the émigré community, which explains why witnesses have refused to come forward or to cooperate with the police.

As has been true in U.S. drug markets involving other criminal groups, Soviet émigré violence is also believed to be an aspect of the unregulated competition that exists in their criminal ventures. An example of this is the history of Monya Elson as recorded in the records of the Tri-state Project. Elson has been involved in extortion and homicide since the early 1980s. His extortion initially was centered in the diamond district of Manhattan, but he later expanded to other areas. He was arrested overseas for drug smuggling and served six years before returning to the United States to put together a crew and carry out a new wave of crime. Among his activities was providing protection for participants in fuel-tax scams.

Elson has been connected to a number of murders, some for hire and others for revenge:

◆   In 1991 he contracted with an Azerbaijani to place a bomb in a car belonging to another émigré. This victim was an associate of a reputed *vor v zakone*. The bomb failed.

◆   Vyacheslav and Vadim Lyubarsky, a father and son, were murdered outside their apartment in 1992. Officials believe that these murders probably were committed at the direction of Elson because the father supposedly was responsible for having Elson shot in 1991. Elson and others were charged in a federal indictment with these murders. Elson was also implicated in the earlier attempted murder of the same Vyacheslav Lyubarsky in 1991.

◆   Elson himself was shot and wounded in Los Angeles in 1992, and another émigré, Leonyard Kanterkantetes, took him to the hospital. A third individual was injured two days later while trying to put a bomb under Kanterkantetes's car.

◆   Said Amin Moussostov, a reputed Chechen enforcer, was murdered in New Jersey in May 1992 by two individuals. He had earlier represented his boss at a meeting with Elson at which Elson attempted to extort money. Investigators suspect Moussostov would not succumb to Elson's demands and that, because two men with similar descriptions as the murderers attended the same meeting, Elson was involved in Moussostov's murder. It should be noted that Moussostov is reputed to have been involved in the murder of Fima Laskin, a leading Soviet crime figure in Germany in 1992.

♦ An Armenian who was an associate of Elson's was found dead in Nassau County in early 1993, possibly killed as revenge for the shooting of another émigré who was involved in the fuel-tax scams.

♦ Elbrous Evdoev, a Soviet émigré, was found murdered in a New Jersey salvage yard in March 1993. He had been shot and wounded twice in 1992 and had told authorities after the second attempt that Elson was behind it.

♦ In July 1993, Elson, his wife, and a bodyguard were shot and wounded in front of Elson's residence. One of the perpetrators, who had been a bodyguard for Elson in the past, was shot in the course of the incident. The attackers were enforcers for a reputed *vor v zakone* who had a falling-out with Elson. When the wounded perpetrator was murdered a few weeks later, in-vestigators assumed that it was at the direction of Elson. The wounded bodyguard was shot and killed outside his home two months later.

♦ A bodyguard for Elson was implicated in the 1994 murder of a Soviet organized crime figure. The same bodyguard also wounded another émigré by shooting him several times in the head after disagreeing about financial dealings.

Elson has had several associates who at times served as his bodyguards. These associates have also been involved in their own extortion, fuel tax-evasion, and credit-card fraud activities. When Al-exander Levichitz, also known as Sasha Pinya, a major Soviet crime figure reputed to be a *vor v zakone,* arrived in the United States, Elson threw a party for him at a Brighton Beach restaurant. Elson also re-portedly turned over his partial ownership of a restaurant to Levichitz.

Other forms of violence or threatened violence have also been common. Kidnapping is one example. Extortion of businesses in exchange for protection is widely practiced by Soviet émigré criminals. The latter may represent the importation of the kind of extortion that operates in the former Soviet Union, in which both legal and illegal businesses are allowed to operate without disruption by either the state or criminals only if they purchase "insurance" against such disruption. One form of protection in Russia involved the *kryshas* ("roofs") described earlier, who offer protection and security to businessmen and their associates and, in return, demand a share of the business profits. This term is also used by Soviet émigrés in this country. It is not yet known, however, whether the term is being used to describe the U.S. extension of Soviet-based criminal organizations or whether it has simply been appropriated to distinguish a hierarchy among Soviet émigré crime groups here. Several substantial cases of extortion have been prosecuted in the tristate region, including the case against Vyacheslav (Yaponchik) Ivankov, who was convicted of the attempted extortion of two Soviet émigré businessmen.

Criminal Enterprises

Most of the offenses we have described so far focus on one or another specific type of criminal activity. With some of the major offenders, however, there is evidence of broad criminal enterprises in a number of separate areas that more clearly resemble organized crime and have the trappings of a sophisticated criminal organization. In particular, the case of the Goldberg crime group provides an example of this type of criminal enterprise. In 1989 Boris Goldberg was indicted under the Racketeer-Influenced and Corrupt Organizations (RICO) statute in the U.S. District Court, Eastern District of New York, for heading a criminal enterprise. The general charges were trafficking in cocaine, attempting to commit murder, committing armed robbery and extortion, extortionate collection of credit, commission of acts of fraud, use of weapons and explosives in the commission of unlawful activities, and preserving and enhancing the power and profits of the group by committing acts of violence.

Specifically, Goldberg and his confederates were charged with the following criminal activities:

◆ As a result of meetings in April 1982, Boris Goldberg and others conspired to murder Robert Ferrante, who was shot on April 12, 1982, in Redondo Beach, California.

◆ Members of the Goldberg crime group traveled across state lines to carry out an extortion of the owners of the Baja Seafood Company.

◆ The Goldberg crime group conducted a form of interstate commerce in distributing drugs, particularly cocaine, between 1982 and 1984.

◆ During 1983 the Goldberg crime group planned an attempt on Soviet crime kingpin Evsei Agron's life. On January 24, 1984, Agron was shot and seriously wounded.

◆ In December 1983 Boris Goldberg used extortionate means to collect extensions of credit from one Arkady Khimovich.

◆ Boris Goldberg and others conspired to take property by force from Ira Hershey, an employee of the Zale Corporation. The property was a quantity of jewels and precious metals, and the force used was violence and the fear of physical injury.

◆ Boris Goldberg and others committed mail fraud between 1983 and 1988 when they defrauded insurance companies by making false claims by mail.

Although it is clear that this network was involved in a variety of offenses and continued over a long period of time, its structure appears to be more that of a gang or team centered around the leadership of a single individual, rather than an ongoing organized crime structure that could continue without the presence of its main organizer.

The Organization of Soviet Émigré Crime

Across a wide variety of offenses, the schemes carried out by Soviet émigrés require extensive coordination between actors and infiltration of legitimate areas of the economy. The organization of these offenses, however, is responsive to the specific nature of the criminal opportunity—for example, the need to mimic the operation of legitimate businesses—and does not simply follow the structure of any existing criminal organization. Criminal entrepreneurs respond to specific opportunities and form the crime networks described by the Tri-state Project reports. They do not look like existing organized crime structures, which maintain operations or branch into new areas. Of the types of harm that are associated with organized crime— violence, monopoly, and corruption—the one most clearly evident in these data is violence. The violence is used mainly to intimidate the public, potential competitors, and group members who might be seen as disloyal. In this respect, the crime networks described here do resemble traditional organized crime. There is, however, no indication that Soviet émigrés have established any criminal monopolies. Instead, their offenses take place in a variety of areas and do not represent the total domination of any markets. Further, at this stage, Soviet émigré criminals in the tristate area do not appear to use systematic corruption to protect their enterprises in the United States. The Goldberg crime group, the clearest example of a wider criminal enterprise, was centered on one individual and was not an ongoing criminal organization that would have enough continuity to survive the loss of its leader.

Soviet émigré criminals operating in the United States have been described by some law enforcement authorities and by some in the media as being structured much like La Cosa Nostra. When Yaponchik was arrested in June 1995, he was labeled the "capo di tutti capi" of Soviet émigré crime in the United States.[17] His arrest was taken as proof of a centralized Soviet émigré criminal organization, along the lines of La Cosa Nostra, a view that was strengthened by his known association with the *Solntsevskaya* gang, the largest gang in the former Soviet Union.[18] An opposing view is that Soviet émigré crime networks have no defined organizational structures or hierarchies that look anything like La Cosa Nostra.[19] Instead of the hierarchical structure associated with continuing criminal enterprises, Russians, according to this view, operate mostly as individual specialists. As such, they have very fluid groups that occasionally come together to commit a crime. They are not rigidly authoritarian, and the people involved do not answer to anybody in particular. When organized, they operate in a marketlike manner, choosing others to work with strictly on the basis of the anticipated return of such cooperation.

It is our assessment that neither of these opposing positions is accurate. Our analyses of the Tri-state Project data indicate that there are large, ongoing networks of individuals identified by law enforcement as involved in or suspected of criminal activities who are directly or indirectly connected to each other. There is no evidence, however, of a complex hierarchy or set of hierarchies. Instead, ad hoc teams of specialists are mustered for specific criminal ventures in an opportunistic manner. They may move across ventures and sometimes work on the basis of referrals, vouching for each other. They often create flexible, project-oriented structures that enable them to carry out particular crimes. In this they do not differ greatly from current trends in licit organizations, where there are indications of a decrease in the amount and degree of hierarchy, an increase in reliance on strategic partnerships and task groups, and a growing reliance on third-party service providers.[20] At times, particularly active and effective individuals may work with ongoing teams, but even these often shift.

The predominant structure is one in which individuals who knew each other in the former Soviet Union, or who know people who know each other, join for some particular criminal opportunity. The backgrounds of these individuals vary, but overall, the professional—but non–*vory v zakone*—criminals and the opportunists who currently dominate Soviet émigré crime in the United States typically mistrust each other. Few references can be found to loyalty based on shared ethnicity or culture, despite the fact that some of the players knew each other prior to emigration. With the exception of the gas-tax scheme and rare other occasions, however, Soviet émigré criminals seem to associate mainly with each other, both criminally and socially.

CHAPTER 8

THE STRUCTURE OF
SOVIET ÉMIGRÉ CRIME

Detailed qualitative information from a variety of sources led us to believe that Soviet émigré crime in the United States is not tightly organized and cannot be conventionally defined as a mafia. Here we use a quantitative technique known as *network analysis* to develop a detailed and systematic understanding of how this crime is organized. Based on the results of these analyses we conclude, as we did when we examined the descriptive material in Chapter 7, that Soviet émigré crime is neither organized crime nor a mafia. We also reject the idea that Soviet émigré crime is organized through isolated small groups and individuals operating on their own. Only a relatively small portion of Soviet émigrés who are involved in criminal activities operate as individuals or through small groups. Much more important are extended networks of actors who know each other directly or through other people. Some actors are clearly more important than others, but none totally dominates or controls the entire network, although some may dominate parts of it. In this sense, the organization of Soviet émigré crime is not very different from the organization of a variety of other economic activities. In many sectors of the legal economy, short-term teams of what are essentially freelance operators come together to carry out short- or medium-term projects but then disband when the project is completed.

To understand the structure of criminal networks and whether they fit the definition of organized crime, it is necessary to examine more than just the crimes that come to the attention of the authorities and result in an arrest or conviction. Such officially recorded information, with a few exceptions, focuses on specific events rather than ongoing organization. It ignores the existence of noncriminal relationships between those involved and, by taking a snapshot of what may be one part of a criminal network, gives the impression that the network in question exists separately from other criminal networks. Although in some instances the picture obtained in this way may be fairly accurate, in many other instances it is incomplete and inaccurate. This may be even more true in organized crime cases than in cases that involve other types of crime. Because prosecutors need to present cases in a way that tells a complete story to grand juries, judges, trial juries, and the media, this tendency to reduce and simplify may be even stronger in those high-profile, often complex, organized crime cases that come to trial.

Unlike prosecutors who seek to create a coherent story, investigators seek to collect large amounts of information about the people and organizations in which they are interested. This is especially true of those who collect criminal intelligence and those who develop cases through ongoing investigations rather than following a specific crime incident reported by a victim. Intelligence information comes from existing documents, ranging from articles in newspapers and magazines, to corporate filings with the state, to interviews with victims or experts, to surveillance. This information, it is believed, may eventually prove useful in understanding developing alliances or divisions, solving particular crimes, or allowing a prosecutor to bring a conspiracy case. In its raw form, however, it is simply information waiting to be put to use. For the purpose of developing a complete understanding of the nature of criminal networks, this raw information is much more useful than the processed information given in some sources. There is also a critical distinction between a prosecutor who needs to follow the rules of evidence while presenting a coherent story, and investigators and intelligence analysts who can use whatever information they have, regardless of the source, to flesh out their theories and test their hypotheses. The latter process is more akin to social science, in which evidence is evaluated in terms of reliability and validity but does not have to meet legal evidentiary standards.

We were fortunate to have the cooperation of member organizations of the Tri-state Joint Soviet Émigré Organized Crime Project, which allowed us to have access to virtually all the raw information on Soviet émigré crimes collected by that group. Their data allow us to paint a much more complete picture of Soviet émigré crime than would be possible if we relied on court cases alone.[1]

The Tri-state Project's Information Sources

The information from the Tri-state Project came in seven basic forms, each one of which has strengths and weaknesses as a source of information:

♦   *Indictments* Participants in the Project shared indictments of individuals and organizations that were charged with crimes by grand juries. These concerned cases in which they were involved directly and occasionally cases investigated by others, including several from federal courts and jurisdictions outside of their region. The indictments include some of the best-known cases involving Soviet émigrés, such as some of the motor-fuel tax-fraud indictments, as well as less well-known cases.

♦   *Newspaper and magazine articles* Participants in the project collected and exchanged clippings from various publications about their cases or any type of crime involving Soviet émigrés. Two Russian-speaking investigators also followed the Russian-language newspapers from New York City and elsewhere and translated articles thought to be relevant to an investigation. Advertisements were of particular interest to investigators, especially those that may have involved fraudulent activities, such as ads for medical services and equipment and ads that promised to provide services at no cost to the recipient. Announcements—usually memorials placed in honor of murdered figures who were known to be involved in criminal activity—were monitored, as well. These announcements, along with the corresponding deaths, allowed investigators to examine alliances and splits among Soviet émigrés active in crime.

◆ *Phones* The Project collected phone records of individuals who were targets of their investigations. These records provided information on the toll calls made from the targeted telephone number and, in a few cases involving major figures, records on incoming calls. These types of phone records are problematic in that they do not identify who is actually speaking on the phone (or even that a call involves two people speaking and not the operation of a fax machine). Certainly, many phone calls did not involve any criminal activity. Yet with all their limitations, these records provide useful information about connections between actors and the names of organizations that might be involved in illegal activities.

◆ *General surveillance* Certain documents summarize the results of general surveillance of targeted individuals or locations based on direct observation by investigators, although they may add other information, such as the fact that an observed person is the child of someone being investigated. Investigators often watched a person (or his or her house or car) on a regular basis over several weeks or months to understand who had contact with the person, what locations he or she visited, and what his or her routines were.

◆ *Social surveillance* Reports from the surveillance of social events, such as weddings, were analyzed separately from general surveillance reports because they target events rather than individuals or organizations. Surveillance methods included, for example, recording the license plate numbers of all cars in the parking lot without knowing which ones belonged to targeted actors. Because this form of surveillance casts a wide net, the reports often included the names of individuals whose only connection to the targeted person was that they happened to attend the same social event. If the same person appears again at some later point in the investigation, he or she may be incorporated in the criminal network investigators are creating, but the information that a person attended a social event would seldom be crucial to a prosecutor's case. In analyzing these data we took two approaches when cars were identified—treating them as separate entities and treating them as proxies for their owners.

◆ *Confidential informant reports* Investigators worked with confidential informants who had some knowledge about criminal activities, often by themselves engaging in such activities. Informants usually receive some type of benefit—such as immunity from prosecution for their own crimes—in exchange for the information they supply. Because informants may fabricate or exaggerate information to obtain such benefits, depending on the information they provide is controversial. However, investigators often value the information such informants provide.

◆ *Reports* A variety of other reports were produced in the course of investigation. Investigative reports involved continuing investigations and described new information or summarized investigative activities. Intelligence reports provided background information on a number of topics. Interview reports summarized interviews of people in custody, prospective confidential informants, interested citizens, and others. Arrest reports described the circumstances, charges, personnel, and subjects of arrests. Incident reports described crimes and other activities. Search reports summarized the results of searches of facilities conducted by law enforcement personnel. Meeting reports summarized meetings with specific individuals. So-called routine reports described the service of a subpoena or similar actions.

Company reports described a company of interest to the investigators, often including a listing of the officers and managers, information available from public corporate records or from commercial firms that provide such information, detailed descriptions of corporate structures, and outlines of the interrelationships between a number of companies.

Each of these seven sources of information has deficiencies, but together they complement one another and provide information that has more reliability and validity than any one source alone. For example, phone call information is accurately recorded twenty-four hours a day, seven days a week, and includes a large number of individuals, families, and businesses, but we can never be certain of who is speaking to whom or what was said. The information obtained through direct surveillance is accurate about who is with whom, but because it is expensive, surveillance rarely takes place full time over a prolonged period. It is, therefore, only a hit-or-miss sample. Reports from confidential informants often provide detailed information about individuals of interest, but the suppliers of this information are often far from disinterested observers and cannot be considered completely trustworthy. If, however, two individuals can be connected through phone records, direct observation, and a report from a confidential informant, we can more confidently conclude that a link between them exists.

Just as prosecutors sort through and selectively use the information collected by investigators to build successful cases, we have sorted through our information from the Tri-state Project to develop a picture of the organization of Soviet émigré crime in the tristate region. This picture includes the nature and extent of criminal activities in which Soviet émigrés are engaged, whether as members of criminal organizations, as partners in networks, or as individuals. To protect the confidentiality of people and organizations not involved in crimes, we use the names of individuals, organizations, and other entities only when they have appeared in an indictment, accounts in the press, or other publicly available documents. Some of these people are not involved in criminal activities and may actually be victims. Others are represented in the figures in this chapter by the code numbers they were assigned when we collected our network information.

Crime Networks

Networks are defined by the relationships among individual actors rather than, for example, by the names of the particular positions or roles—such as treasurer or assistant—that individuals occupy. Networks consist of the actual (although perhaps subjective) relationships among individuals rather than the relationships that are formally supposed to exist. This emphasis is particularly useful for the study of crimes involving formal organizations or involving the legitimate economy because the nominal roles that people occupy—such as president of a fuel-oil company—often have little to do with their actual positions. In one daisy-chain scheme, for example, a janitor was designated the head of a burn company. Because of their emphasis on the relationships among actors, networks are distinct from other forms of social organization.[2] Markets, for example, are characterized by individualized behavior based on competition, and actors who have transactions with each other are adversaries. Formal organizations, on the other hand, coordinate goal-directed activities through adoption of explicit procedures and have official boundaries.[3] Often, formal organizations incorporate elements of hierarchy, featuring well-defined authority of some over others and centralized administration.[4]

That crime is not usually organized through either formal organization or markets may seem obvious, based simply on the fact that the activities are illegal.[5] Clearly, people do not set up formal organizations with the publicly expressed goal of carrying out criminal activities. Further, even setting up a formal organization with noncriminal public goals and secret criminal goals may involve increased risk of exposure for all those involved in the organization, if its criminal nature is discovered by the authorities. Similarly, an individual, network, or organization providing illegal goods will not follow true market practices and make public the necessary information that would bring in the largest potential number of customers.[6] Even if such market activities could be invisible to all but active criminals, the risk of detection by the authorities may remain high (if, for example, informing has low costs and high benefits for those participants who do the informing). Both legal prohibitions and surveillance limit the ways in which crime may be organized. Under these conditions, nonmarket, nonformal organizational structures may be preferred.[7]

Some crimes require particular types of knowledge or skills. Bootleg gas schemes require someone who knows how to make invoices and other records that appear to be legitimate, and Medicaid fraud requires someone knowledgeable about medical goods. Even money laundering and murder for hire require a degree of expertise. The need for knowledge may lead to the creation of a relationship with those who possess it, but this relationship may be short-lived. Because of the special access or know-how necessary for many kinds of crimes, those who possess it are seldom subject to marketlike competition, and they may be unwilling to take subordinate positions in a hierarchy.[8] Thus, a network relationship based on personal ties between two individuals may emerge. Because they can be both started and ended quickly, network forms are often adopted in environments that reward flexibility and that require adaptability to change.[9] The environments for criminal activities may change because of changes in crime prevention strategies, because of differences between potential victims, because of the incarceration of co-offenders, or for other reasons. Specific criminal acts are often short-term,[10] and even in the case of the longer-term criminal activities, such as complex frauds, participants often aim to have the ability to end the schemes quickly in the event that the victims become suspicious.[11]

Finally, network—rather than competitive or coercive—forms may most often appear in legitimate contexts when trust exists among actors. Co-offending generally requires some degree of trust among participants.[12] Powell argues that "networks should be most common in work settings in which participants have some kind of common background—be it ethnic, geographic, ideological or professional. The more homogeneous the group, the greater the trust, hence the easier to sustain network-like arrangements."[13] This selection of individuals like oneself as partners in criminal activity has been found in various studies of offenses involving co-offending and may provide a basis of trust.[14] Independent of homophily, however, co-offenders must have some degree of trust in each other to cooperate in an offense.[15] Powell suggests that network forms of organization, rather than markets or hierarchies, are most likely to be adopted to organize legitimate economic activity when there is the need for specific kinds of knowledge or abilities, speed, and trust between actors.[16] Because these requirements are often present when actors come together to commit crime and when environmental constraints limit the use of other forms of organization, networks may emerge as the most common form of criminal organization. This does not mean that elements of other forms of social organization are never present when offenders cooperate. Even when an offense operates through a formal organization, however, the personal relationships between individuals are at least as important as the organizational structure. Thus, within organized crime personal ties and loyalties between offenders have great importance, even though there may be a hierarchical structure and a separation of role from actor.[17]

The Tri-state Project files and other documents identified individuals, organizations, places, and other entities. The greatest number of these identified entities (1,851) came from the phone information, followed by general reports (1,738) and general surveillance (667).

Newspapers and magazines provided the smallest number of entities (137). The other sources of information (social surveillance, confidential informant reports, and indictments) had between 250 and 400 entities. To examine the organization of these entities into a network, we recorded all information in the documents that linked any one of these entities to any other. A total of 34,484 ties between pairs of entities were recorded. The challenge then was to make this vast quantity of information intelligible and interpretable; to do this, we used a set of techniques known as *network analysis.* Network analysis uses a set of mathematical techniques to analyze and interpret relational data. Although the term *network* is widely used by both law enforcement officials and scholars who deal with organized crime, the use of the formal techniques of network analysis is relatively rare.[18] Because of this, we briefly explain some of the techniques that we used and our approaches to the data analysis task.

As pointed out earlier, each of the seven types of data that the Tri-state Project collected has its own strengths and weaknesses. We examined the sources separately and together, and we also explored different approaches to the same information. For example, when we have information that cars belonging to two individuals were seen parked in the same parking lot, we had to decide whether to treat that information as though it indicated that those two individuals were actually together. This is further complicated by the fact that the cars that people drive may not actually be registered in their names. For example, investigators pointed out to us that many of their targets drove cars that were registered in the names of their spouses or children. A similar situation exists with the phone data: we know only that a phone call was made between two phone numbers, not who actually spoke during a particular call. This problem was partially addressed by systematically coding all information on connections between individuals, including that between family members. Therefore, if two cars were parked together—one owned by the child of its driver and the other owned by the spouse of its driver—the two driv-

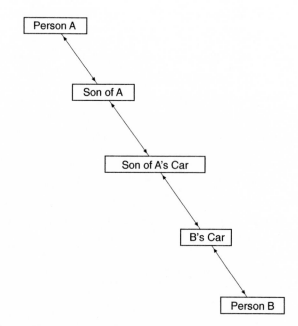

Figure 8.1 An Indirect Relationship Between Person A and Person B

ers would be connected indirectly in our network through their family members even if they were never seen together in person. This is illustrated in Figure 8.1.

At times, specific individuals were observed in specific cars, and the individuals did not include the registered owners of the cars. Many cars were registered to car leasing companies. To address this, we did some analyses in which the cars were treated as entities separate from their owners, and other analyses in which they were treated as proxies for their owners. For the phone information, it was assumed that the person to whom the phone was listed was the person speaking on the phone. Here, too, the coding of the relationships between the listed name and other people, including family, amorous, and business relationships, ensured that indirect connections between entities were identified.

Because the information sources were so diverse, we analyzed them in two ways. First, we combined all of the sources of information into one large network. We then looked at each source separately. Not surprisingly, the results were very different on a number of dimensions. The separate analyses each reflected, in part, the nature of the information included and the process through which that information was collected. The analyses using the combined information are quite different from the separate results. Although one could criticize this strategy, which seems to combine the apples of information on phone calls with the oranges of newspaper reports, this pooling is quite similar to the process through which investigators develop their models of what a criminal network looks like.

What Does the Structure Look Like?

The primary goals of our research project were to develop a broad picture of Soviet émigré crime in the tristate area, to systematically describe how it is structured, and to determine whether it is organized crime. Using techniques, described in detail in Appendix C, that are drawn from the larger set of approaches known as network analysis, the objective of our analysis was to describe the structure in terms of its overall characteristics, the locations of specific actors, and the number and characteristics of subgroups.

Overlap Analysis

A first step in comparing the information obtained from different sources is to assess the degree to which the same actors are identified in several sources and what, if any, patterns can be discerned in these overlappings. It might be hypothesized that key network members—or at least ones who are thought by the investigators to be key—would appear in more than one source. This involves a two-step analysis: first, we identified actors appearing in multiple sources of information, and then we examined their ties to each other to understand whether and how they are arranged.

Of the 4,798 individuals, organizations, and other entities that appear at least once in the Tri-state Project files, just thirty-seven were represented in four or more sources of information. Almost three times as many, 104, appeared in three or more sources, and 331 appeared in two sources. (Of course, many actors appear two or more times within the same source; for example, the one person may have phoned five or six other people.) Overall, then, there is very little overlap, in absolute terms, across the sources of information.

Not surprisingly, the actors who appeared in many sources tend to be among the most important according to the investigators. For some of these actors, there is a kind of chaining, in which an actor appears in one source, which leads investigators to initiate an investigation in another area. For example, in the course of watching one individual, another may be identified as meeting with him or her several times. This may lead to a background check, surveillance, or even a request for toll-call information about the new actor.

Figure 8.2 shows the ties between those actors who appear in four or more sources.[19] It contains many of the individuals and organizations that were mentioned earlier along with some new ones. Elson, Agron, Boris and Benjamin Nayfeld, Balagula, Ivankov, and Shuster are all included. Although not all directly connected to each other, they together form the center of the network. The network also includes a number of the locations and organizations with which they are identified. For example, many meetings and social events took place at the Paradise, Odessa, and Metropole restaurants, Cafe Kalinka, and Rasputin Catering, which, as a result, were also the subjects of surveillance by investigators. Two confidential informants are also included. The investigators used many informants, but these two indicate the complexity of the informant role. Not only do they provide information about other people, but they may also be surveilled in the course of other activity by investigators or be called by someone else

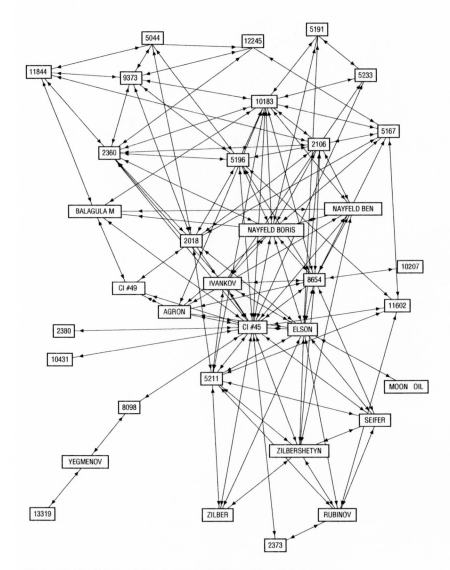

Figure 8.2 Ties Between Actors Appearing in Four or More Data Sources

who is being investigated. If they were not active in these networks, they would be of little use to investigators. From the structure found here, it is perhaps not surprising to know that confidential informant 45 was murdered during the course of the Tri-state Project investigation. This analysis does not provide a picture of Soviet émigré crime that appears particularly hierarchical or centered on just three or four individuals.

The information about those who are found in many different data sources also provides a map of how investigators viewed the organization of Soviet émigré crime. Because investigators did the data collection and prepared the reports from which we drew our data, their documents served both to reflect and to create their understandings of the structure of the crime networks. The actors represented are often those whom the investigators sought to prosecute because they had received a great deal of information indicating that these actors were important. Those who appear in many sources were mentioned most often in reports. Phone information, general surveillance reports, and confidential informants' reports were the next most important sources. Just nine of those individuals mentioned in four or more sources were mentioned in newspaper or magazine reports. Only eight were actually indicted during the time we gathered our data.

Analysis of All the Sources Together

The next phase of our analysis was to put together all the information from all the sources into one analysis. Because of the inclusiveness of this analysis, it should be considerably less filtered than the analysis of overlapping individuals. We analyzed this information in a number of ways. For example, we treated cars as proxies for their owners in some analyses but as completely independent entities in others. This distinction had no substantive impact on the results of the analysis. We also performed separate analyses using information on actual individuals only and then using information on people, organizations, locations, and other types of entities. The latter included such general concepts as "the Gambino crime family," which, while not physical entities, appeared important in the understandings of the organization of Soviet émigré crime held by investigators, prosecutors, journalists, and others. Many of the results were consistent from one analysis to another.

Each way that we analyzed the data, we found that there were more than 130 connected networks, called *components* in network analysis.[20] It is clear, however, that one very large component dominates. This component includes between 75 percent and 85 percent of the individuals and entities in the network, whether we look at individuals alone, all entities and individuals together, or some other configuration. The overall densities of both the network and the largest component are low, but this is not surprising given their sizes. The many smaller components—which often contained just two or three individuals or entities—were, of course, more densely connected. There were a small number of people with very many ties (as many as 311 in the case of confidential informant 45, when all types of entities are counted), and many more people with relatively few ties. Some of the other people with very many ties were also confidential informants, and this reflected the fact that they claimed to have direct knowledge of a large number of people. A substantial number of people were also tied to only one other actor in the network. The major actors identified in the overlap analysis tended to have a moderate, rather than very large, number of ties. Despite the size of the network in terms of numbers of members, the diameters are small. For example, with all entities treated separately, the diameter (or longest distance between any two members of the component) is 12. When people only are used, it is 13.

Because the networks were so clearly dominated by one large component, we focused on that group as the most likely to contain information that would indicate the existence of a centralized or hierarchical structure. Because it still contained thousands of actors, it

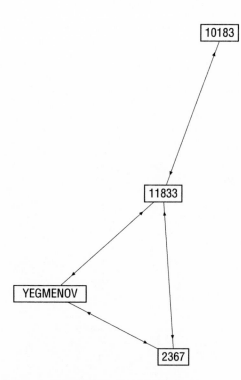

Figure 8.3 Jordan Center of Combined Sources for People Only

remained impossible to examine the structure visually. Therefore, we carried out two types of analysis: first, we examined what is known as the Jordan center of the component to identify the most central actors and entities, and then we used cluster analysis to describe the overall structure of the component.

The Jordan centers of the large components included nodes with maximum geodesics of 6 or 7, and they identify relatively small groups of actors. In the case of the analysis including people only, there were four actors in the Jordan center (see Figure 8.3), while all of the data combined yielded a Jordan center of sixty-one individuals and other entities (see Figure 8.4). The Jordan centers, as with the overlap analysis, identified people who were relatively important in the view of investigators. Although they did not contain the same

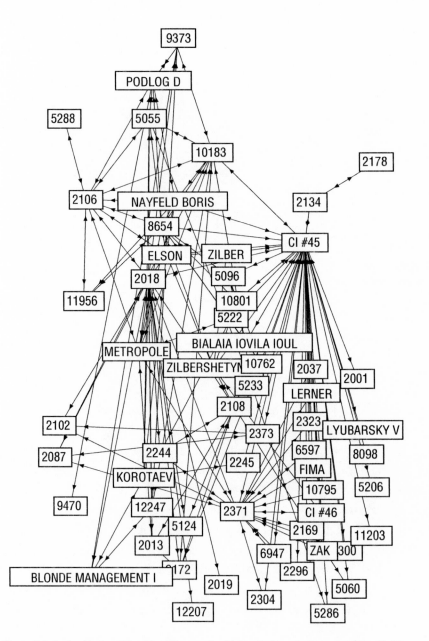

Figure 8.4 Jordan Center of Combined Sources for All People, Organizations, and Other Entities

individuals, all the individuals who were part of the Jordan centers of the networks were among the most important in terms of other network measures in all of the data sets.[21] That is, the overall centers of the networks were consistent.

Examination of Figure 8.4 reveals that it contains some of the actors that we saw in the overlap analysis. These include confidential informant 45, Elson, Zilber, Balagula, and Boris Nayfeld. Also included in both were some of the same organizations, such as the Metropole restaurant and Blonde Management. On the other hand, well-known actors such as Podlog (a convicted drug dealer) and Korotaev (a boxer and enforcer who was murdered outside a restaurant in Brighton Beach), who were not prominent in the overlap analysis, are included in the Jordan center. Interestingly, Ivankov (Yaponchik) and Agron, who have been at the center of many of the most important newspaper and magazine stories about Soviet émigré crime, do not occupy central positions in the network. It is important to remember, however, that there are ways to be important in a network without being at the center of it. It could be, for example, that unlike the idealized family organized crime structure in which key actors connect directly with each other, here they use intermediaries to connect with each other.[22] This is why it is essential to examine both the overall structure of the network and the individual-level characteristics such as number of ties or whether an actor is in the Jordan center.

To describe the overall structure of the network, we use a technique known as *cluster analysis,* which looks at each individual's and entity's connections and lack of connections to others in the network, which in this case was the largest component. The analysis then divides the network into clusters that contain individuals or entities with similar patterns of connections (and lack of connections). Thus, individuals in the same cluster are not necessarily connected to each other, although they often are; rather, they should be connected to the same other people or entities.[23] The analysis may find that there are no clearly defined clusters, and such a finding for our research would

mean that there was little or no organization of Soviet émigré criminals in the United States.

The cluster analyses identified clear clusters, and these clusters
were generally consistent for the analyses using only people and all
entities and treating cars as cars or as their owners. All the cluster
analyses found one large cluster that contained a broad spectrum of
people and, when they were included, other entities that appeared a
small number of times in the data and whose connections were to
other entities or actors that were similarly marginal. In a few instances, some seemingly important actors are included in this cluster,
even though they often appeared just a few times in the data. The
cluster analyses—regardless of how the data set was treated—tended
to place some actors into clusters by themselves and other actors into
small, consistent clusters. For example, in the twenty-four-cluster solution for all entities and the twenty-cluster solution for people only,
Yegemenov, Schteinberg, Elson, Grinbeyn, Komarov, and Boris
Nayfeld were all placed in clusters by themselves.[24] This befits their
distinctive patterns of relationships with other actors. In some analyses, Ivankov and certain key organizations were also placed in their
own clusters. David Podlog was consistently placed in a cluster in
which other people involved in his drug-smuggling conspiracy were
also located. The cluster analyses that included all entities also consistently yielded clusters that connected a single restaurant—such as the
Rasputin, the White Palace, and the Metropole—to a set of cars. A
consistent cluster containing three individuals emerged in virtually
every solution.

In general, the cluster analysis was successful in identifying
key actors and yielded important information about the overall organization. The key actors were each placed in clusters by themselves,
which indicates that they had distinctive patterns of relationships—
that is, they were tied or not tied to different members of the network
and also were not generally tied directly to each other. At the same
time, generally six or more individuals had distinctive positions,

which indicates that a simple hierarchical structure is not present. It may be that, as was the case for the Goldberg crime group described previously, ongoing structures are more personal and centered around individuals who through physical force, force of personality, or some combination of the two bring together a number of other actors to engage in a variety of criminal enterprises.

Analysis of the Separate Sources of Data

Research on organized crime has traditionally relied on a small number of data sources. For example, much use has been made of public hearings, court documents, newspaper reports, and interviews with investigators. Other research has relied mainly on interviews with participants in the organized crime network being studied. Because we had a diverse set of sources available, we were able to use each of these sources separately to compare what the structure of Soviet émigré crime looked like. The results of the separate analyses are in many instances quite different from those we obtained from our simultaneous analysis of all of the sources of information combined. The image of the structure drawn from each of the separate sources reflects the distinctive characteristics of the data source and may, in itself, explain some of the discrepancies between various commentators over the extent to which Soviet émigré crime is hierarchically organized.

Because the numbers of individuals and other entities included in each of the sources varied widely—from 1,851 for telephones to 137 for newspapers—we take somewhat different approaches to presenting the results of each separate analysis. We should note, however, that this big difference in numbers itself reflects the nature of the data sources. Newspapers and magazines almost inevitably focus on a smaller number of actors who are part of the most interesting or dramatic cases. Phone information, on the other hand, includes both important communications between key actors and mundane calls to a child's school or a catalog company. Thus, in the case of newspaper and magazine articles we can present an image of all the information in a single figure (Figure 8.5), whereas for other sources of information this is not possible.

As was true in the combined analysis, one large component contained over half of the network members in each of the sources (except newspapers, for which the largest component still contained 41 percent of those mentioned). In the case of phones, 98 percent of all of the actors and entities were contained in the largest component, while in the case of surveillance 56 percent were. The number of separate components in each data source ranged from eighteen or fewer for indictments (five), confidential informant reports (six), phones (nine), social surveillance (twelve), and newspapers (eighteen), up to fifty-five for general surveillance and 132 for reports.

The division of each data source into components reflects the nature of that source. Indictments are clearly meant to identify a set of actors involved in particular acts. They are not wide reaching and do not include information about unrelated acts. On the other hand, they are fairly dense within each component because all the people indicted together were accused of related criminal activities (Figure 8.6). The four small components represent the Podlog drug conspiracy, the Yegemenov and Syroejine false documents scheme, the Goldberg crime group, and the two crack vial manufacturing conspiracies. Each of these structures is well defined. The Goldberg crime group clearly centers on him, while the Podlog group contains a set of actors who all work directly with one another. The false document conspiracy centers on the two main actors and the organizations that they used in carrying out their schemes, including the banks in which they deposited the proceeds. The crack vial conspiracy at first seems more complex, but this turns out to be because there are actually two dense conspiracies with three actors linking them. The companies at the edge of that diagram were involved in the retail distribution of the crack vials.

The largest indictment component, representing a series of

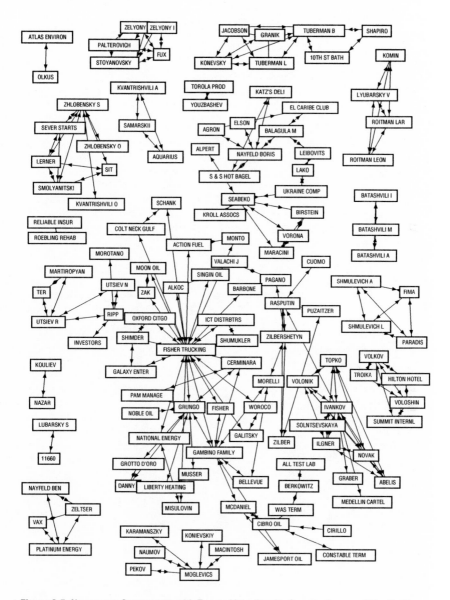

Figure 8.5 Newspaper Components with Two or More People, Organizations, or Other Entities

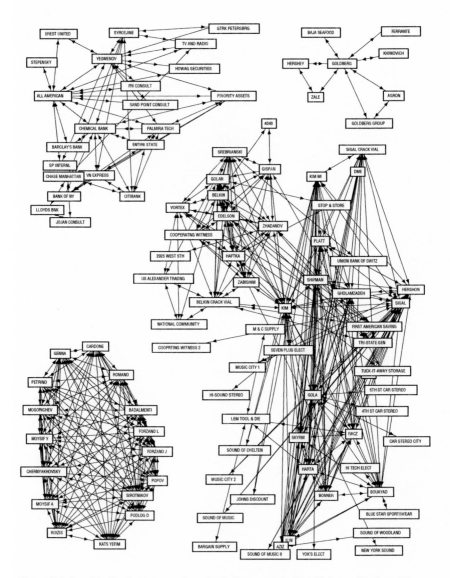

Figure 8.6 Four Smaller Components from the Indictment Data (Not All Actors Mentioned Have Been Indicted)

cases involving the motor-fuel tax-evasion schemes, is itself too complex to present in a simple diagram. Using a network analysis technique known as *block modeling*, however, we were able to determine
that the component actually consisted of seven very dense conspiracies, which were then connected to each other through a much smaller
number of individuals and companies. One reason these networks
were so dense was the nature of the fuel-tax scheme; a large number
of companies were named in each indictment, but many of these companies existed only on paper. An example of these networks is given
in Figure 8.7.

In contrast to the indictments, newspaper reports tend to be of
two types—the coverage of a specific incident or trial and general
coverage of the problem of Soviet organized crime. The latter provides less information about the actual ties between individuals and
more general structural characteristics as reported by experts
(whether law enforcement officials or criminologists), while the former provides links between actors but not across incidents. Therefore,
it is not surprising that considering the small number of members
of the network, a relatively large number of separate components of
moderate size are identified. It is also not surprising that an entity
such as the Gambino crime family plays an important role in this
network, occupying the Jordan center of the largest component because it serves as a link between several separate schemes. Such a
link is important because it builds a connection to existing stories on
other criminal organizations. Indeed, reporters covering the "Soviet
organized crime" story often also cover other organized crime stories.

Other data sources are also distinctive. Social surveillance focuses on well-defined events and therefore identifies clumps of people
attending the same events. At times these events overlap, but at other
times they do not, and each event identifies a new component. Other
types of surveillance and reports often involve investigators following
links between actors wherever they go. This leads to chaining of
actors and to broad components. Information from confidential infor-

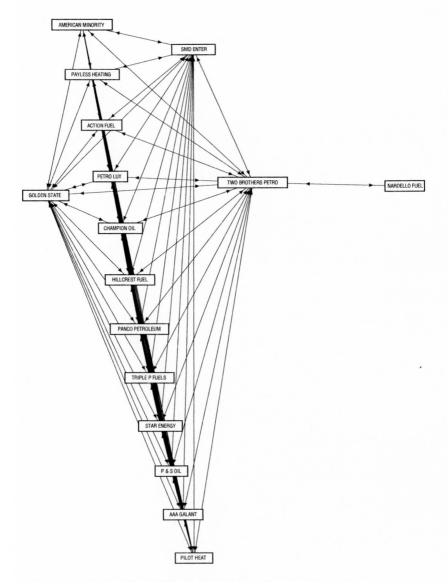

Figure 8.7 A Block from the Fuel Tax-Evasion Indictment Component

mants tends to focus on actors about whom the informant has direct or close indirect knowledge. Further, the informants often have or give information about each other. Finally, informants are, of course, being asked questions about relationships between actors by the investigators. As a result, their components tend to be, on average, relatively dense. The phone information is, for the individuals who are investigated, the least biased of any data. That is, all toll calls were entered without any further judgment being made about the importance of the actors calling or being called. These data yield one extremely dominant component and eight very small ones. In this they reflect, in part, investigative chaining (that is, places that received calls from a monitored phone may themselves be investigated) but also the characteristics of the network. As one investigator put it to us, "They all have each others' phone numbers."

That nearly all the investigative data sources produce a very large component itself provides important information about the nature of the Soviet émigré crime networks. It is incorrect to say that Soviet émigré crime consists mainly of totally distinct individuals or small groups of actors engaged in completely separate offenses. Rather, it indicates that, at a minimum, there are large networks of actors who have, through their networks, access to a variety of network resources. In the remaining analyses we focus primarily on the large components in the investigative sources.[25] This is indicated by the diameter of each of the components.

In the indictments, all actor(s) are no more than seven steps away from the farthest person in their component. In the largest phone component, with 1,816 actors, none is more than ten from any other, and some are no more than six from any other. This indicates that despite the low density of the network, it is still relatively tight, especially considering that 774 actors within the phone component have ties to only one other actor. General surveillance, reports, and newspapers have relatively spread-out structures with diameters of fifteen, seventeen, and ten, respectively. As would be expected by the nature of confidential informant data, the diameter of the largest component was just three.

In some instances, the Jordan center of a largest component contained only one actor. For reports, this was Zemnovitch, who was the owner of the Paradise restaurant. In the case of confidential informant reports, Levchitz (Sasha Pinya) was the Jordan center, while for general surveillance the center is Eugene Bendersky. Figures 8.8 and 8.9 (which include not only the Jordan centers for confidential informants and reports but also the network members whose maximum geodesics were one greater than theirs) indicate that their positions in the network are important but not dominant. Figure 8.10 contains all of the members of the largest component of the general surveillance network who appear more than once. Bendersky clearly plays a key role in linking together a set of separate observations, yet others in the same component—for example Yegemenov, and individuals associated with the Verrazano social club—appear to be important in other respects. The fact that Levchitz and several others also appeared in the overlap analysis indicates that they are of great interest to investigators and play possible coordinating and connecting roles. Of the three, however, only one is in the overall Jordan center.

Examining each of the data sources separately clarifies the nature of the structure of Soviet émigré crime networks and also illustrates the problematic nature of drawing conclusions based on just one or two types of information. Some sources of information, such as indictments, show structures that are dense, separate, and not very centralized. Other sources, such as newspaper coverage, produce centralized networks of key actors that often emphasize the importance of connections to other organized crime structures. Reports from confidential informants produce structures that are somewhat limited in their reach and centered around the informants themselves. If, however, several informants cover overlapping material, a more general understanding can be developed. We suspect that what is true for these

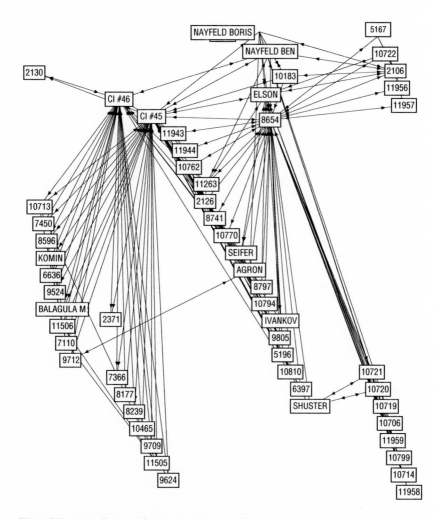

Figure 8.8 Jordan Center of Confidential Informant Reports

data will also be true in almost all data on criminal organizations. In this sense, issues around the use of these data by both investigators and researchers are similar to those that researchers face in all settings. It is clearly preferable to have information about any subject that is collected in several different ways, each of which can make up for the weaknesses of the other. Reliance on a small number of infor-

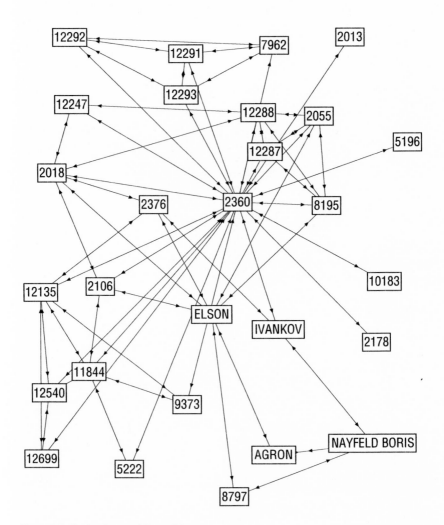

Figure 8.9 Jordan Center of General Reports

mants or a single source of information is likely to produce results that are biased. It is useful, however, to examine each of the sources separately in addition to examining the sources together as we did earlier in the chapter. Indeed, it is essential to understand the nature of each of the data sources to interpret the combined network appropriately.

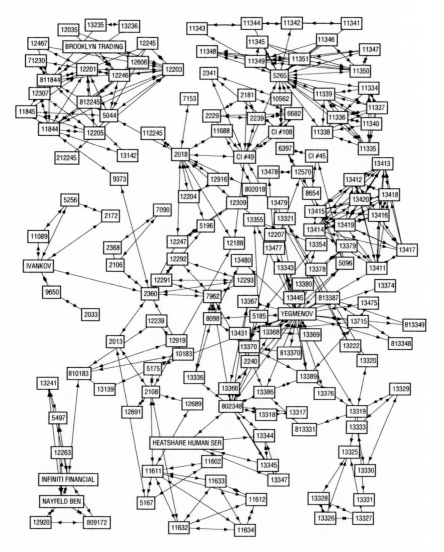

Figure 8.10 Members of the Largest General Surveillance Component Who Are Mentioned More Than Once

The Organization of Soviet Émigré Crime

The qualitative analyses in Chapter 7 and the network analysis here present similar pictures of the organization of Soviet émigré crime. On the one hand, this structure does not look like either what is commonly understood to be the structure of organized crime or a mafia in the conventional sense of those terms. The networks are neither highly centralized nor dominated by a small number of individuals. Those individuals who do have particular influence seem to occupy their positions on the basis of their personal characteristics, and we have seen little to indicate that these organizational structures will outlive the involvement of their central actors. This means that the networks lack the continuing structures associated with, for example, La Cosa Nostra.

On the other hand, it is clear that these structures are not simply small groups of criminals essentially acting independently of one another. Although such groups do seem to exist, they represent a tiny portion of the actors identified in the course of the Tri-state Project. Instead, there is broad connectivity among most of the actors. They may not be directly connected to a large number of others, but they are indirectly connected to many. This allows the networks a great deal of flexibility in the organization of their offenses, which means they can be responsive to the opportunities for illegal undertakings that develop. Given such an opportunity, a member of these large networks can access partners who are either generalists or specialists, can raise capital, and can access other needed resources. In this sense, the structure is very functional. The fluid nature of the structure may also explain the high level of internal violence that the network seems to experience. The lack of a more hierarchical structure means that no one can effectively control the use of violence or mediate disputes. In addition, the lack of more formal subgroupings weakens loyalty to past partners: many of the murders, for example, seem to involve disputes between individuals who once worked together.

This suggests that people from the former Soviet Union who have become involved in crime have been especially opportunistic and, at the same time, lack the trust associated with ethnic identity that is associated with other criminal organizations. Our findings also seem to support the observation of a Russian criminal who testified at a U.S. Senate hearing:

> Some [of the criminals who have come to the United States] are thugs who worked as enforcers or muscle in criminal groups based in Russia. These men are responsible for much of the violence that has taken place in Brighton Beach and other communities where Russians are concentrated in this country. These men are also disorganized and looking for a leader to devise a profitable criminal venture—someone like Ivankov. These are dangerous men, but would be far more so behind a clever leader.[26]

The analysis of both separate data sources and combined data sources provides useful information about the nature of Soviet émigré crime networks and, perhaps most important, provides systematic approaches to the use of relatively unfiltered data that would not be possible if only descriptive methods were used. It is important, however, that the limitations of these approaches be kept in mind. Both the descriptive and the network analytic approaches that we have used rely on information that is collected by the investigators from a variety of agencies, but these analyses do not incorporate information on other activities that may be taking place or on structures that exist but of which investigators are unaware.

In the end, these analyses must always be viewed with the caveat that they represent not *the* structure of Soviet émigré crime networks but a structure of Soviet émigré crime networks as seen by the investigators of the Tri-state Project. Although this is a research caveat, this situation also represents the real world of investigating and prosecuting organized crime. The investigators themselves do not necessarily view the networks in the same way that network analysis leads us to see them. There is simply too much information from too many sources for any one individual to process, and different analysts might take different approaches and reach different conclusions. Therefore, it is useful to explore the views of others who have observed the activities of Soviet émigrés. To that end, we next examine the perceptions of the ordinary Soviet émigrés—those not involved in crime—who live and work in the same communities as the criminals in whom we are interested.

CHAPTER 9

HOW SOVIET ÉMIGRÉS VIEW
SOVIET ÉMIGRÉ CRIME

Brighton Beach, Brooklyn, is perhaps the largest Soviet émigré community in the world. These few miles along the Atlantic Ocean contain a world of people and stores in which Russian is the most frequently heard language. Foods and other products reflect Russian, Ukrainian, and other cultures of the former Soviet Union. According to the 1990 census, some 23,656 of the 59,917 people in Brighton Beach and the surrounding area claimed Russian, Ukrainian, or Lithuanian ancestry. That population continued to grow in the years following the 1991 collapse of the Soviet Union.[1] Feature articles in the press regularly describe the neighborhood's food shops, restaurants, and streets as exotic destinations for the adventurous to visit.[2] The neighborhood is sometimes referred to as "Little Odessa" or "Little Russia." In the press, especially in New York City, it is frequently cited as the center for Soviet émigré organized crime.[3] Many of the same restaurants and clubs—such as the Odessa, the Rasputin, and the National, mentioned earlier—are regularly featured in both types of articles.

Although Brighton Beach has long been home to Jewish immigrants from Russia and elsewhere, most of the Soviet émigrés living there today are relatively recent arrivals.[4] Of the foreign-born population of the Brighton Beach area included in the 1990 census, two-thirds have arrived since 1975. The Soviet émigré population consists mainly of those who arrived in the late 1970s as part of the movement of Jews out of the Soviet Union (19 percent arrived between 1975 and 1979) and another wave that arrived after leaving the USSR became easier in 1985. Yet a third wave of migrants began to arrive after 1991, making immigrants from the states of the former Soviet Union one of the largest groups of new arrivals in the United States in the early 1990s.[5]

Because of Brighton Beach's importance for the Soviet émigré population both nationally and in the tristate region, a closer look at who lives there and how they view the criminal activities of their fellow émigrés is useful for the understanding of Soviet émigré crime. To this end, we carried out a set of interviews with "ordinary" Soviet émigrés. Because we asked potentially sensitive questions about crime and organized crime, obtaining a scientific, random sample of Soviet émigrés living in the United States, New York, or even Brighton Beach itself would have been extremely difficult. Many in the émigré community were hesitant to be interviewed on any subject and were especially wary of questions about organized crime. We also asked subjects open-ended questions about themselves and their experiences. This meant face-to-face interviews during which the interviewer could ask follow-up questions to clarify answers. We preferred this approach to a mail or telephone survey in which the subjects would have been given a large number of narrow questions with a fixed set of answers from which they could choose.

Instead of taking a random sample of émigrés, we found subjects through a process known as *snowball sampling,* in which the interviewer starts with a small number of subjects who are willing to be interviewed and then asks those subjects for suggestions of other people who would also be willing to be interviewed. A total of twenty-five people were interviewed. The interviewees were not paid.

We cannot generalize from our results to any broader population in any statistical sense. We do believe, however, that the results of the survey reflect broad patterns within the Brighton Beach community. A university student who had herself emigrated from Moscow conducted all the interviews in Russian, recorded them, and translated them into English.

As part of the snowball sampling process, the interviewer sought people with a variety of perspectives. Sixteen of the interview subjects were men, and nine were women, ranging in age from eighteen to seventy-two. The respondents included students, teachers, a salesperson, and a taxi driver. Most were originally from Ukraine and Belarus, especially the cities of Kiev and Minsk. All were self-identified Jews. The earliest had arrived in the United States in 1979, and the most recent in 1994. Slightly more than half lived in Brighton Beach itself, while the rest lived in the immediately surrounding areas. We had no reason to suspect that any had been involved in criminal activity.[6] To understand their perspective on crime in Brighton Beach and among their fellow émigrés, we first needed to understand their experiences in the Soviet Union and the United States.

Why Émigrés Came to the United States

The Soviet émigrés we interviewed gave several types of reasons for having moved to the United States. These reflected the conditions in the Soviet Union—especially the anti-Semitism faced by Jews—at the time they left, their family situations, and other concerns such as their future prospects and the health of their families. By far the most common reason—given alone or in combination with others—involved anti-Semitism. This took several different forms. For some anti-Semitism was experienced as an inability to advance in their careers or a belief that discrimination against Jews was common. A waiter in his twenties said, "I left Russia because I had no future there. No matter how hard I tried or strived for success, I would not reach my goal. Jews were discriminated against for many years. My father did not get the promotions that he deserved. I did not want the same thing to happen to me." A businessman said, "I felt there was a lot of prejudice in Russia. I did not like the way people talked about the Jews. I did not feel I did something to upset those people. I thought it was very unfair to me. Not only was I denied the basic opportunity to practice my religion, but I was also denied a chance to advance in [my] career."

Other émigrés feared physical violence. A woman in her fifties commented, "I wanted to take my children away from that country. I remember the fear when the anti-Semitism was developing. Finally, I realized that I would not be able to live and know that my grandchildren were safe unless I took them away from this country." Many of these respondents had left after the collapse of the Soviet Union and argued that the situation had grown worse since then. A schoolteacher in her late fifties said the following:

> We came here because there was a great deal of anti-Semitism in Russia. During the last years when the democracy was associated with our life, it became very scary. They could insult you on the street or in the store; they could say nasty things virtually anywhere. Several times we came across cases when we had to run to avoid scandal and fighting. I was retired by that time. When I went to work, I never felt anything like that. My husband and I were teachers. He taught music, and I taught literature. It is possible that some people didn't like us, but we worked hard, and they were satisfied with our work. So when we retired it became very scary. We were afraid for our children and grandchildren. We were afraid that the situation was going to develop into God knows what. There were many representatives of Pamyat [a right-wing nationalist movement with strong anti-Semitic ideology] in Minsk. They used to arrange meetings. We were even warned that if there was a sign of a coming pogrom [an organized massacre], we had to call a certain number.

Others focused more specifically on their inability to practice their religion. A computer programmer said, "I was not allowed to practice my religion. I come from a very religious family." Another said, "Religion has always been very important to me. I was not allowed to have any information concerning Jewish religion."

The second theme that emerged in discussions of why they had left the Soviet Union focused on economic opportunity. Of course, some of those who reported anti-Semitism also spoke of how this discrimination limited their chances in their occupations. But a smaller number of émigrés were attracted strictly by the opportunities in the United States. A nineteen-year-old student who had arrived in 1992 said, "I came here because I wanted a better life for myself. Don't get me wrong. My parents were pretty well off in Russia. I lived well, but I hoped that I would live even better in the United States. There are no other reasons—neither political nor religious— for me to be here." Another man, in his forties, said simply, "I wanted to live better." Each of these themes would also have been expressed by the millions of immigrants of all nationalities coming here since the founding of European settlements in North America.

The third theme that emerged involved family ties. Often the younger respondents reported that they had no role in the decision to emigrate and that their parents made the decision for them. Many of the people we interviewed said that they came because their families were coming or because other members of their families had already migrated. This was, of course, especially so for those who had migrated as children. Some of these younger respondents said that they would have chosen to stay with their friends in Russia. Similar reasons were also given by some of the older respondents, including one who was seventy-two years of age. As one person put it, "The sole reason was that my whole family lives here. I, personally, would prefer to stay in Russia. There is more money there, and you don't have to work as hard."

Two other explanations were also given. Two respondents mentioned that the contamination caused by the Chernobyl nuclear disaster near Kiev made continuing to reside in Ukraine impossible for them. As one put it, "Chernobyl was there. We were trying to save our children and grandchildren. The level of radiation was very high." Whatever its role in the thinking of others, only one person explicitly mentioned wanting "to live in a free country." "Freedom," said this émigré, "was something I was never going to enjoy in Russia no matter what party was in power. Russian Jews were not welcome in Russia. Even native Russians did not enjoy full freedom. America was a perfect place that gave me the opportunity to be free."

Brighton Beach as a Destination for Émigrés

Most of the respondents had heard of Brighton Beach before emigrating. They knew that it was an area where many Russians lived and where Russian was spoken. As one put it, "I heard it was a little Odessa. Most of the population was Ukrainian Jews. It was a Jewish reservation consisting of new immigrants from Russia." Their information came from various sources, including letters from relatives or friends living in the United States and radio, newspapers, and television in the Soviet Union. One mentioned that Brighton Beach came up in jokes told by comedians. As a student put it, "I cannot narrow it down to one person or one paper that I read it in. It was a well-known fact among Russians. Some of the information came from the people who live in America, but most of it came from casual conversations that I had in Russia." Many mentioned that they felt comfortable being in a community where Russian was spoken and "the signs on the street were written in Russian."

The language issue was central for many of those who chose to live in Brighton Beach. Language problems were the biggest barrier that they faced in the United States. One said, "When you first come to a new country and you don't know the language, it is always better to go somewhere where you can communicate the best. You have to be able to tell the salesperson what you want to buy. The only place offering these kinds of opportunities is Brighton Beach. The fact that most of the Russian population lives there allows me to lead the same lifestyle that I am used to leading in the former Soviet Union." The desire for familiar cultural surroundings can last far beyond the initial move to a new country. As a twenty-six-year-old paralegal put it, "Well, actually we used to live in Buffalo, but it was too boring there because we were the only Russians living there. The thing is that we are Russians after all. We need some communication, and we couldn't get it there. We wanted to go somewhere where there is action. Brighton Beach is a perfect place for it. It is filled with life." Several said that they were surprised that Americans "would allow" people to speak only Russian. Seeing images of Brighton Beach while still in the Soviet Union, a schoolteacher remembered, "Brighton Beach for us was like the American legend. We didn't hear anything negative about Brighton Beach."

Others had heard negative things about Brighton Beach, especially about crime there. One mentioned, "I also heard that a lot of people who used to make money through extortion come to Brighton Beach to continue doing the same. Being in the Soviet Union, I heard that Brighton Beach was not the best place to live in." Others had heard about conflicts between the Russian immigrants and African Americans. One recalled, "There were a lot of rumors about Brighton Beach—some true, some false. I found out a lot from the letters from my son. He told me a lot about the war that took place between the Ukrainians and the blacks who were living in Brighton Beach at that time. I have heard a lot about the crime in Brighton Beach." Others mentioned a general fear of crime in America. For example, "We heard that America was a very horrible place to live in. We heard that people were often robbed and killed there. So the only area where one could feel safe was Brighton Beach." Others had negative impressions of Brighton Beach for other reasons. For example, a student in his thirties said, "I heard that mostly old people lived there. It didn't sound like a place for successful people. I also heard something about the crime problem here, but I did not pay too much attention to it. Besides, I didn't know how bad it was."

Many émigrés also had friends or relatives already living in Brighton Beach or nearby areas, and this led them to settle there. For example, a student in his twenties remembered, "It just so happened that our relatives lived in Brighton Beach. They were the ones who helped us settle here. So they just rented us an apartment that was close to where they lived. They didn't exactly ask me where I wanted to live. I think that if our relatives lived somewhere else, we would end up living somewhere else." Others found it simply convenient at the time of migration. For example, a computer programmer said, "I didn't really decide to live anywhere. When I first came here, I had no money, no transportation. We were sort of dumped here. I had friends who told me they rented an apartment for my family in Brighton Beach. There were three families of our relatives that came at the same time. We had to communicate somehow and see each other. Without transportation it would have been hard to do. It was hard to find three apartments together. We were able to do it in Brighton Beach."

Some respondents did not want to live in Brighton Beach. A nineteen-year-old female bank teller who used to live in Brighton Beach commented, "I don't like this place. It is too loud and too dirty. And it is not just the dirt and the Russian cursing everywhere. Brighton Beach is becoming a very dangerous area. It is scary to hear about all the crimes that are being committed there." The student who claimed to come only for economic reasons declared, "I did not come to this country to be the same kind of Russian and live with the same Russians in America. Brighton Beach is an exact copy of Russia— same stores, same people, same food, same lines in the grocery shops. It may be a little better than the Soviet Union, but I would not like to live there." A twenty-two-year-old college student who had been in the United States for three years said, "I don't like to live among Russians. I don't know why, but it is annoying for me to come to America and live among Russians. Don't get me wrong. I have a lot of Russian friends, but I wouldn't want to live in that environment all my life. If you came to America, you are better off starting out among Americans." Others became disillusioned with the neighborhood. A forty-nine-year-old cook who had lived in Brighton Beach for a year moved out. She commented, "I don't like Brighton Beach because it is too loud, too dirty, and there are too many people there. I want to live in a place that is quieter, somewhere where you can relax after work. I have lived in Brighton Beach about a year after I came here. I didn't like it at all."

Problems Émigrés Felt They Faced in the United States

Like all immigrants, the people we interviewed faced various problems and challenges when they came to the United States. These problems may, themselves, serve to strengthen the Brighton Beach community as a center of Russian émigré life. Discussion of these problems required some prompting. Often when asked simply if they had had any problems, they would reply "not really" or with some similar phrase. When asked what specific problems they faced, however, many could name some. Some mentioned cultural problems having to do with the differences between living in the United States and living in the Soviet Union. One woman commented on the strangeness of many situations here: "We had to get used to the order of things over here. We had to find out about America and learn how to live here. We even had problems with shopping. The variety is so great that you don't know what is more profitable to buy." A woman now in her mid-twenties who had arrived as a child in 1979 remembered, "[W]e were sticking out because we couldn't dress like everybody else. At that time conditioners cost less than shampoos, so we washed hair with it because we thought it was the same thing. That was very rough for people who just left everything in pursuit [of a] better future." Simply learning the ways of American culture, even when living in a largely Russian community, was difficult.

Not surprisingly, the most frequently mentioned difficulties centered around language and the difficulties that not being able to speak fluent or unaccented English created for adjustment to the

United States. This made it especially difficult to obtain a job. A fifty-six-year-old librarian commented, "The main problem was a language problem. We felt very helpless and therefore depressed. Our children lived far away from us, and we were unable to communicate so that we were understood by Americans. It was very depressing. Now, with time, we got used to the country, its laws and traditions, its language. We can explain what we want using basic signs. That's all we need." A taxi driver told us that when he had first arrived, "I could hardly speak, but I did not understand a word of what those people were saying. I had to drive to earn money, and it was really stressful not to be able to understand where they wanted me to go." Another remembered feeling embarrassed when customers complained to his manager that they could not understand him because of his accent. Others felt that language problems meant that getting a job outside of Brighton Beach would be very difficult. A forty-seven-year-old businessman said, "When people heard a heavy Russian accent, they were not willing to give us a job." At times this made the émigrés feel very frustrated. One commented, "People did not understand us and, quite honestly, did not want to."

Many of the émigrés reported that they felt discriminated against, in part because of their accented English, and this was seen as part of an ongoing cycle that limited their ability to improve their English. One woman in her thirties commented, "It was hard for me to get a job anywhere outside Brighton Beach. Even after so many years, I still cannot find a job in Manhattan. I do not have any proof, but I feel that I am discriminated against. My English has improved over the years. It would improve even more if I could get a decent job in Manhattan. Due to the nature and location of the [company] I work in, I mostly speak Russian. My [company] does not make a lot of money. I think I am denied certain opportunities because of my Russian accent and national belonging." Another expressed frustration at what he perceived as the attitudes of Americans toward the émigrés and also at his own difficulties: "In the Soviet Union the Jews were not welcome. When I came here, I became Russian and have the same problems. I feel as though I am not welcome here. Americans don't want any Russian immigrants living with them in the same country. Although I knew the language when I came here, I am still embarrassed to speak it in front of other people. I realize that I will never get rid of the accent, but I don't think this should bother people who were born here as much as it does."

Beyond the workplace many felt they were subject to stereotypes as either criminals or people living on public assistance. A student in his thirties commented:

In every society there are certain people who love creating stereotypes and attaching stigmas to people. They think that all Russian immigrants are the same—that they don't want to work. According to those people, Russians just sit at home and collect public assistance. Another stereotype that bothers me a lot is the one that is particularly popular in Brooklyn—that most Russians belong to the mafia. Lots of American students at my school come and ask me these stupid questions. This bothers me a lot. What can I tell them? Of course, there are some people like that, but the majority of Russians want to work, get a good education, and pay taxes like everyone else. Why is it so hard to comprehend?

Another said that his younger brother, a middle-school student, had been beaten up in school because he was Russian.

Several respondents mentioned their feelings that the police were biased against people from Brighton Beach and Russian immigrants in general. They felt that police officers were rude and unnecessarily rough—complaints heard from many communities in New York City. Several respondents referred to an incident in which the police were called to a restaurant when a fight was going on: "When the police arrived, they arrested the whole family and beat up a guy who was drunk. I remember reading about a strike after that incident. Peo-

ple were protesting against the cruelty with which the American police officers treat people in Brighton Beach." Although none seemed
to have direct knowledge of the incident, and they did not all agree
on its details, they all felt that the police had overreacted and that this
was due to their negative feelings about Russians. Strained relations
between the émigrés and the police, which are exacerbated by language difficulties, have at times been severe enough to lead to mainstream press coverage and the organization of "sensitivity sessions"
at the local precinct.[7]

For some, there was a racial dimension to many of their feelings
of discrimination. Four respondents volunteered that they felt that the
people who work in social welfare offices discriminated against Russians: "I felt strong discrimination in offices of public assistance. I
am not sure if it is discrimination against Russians or against whites
in general, but blacks who sit there do not show any respect to new
Russian immigrants who need that money only for a couple of months
to survive before they get a job." Another said that the welfare workers assumed that they would be "like the blacks" in terms of their
dependency on welfare. They could not understand how welfare
workers could not be more sympathetic to their individual plights.
More specifically, several of these respondents insisted that welfare
benefits for "blacks" were better than those available to Russians: "I
have no definite information about how the welfare system works in
the United States, but I am pretty sure that Russians are discriminated
against in welfare offices. We get less public assistance than anyone
in the state." A student said that his parents told him that they received less welfare than blacks.

For Russians—coming from a state that provided social support
in the form of subsidized housing, food, medical care, and employment—the well-known hostility of American welfare workers to applicants and the stigma attached to welfare dependence may have
been particularly surprising. Further, as the 1997 reforms to the welfare laws indicate, it is clear that there is broad hostility to the very

idea that immigrants should be entitled to transfer payments of any kind. The fact that they identified this as a racial issue may be a result of their location in Brooklyn, where African Americans make up more than one-third of the population and nonblack Hispanics account for an additional 20 percent of the population.[8] It would not be surprising if most non-Russians they came into contact with on a daily basis—in school, in public areas, and in government offices—were also African American. Another important factor may also be the use of the term *black* in Russian areas as a description for Chechens and others from the Caucasus region of the former Soviet Union, who are also treated with hostility and stereotyped as criminals.

Not everyone described these sorts of problems. As one seventy-two-year-old put it, "We received financial assistance right after we came here. As far as the emotional part goes, we had no problems. Of course, it is hard to live without knowing the language, but that has nothing to do with us being Russian immigrants." Another person described the support she received from neighbors and agencies after having a fire in her family's apartment.

Perceptions of Crime in Brighton Beach

Those interviewed were evenly divided on the question of whether there is a general crime problem in Brighton Beach. Those who believed that there was not a problem generally argued that the crime that goes on in Brighton Beach is no worse than that in other parts of New York. As one man put it, "Crime is everywhere, whether it is Brighton Beach or Beverly Hills. . . . Brighton Beach is far from leading the charts." Several blamed the media for creating the impression that Brighton Beach was crime ridden. A waiter said, "I think the media blows the whole thing out of proportion. The statistics would show that reporters greatly exaggerate the level of crime in Brighton Beach to make a sensation." A few contrasted life in Brighton Beach as they know it with the image that they believed that the media created. A cook said, "My friend and her family live very peacefully. Their children play outside day and night. They don't seem to have any problems with Brighton Beach. My friend's father sits on the boardwalk and plays chess all day. He never had any problems either."

Others felt that there was a crime problem, but many of them focused on street crime as a major issue. In this, their comments were probably not very different from those you would hear from residents of many neighborhoods in New York City. Many blamed the crime problem on residents of nearby, non-Russian neighborhoods. One said, "It has become worse with time. When we first came here, it wasn't that bad. We are very close to Coney Island. The crime rate is pretty high there. That's why it bothers me. I feel a little better in the summer. There are lots more police in Brighton Beach in the summer. I think we should have more police officers in winter too." Another said, "We don't come across anything serious. Of course, you should not walk alone at night because someone else from the other neighborhood can come in at night and you will get yourself in trouble. . . . Our own people don't give us problems." For these people, the discussions of crime were part of larger discussions—often incorporating racial and ethnic themes—about the difficulties of living in New York. It is not surprising that those who reported having problems when they came to the United States were more likely to report that Brighton Beach had a crime problem.

A third group said there was a crime problem but explicitly connected the problem with organized crime or the Russian mafia. A nineteen-year-old bank teller said, "Brighton Beach is a very dangerous area to live in. I don't know whether it is due to the fact that the Russians and Puerto Ricans and Italians live there and they fight for the territory or because there are so many immigrants there who used to belong to the Russian Mafia in the former Soviet Union." One said, "All the murders and fights scare me. When we first came here, a couple was killed. Nothing was taken away from them. I am sure it was not just an accidental death. The mafia knew who they were aiming at." Some of those in this group expressed views that reflected a number of separate themes. For example, one said, referring to the crime problem, "This does not only include crimes that are publicized by the media and attributed to the Russian mafia but also regular crimes, victims of which we often become. Besides, in the last couple of years, there were quite a few mafia conflicts that were resolved through murder. I think this indicates a problem."

For a small number of respondents, usually somewhat older than the others we interviewed, their perceptions of crime had a serious impact on their lives. The seventy-two-year-old woman reported, "We are scared to walk out on the street. It is not a good feeling to be scared. Sometimes we don't get a chance to go for a walk for seven to ten days. We really want to, but we are afraid someone is going to hurt us." Another said, "I have to walk my grandchildren home from school because I am afraid they will get kidnapped." A fifty-nine-year-old teacher reflected the atmosphere of fear that some felt:

> We constantly hear about crime. . . . Basically, we never had anything to do with the Mafia, thank God, because we are too insignificant for them, but we constantly hear about it, and the sense of fear is in the air. It is constantly there. It puts an extra strain on us. It seems to me that if there were no crimes in America it would be an ideal place to live. We also hear on TV and on the radio that even police officers say that 100 percent of juveniles are armed. They also have their own gangs, debts, fights, etc. . . . We constantly hear about that. . . . Even in the Jewish centers that we attend there are handouts that warn us against entering our own house without first ringing the bell a couple of times to avoid a tragic situation if the burglars are still in the house. They teach us how to act when someone knocks on your door, how to act when you feel that someone is about to attack you. In other words the danger is so clear that the Jewish center and even the media warn us about it.

She was able to give an extensive list of crimes that she had heard about.

Asked who was committing crime in Brighton Beach, the respondents were evenly divided between putting most of the blame on Russians and putting it on people from other ethnic groups. A number argued, as did one businessman, "If we are talking about the Russian organized crime, I would say that most of the people are Russian. If we are talking about the street crimes like pocket picking and prostitution, I believe that Latinos and non-Russian immigrants are responsible for it. It is at least 60 percent non-Russian." Another said, "Blacks commit most of the street crimes. Russians are involved in higher, more profitable types of crime." Similarly, a twenty-one-year-old student commented, "I believe that others are responsible for crimes in Brighton Beach. Russians would be involved in more universal crimes—crimes that are more serious. Stealing, vandalizing cars is not something that a Russian criminal would do, in my opinion."

A number, however, focused on Russians as the main group involved in crime in Brighton Beach. They often stressed, however, that the Russians involved in crime either were not real immigrants— "they don't live here permanently"—or were of different ethnic backgrounds than they were. Some said that the Russians involved traveled back and forth between New York and the former Soviet Union. According to a student in his thirties,

> The people who are responsible for most of the crime are Russian tourists who have temporary visas. They live in Russia and just come here to finalize the deal or to get rid of someone. Most of the business visas that they have are fake, but no one cares. So these people keep commuting back and forth. They are the ones committing most of the crime. They work for the Russian Mafia over in Russia, not in Brighton Beach. They just need connections here. They need banks to hide money. They need to invest that money here, so that no one could take that away from them.

As one twenty-six-year-old woman put it, "As far as organized crime goes, most of the members of the mafia are Russian and live in Brighton Beach. Some of them are here illegally, but most of them are not Jewish; they are Christians, and they are not like us. They are more cruel." Another argued that those Russians involved in crime were criminals in the Soviet Union "who come to America to escape the punishment. They continue committing crime as they used to do. On the other hand, engineers, teachers, doctors do not come here to kill people."

When asked what types of crime Russians were involved in, murder for hire was the most frequently volunteered offense. There was a particular emphasis on the hiring of people from the Soviet Union to come and commit murder and then leave. This may reflect a series of stories in the media about such incidents. A gym teacher gave a more detailed description than most:

> I think the most popular type of crime is murder for hire. That is what Russians do the best. They have been trained to do so in Afghanistan and in World War II. Russians are ready to do anything for money, especially when you do not have the brain to make it any other legal way. Murder for hire is the simplest kind of crime for Russian criminals because of their Russian background in a lawless country. . . .
>
> Russian murderers are being ordered and brought from Russia to complete a specific task of killing someone. The [Russian] mafia shows them who to kill, and that is the end of it. It is planned and organized pretty well. However, I don't think that Russians occupy any of the higher positions in the criminal structure.

Many people mentioned drugs, including one student who said, "There are a lot of kids even in my school who sell and do drugs." Others talked about the easy availability of drugs on the boardwalk and the opportunities for drug selling provided to young people.

Several respondents mentioned that Russian criminals were involved in a wide variety of scams and financial crimes, including false lotteries in which the supposed winners ended up losing their money, fraudulent credit cards, and gas scams. In the case of the gas scams, several mentioned that the gasoline sold might contain water or other additives, which makes these stories different from the major gas scams reported by law enforcement. Others described the extortion of businesses in Brighton Beach. Money laundering, especially at the large restaurants, was also mentioned repeatedly. Other types of crimes mentioned were rape, pickpocketing, car theft, prostitution, robbery, and burglary. The respondents did not, however, usually base responses to this question on direct, personal experiences. Rather, they seemed strongly influenced by the media and stories heard from others. The mention of rape by several of the émigrés may be a reflection of this. In the period prior to the interviews there had been a highly publicized rape of a Russian woman under the nearby Coney Island boardwalk.[9] The assailants arrested by the police were not, however, Russian.

Every respondent reported having heard of organized crime in Brighton Beach either in the media or from other people, but only six reported that they had been the victim of any type of crime in Brighton Beach. The same number reported that they knew a victim of a crime. In most cases, these crimes were not attributed to organized crime but were viewed more as ordinary street crimes that may or may not have been committed by other émigrés. For example, one woman reported that she had had her wallet stolen, and a student recalled that he had been robbed of $20 at knife point while delivering pizzas. A third person had his car broken into. One woman reported that "a psychotic Puerto Rican woman, who got mad because the landlord kicked her out, . . . showed up and burned her apartment. My family and I were right above it." She was not certain, however, that she should classify herself as a victim of a crime, since her family's apartment was not damaged deliberately by the arsonist.

Only two people spoke of themselves as direct victims of organized crime. The owner of a small business said he was required to change the fire extinguishers every two years. He said, "Once, I oversaw that the people were simply changing the labels and charging about $250 for each time. So I told them I was not going to pay them anything. If they ever came back, I would call the police. Most of the people were Russian." He apparently suffered no consequences for this defiance. Another described an incident in which he bought a ticket to Russia for his grandmother through a Russian travel agency but never received the ticket. A detective told him that it was a fraudulent agency that had disappeared and that there were quite a few people who were victimized as a result of this scam. Although in these crimes groups of individuals were acting together, there is no indication that either was a part of any overarching organization.

One woman in her twenties spoke about a boyfriend who was "in the mafia." She reported, however, that "he kept me strictly out of it. He never talked about business at home." She did recount several incidents in which he was able to intimidate people who were causing trouble for her or others, although she was not sure what form this intimidation actually took. One incident was described as follows:

About seven years ago I was at a party, and I had a conflict with a girl who I previously knew. I knew she was using drugs. I was also aware that she was using them for a long time. She was out of control. In the middle of the night her boyfriend found a moment when I was alone, and he told me in a very threatening tone of voice that I was not going to come out of this restaurant alive. He put a knife to my throat and pulled me by my hair. I managed to get away from him and ran to the bathroom. Thank God, I had a cellular phone that I used to call my boyfriend. In three minutes my boyfriend and three big guys entered the restaurant and forced the guy, who put a knife to my throat, into a limo. He took him to the boardwalk, and I never saw the guy since then.

In another incident the boyfriend stabbed a man who was bothering her at a restaurant.

Crimes experienced by people known to the respondents were similar to those they had experienced themselves. Most involved theft or robbery, and one involved vandalism of a car. A friend of one was burglarized three times in the last two and a half years. Another woman had a friend who was pistol whipped during a robbery in the fur store in which she worked. One of the three robbers was Russian; the other two were Latinos. Another had a friend who was struck on the head in the elevator of her building and had her food stamps taken. One reported that a friend was a victim of a common form of pickpocketing in which "a guy, passing by, spilled something on him. Right away a woman came up to him and started helping him and cleaning his coat. After she left, he realized that both the food stamps and the money were gone." Respondents who knew crime victims were, on the whole, older than others in the sample and had lived in the United States longer.

Three people reported crimes that have, in their opinions, involved at least elements of organized crime. One told of a friend who started a small business: "As soon as he started making some money, a couple of guys came up to him asking him for money. They said that he has to pay if he wants to have his business and family to be safe. Since then, he pays them promptly every month on a certain day. He never reported anything to the police. If he ever did tell the police or refuse to pay the money, there would not be business at all. There's a good chance he would be killed or at least crippled so that he would remember that and never mess with those guys. He started paying about a year ago, and he does not intend to report anything to the police." Another person reported that the father of a friend owned a business, and people asked him for protection money. Another person spoke of a neighbor who was a prosperous businessman who was involved in business in Russia. He was murdered, and the respondent attributed this to the mafia.

Twenty-four of the twenty-five people we interviewed reported getting information about Russian organized crime from the mass media, including both English- and Russian-language newspapers and television. The importance of these sources of information for ordinary Russian immigrants illustrates the degree to which any direct experience with organized crime is atypical. The knowledge of the Russian mafia that residents of Brighton Beach have is therefore not very different from that available to either the general public or law enforcement officials who rely on the media for leads. The exception is that the Soviet émigrés have easy access to the Russian-language media, which many law enforcement agencies do not have—or at least not readily. As a businessman put it, "I have no inside information. My friends have the same information as I do. I get all the information from the media." A forty-year-old man reported that his aunt reads all the Russian newspapers that are printed in Brighton Beach and keeps him up to date on crime in Brighton Beach. As with many others, these articles informed him about activity at the Rasputin restaurant and the gas tax-evasion schemes. Some also reported that their information came from television reports they saw before leaving the Soviet Union. They also hear about murder for hire from news reports.

Many of the immigrants believe that the media exaggerate in their descriptions of crime in Brighton Beach, and they say that the stories in the media do not match their experiences. As one man put it:

> They always have an article in a Russian paper about the cruelty of the Russian mafia. There are too many of them, and they are often stating quite opposite facts. They say that the Russian mafia terrorizes Brighton Beach. They say that the Russian mafia suffocates the businesses by making them pay large sums of money.
>
> I believe that reporters blow the whole deal with the Russian organized crime way out of proportion. That is why they are reporters;

they get a small fact and create many small details so that the reader would have more to read in the morning. Some of it may be true, but a lot is just in the imagination of the people writing those articles.

Of course, due to my profession [gym teacher], I do not deal with it too often, but as far as I understand it, no one is terrorized, and I am not even sure if all stores are paying the extortion money.

In reality, most of the information that these residents of Brighton Beach had about crime in general, and organized crime in particular, came from a combination of personal observation, media reports, conversations with people they knew, and other indirect sources. As a student put it, "Every time I go to a Russian supermarket or restaurant, I hear people talking about the mafia." It was often difficult for them to identify where a particular piece of information or an impression had come from. Since even information from people they know may have originated with a media report, this is hardly surprising. When a story—such as those about the Rasputin and other restaurants or a murder for hire—is particularly dramatic, it takes on a life of its own with information and interpretation coming from a variety of sources. A good example, involving non-Russian crime, is this report from a nineteen-year-old student:

I know that one Russian guy had a body shop where he repaired windshields. One of the people overheard the conversation that took place between the member of the Italian mafia and the Russian guy. The member of the Italian mafia told him not to repair windshields on cars any more. When the guy didn't take his "advice," a garbage truck ran into his shop tearing everything. . . . I actually saw the body shop after it was torn apart. It sure didn't look like an accident to me. I am sure it was intentional.

Several others whom we interviewed also mentioned having seen the aftermath of a crime, such as a crowd gathering outside the

Winter Garden restaurant and surrounding a gun. The respondent was told that someone was trying to shoot the owner. Another mentioned that the previous occupant of his apartment had been murdered. A twenty-three-year-old student recounted this series of events:

> Five months ago, a guy got killed right before my other friend's eyes. Well, it happens. Of course, it had something to do with the organized crimes. I don't think he was killed by accident. The guy was beaten by five guys right in front of the restaurant. They beat him till he fell unconscious. He died a couple of hours after that. Last summer another guy was shot across this building at six o'clock at night. Broad daylight. He survived although he was shot three times. I, personally, thought that it was somebody having a loud party. This is obviously an organized crime. . . . The organized crime is a problem. This guy was shot three times right next to where I live. This does not exactly make you feel too good about where you live.

Several people mentioned that they had heard of various scams, including falsifying documents for insurance. They believed that these usually did not involve organized crime but rather small groups of criminals acting together.

More than two-thirds of the respondents mentioned that they had heard that Russian-owned businesses in Brighton Beach had to pay a mafia "tax" or similar protection money. The woman with the boyfriend in the Russian mafia said that she was told that "the mafia makes sure that the businesses are safe. The store and restaurant owners pay them a fee so that they protect them from other mafia or single criminals. It is called 'giving roof to somebody.' " Many others gave similar descriptions, including the use of the word *roof,* which has its origins in the practices of organized crime in the former Soviet Union. Keeping in mind the media influence on the views being expressed, if we accept their opinions that the *krysha* system is being practiced in Brighton Beach, it indicates the importation of the same type of protection racket that operates in the former Soviet Union.

A number of the interviewees expressed opinions similar to this businessman: "I think that the Russian mafia has some sort of relationship with every business in Brighton Beach. All business owners have to pay a portion of their income to the mafia. If you pay it, you don't have any problems. Mafia needs businesses. It is in both the owner's and the mafia's interest if the business prospers. If the business makes more money, they can milk it some more." Others said that the mafia focused its attention on restaurants, nightclubs, and stores with expensive merchandise and grocery stores. Some people said that they had heard that members of the mafia owned certain businesses—most often restaurants such as the Rasputin, the Winter Garden, or the Odessa—outright. These places have all been mentioned in media coverage of Russian organized crime.

Three people we interviewed—all between the ages of nineteen and thirty-seven who arrived in 1992—said that the presence of the Russian mafia in Brighton Beach actually served positive purposes because it made it safe for businesses to operate. One said, "I don't think that the businesses that pay the money to the mafia can be called victims. By paying the money, the owner protects himself against all the other criminals." Another said that it helps all business in Brighton Beach to prosper by providing protection from other criminals.

Soviet Émigré Crime as Mafia

When we asked our respondents about crime in Brighton Beach, many of them voluntarily used the term *Russian mafia* that is also often used in both the English- and Russian-language media. We asked our respondents what they knew about the mafia and whether they thought Russian crime resembled the mafia. All but one of the respondents said they knew what the mafia was. As a businessman in his forties put it, "Everyone has watched the *Godfather* some time in their life." Those who went into more detail clearly identified the term *mafia* with Italian organized crime. As the librarian put it, "We heard a lot about it while being in the Soviet Union. We thought that it was the only mafia existing in the world. Only after coming to America we learned from the media that there is [a] Russian mafia too." Clearly, the idea of mafia—regardless of its factual basis—is widespread and provides people with an image of a criminal organization with which they can make comparisons. The use of the term *Russian mafia,* however, may create a self-fulfilling prophecy in which people—whether Russian émigrés, members of the general public, law enforcement officials, or journalists—map their images of mafia onto the crimes that occur in Brighton Beach and elsewhere. Here we use the term *mafia* in the same way as our respondents used it—as kind of a generic label for organized crime.

Asking people to make comparisons to a common structure can be a useful way to have them think about the complexity of an issue. Most of the people we interviewed could think of ways in which Soviet émigré crime—which they sometimes referred to as the *Russian mafia*—was both like and unlike what they thought the Italian mafia was like. Nonetheless, the people we interviewed disagreed about the extent to which Soviet émigré crime resembled their images of the mafia.

Some felt that Soviet émigré crime and the mafia were very similar. One young man had worked for the owner of an Italian restaurant who, he claimed, was a member of an organized crime family. He said, "I recognize the conversations that occurred among the members of the Italian mafia. These are the same conversations that occurred between the Russians. They are all doing the same thing." One person argued that they were similar in that both are "very invisible and its members are very hard to catch." Another argued that both use military-style structures and punishments for those who did not do what they were told.

A number of the émigrés noted that both Soviet émigrés and

what they called the mafia committed similar crimes, including extortion, murder, selling of drugs, and money laundering. Others observed that criminals from both ethnic groups were simply involved in crime to get money in any way that they could. As a student put it, "As far as the crimes go, it seems that human imagination has been exhausted. There is no new crime that the mafia can get itself into. All crimes committed by both the Russian and the Italian mafias are the same. I am sure they would be typical of any mafia. As long as it brings profit to the boss, the mafia is involved in it."

Others believed the Russian crime is less well organized than Italian organized crime on a number of different dimensions. A young waiter said, "I think that the Russian mafia reflects the first stage of development of the Italian mafia. The Russian mafia is way behind. That is why there is less organization among different groups. You can't even call it a mafia yet. There is no core that would plan and be responsible for carrying out crimes." Several others argued that the Italian mafia had influence over a much larger geographical area and had political connections that "are keys to the success of the operation." They argued that the Italian mafia was able to organize much more complex crimes that required greater skills and organization than the Russian mafia had. One argued that the explanation for the better organization of the Italian mafia had to do with the environment in which it existed: "It is like everything in America. Your professional and trade unions are stronger and more organized than the Russian ones."

A third, and in some ways dominant, theme emphasized the ways in which Soviet criminals were worse than the mafia. As one émigré put it, "The Italian mafia is just more civilized." The word *cruel* was used repeatedly by the respondents. As a computer programmer in his forties put it, "I think that the Russian mafia is more cruel and more reckless. People who are in the Russian mafia feel free to take people's lives. They do not have any standards, restrictions." A number commented that the Italian mafia was held together by family or other ties while the Russian mafia had little in the way of internal loyalty or ties to each other. One said, "In terms of structure, the Russian mafia is only bonded by the will to break the law to get the money. There is no respect to the boss as it is in the Italian mafia." These respondents argued that this explained the high level of violence within the Russian mafia.

Others attributed violence in the Russian mafia to the experiences of the Soviet era. One man commented, "Italians have different religious views. Russians are all atheists. They are not afraid of anything. They were always taught that there was no God. They do not respect anyone. Their crimes are more vicious and cruel in nature. Seventy years of poverty made Russians very aggravated. They will do anything for money. There is an old saying that the hungry man is more rude than the one who ate." Another commented, "People who are part of the Russian mafia in Brighton Beach come from a very vicious country having [a] faulty criminal justice system. They are not afraid of anything." Another mentioned the history of violence and war: "Italians don't get themselves involved in a murder unless it is really necessary. Russians, on the other hand, have no problems with that because they have been fighting all their lives—World War II, Afghanistan, internal war. It has made them insensitive to human pain and sufferings."

Many of the respondents mentioned several of these themes as they reflected on the comparison. The comments of a taxi driver illustrate this: "The Italian mafia is an ideal—an example of what a mafia should be like. Russians can only look and learn from them. The Russian mafia cannot commit certain complicated crimes. They lack both the education and the experience. In Russia people were used to the fact that there were no laws and the ones that existed had millions of loopholes in them. In America they cannot compete with Italians. They do not have enough information and experience to play with the law and be able to turn it in their favor. They compensate for it by displaying unusual cruelty that is not characteristic of the Italian mafia."

Émigré Understanding of Crime in Their Community

The picture of Soviet émigré crime that emerges from the interviews with Soviet émigrés is similar to that given in the previous chapters: they believe that there is crime among Russian émigrés, that it is fairly widespread, and that the overwhelming majority of émigrés are not involved. The crime is not highly structured, but there are instances in which some more ongoing and possibly hierarchical relationships are apparent—most notably those involving extortion and money laundering. Restaurants and nightclubs are seen as important foci of these more ongoing relationships, and the actors at their center are often well-known criminals from the former Soviet Union. The level of violence may be high, but it involves mainly those who are already associated with organized crime and does not directly affect ordinary immigrants unless they happen to be witnesses. Most ordinary community residents hear about crime mainly from the media or others in the community, and the crimes of greatest concern involve robberies, thefts, and swindles. In this sense, they are not different from many other New Yorkers.

CHAPTER 10

IS THERE A RUSSIAN MAFIA IN AMERICA?

When we began our research, we considered three general views about the possible organized nature of Russian émigré crime. Putting aside the question of whether there is a single such entity, one view was that Russian émigré crime was arranged as a loose-knit organization without divisions. Another was that it was a confederation of gangs based on geographic origins in the former USSR. The third argued that Russian organized crime did not exist but that Soviet émigré criminals were basically individual opportunists doing anything for money. According to the latter perspective, these criminals were mostly well educated and smart but too mistrustful, lacking in loyalty, and ruthless to be a tightly structured criminal organization. Apart from some anecdotal evidence and considerable speculation, little was actually known about the continuity and internal structures of any criminal organizations made up of persons from the Soviet Union. Likewise, little was known about their ability to commit harms, either in their local communities (such as Brighton Beach and Northeast Philadelphia) or in the larger society. The capacity of these individuals to monopolize criminal markets, to systematically use threats and violence, and to corrupt law enforcement and the legal and political processes was a mystery. In other words, we were basically in the dark about whether the characteristics that best define organized crime were present.

Cosa Nostra as a Model

To further assist our analysis and assessment of Russian criminal activity in the United States, we examine La Cosa Nostra to provide a basis of comparison between the two ethnic groups. We do this for two reasons: it is the most familiar example of organized crime, and it best illustrates and demonstrates the harm perspective that we believe should be taken in assessing organized crime. The information compiled by the Tri-state Project permits us to address whether Soviet émigré crime has the kind of organizational structures and commits the kind of harms that define the special problem of organized crime.

Organizational Structure

The Cosa Nostra structures criminal syndicates as continuing enterprises that conduct a variety of criminal ventures. Some in law enforcement and the media believe that Russian criminals have organized themselves in a similar structure around specific criminal activities, even to the point of monopolizing those activities. Other knowledgeable observers claim that the ex-Soviets do not have the rigidly authoritarian and hierarchical structures of the Cosa Nostra. Both perspectives begin with La Cosa Nostra as the defining model. We believe the truth lies between these two positions and that Soviet émigré criminals have a more amorphous organizational structure than the Cosa Nostra.

We found considerable consensus among the experts that we interviewed that émigré criminal organization is not as well structured as the crime families of the Cosa Nostra are. For example, the Russian undercover agent from Minsk who worked with the Tri-state Project told us adamantly that the "Russians are not organized like Italians."[1] Alexander Grant of the New York–based Russian-language newspaper *Novoye Russkoye Slovo,* who has written extensively on the issue, likewise said that the émigré crime model was different from the Cosa

Nostra families: "They come together around particular crimes and then disperse. Criminals approach other criminals whom they know—at least by reputation—to go in with them." He did not believe that these criminals maintain their involvement in multiple criminal enterprises. Two specialists in Soviet and Russian intelligence described individual criminal enterprises in California that were highly organized but said there was no evidence of group continuity across enterprises.[2] There is certainly no evidence of one or even a few hierarchical groups of participants engaged in specialized activities. Extortion in Brighton Beach is widespread, for example, but not organized on a permanent and continuous basis. The floating structures we have described coalesce around particular criminal opportunities.

A criminal organization may not be structured like the Cosa Nostra but may be well suited to particular criminal activities and may be attractive to the individuals engaging in particular activities at a particular time. For example, criminal ventures that are long lasting or individuals engaged in multiple criminal ventures demand a considerable degree of interpersonal trust among participants. Common ethnicity is one of the elements ensuring this trust. Participants must trust that partners have the ability to perform the necessary tasks in the necessary manner and that the co-conspirators will not give the venture away or perhaps give each other up to law enforcement if they are caught. One of the ways that La Cosa Nostra specifically attempts to ensure this kind of trust is through the code of omertà. Absent interpersonal trust and an insurance mechanism such as the code, criminal networks are likely to be more fluid, more single-venture oriented, and less stable over time. Such is the case with the networks of Russian émigré criminals.

Known Russian criminals fall into two general categories—those who were active criminals before they came to the United States and who simply continue with their preexisting way of life, and those who are opportunists taking advantage of the new opportunities for crime they have found in the United States. Referring in particular to the criminal opportunists, the Russian undercover agent on the Tri-state Project said, "They want to make money any way and any how they can. Every Russian wants to be a millionaire over night." A few of these individuals may perceive themselves as being part of a criminal organization, but the absence of group loyalty and the individual nature of the specialists' participation seem to make them more vulnerable to law enforcement. On the other hand, the organizational entity is not likely to look like the typical criminal enterprise that is targeted for RICO prosecution.

One way to contrast the Cosa Nostra structure and the Soviet émigré organizational structure is to view Italians as having structures—crime families—that are supported by crimes. The family is continuous, and the crimes are functional in the sense of supporting and carrying out the objectives of the family. The Soviet émigrés, on the other hand, create floating structures, on an as-needed basis, to enable them to carry out particular crimes. The criminal opportunities come first, and the necessary structure to take advantage of those opportunities follows.

Use of Violence

The demonstrated willingness to use force and violence to control markets, to discourage competition, and to intimidate witnesses is also one of the mainstays of La Cosa Nostra. This use of violence is usually systematic and functional in that it is a calculated tool that furthers the interests of the organization—to increase business gain, to enforce mediated agreements, and to organize markets. Russian émigré violence, in contrast, is ad hoc and unpredictable. Dozens of murders and attempted murders have involved persons from the former Soviet Union in New York and New Jersey, almost all of which remain unsolved or not prosecuted, but greed and personal vendetta seem to have been the motivating factors in most of these murders. It is also the view of some in law enforcement that the Russians' reputation for violence in the United States exceeds the reality of its use.

There are a violent few residing among the Soviet émigrés, but the nature and magnitude of their violence neither resembles nor rivals that of La Cosa Nostra. But a clear fear and intimidation effect from their reputation for violence is a major factor in all the unsolved homicides in this community. Witnesses refuse to come forward or cooperate with the police. In California, for example, Bryant and Stanny told us that businessmen and others are reluctant to talk to law enforcement about Russian criminal activities. A young couple from Ukraine living in Brighton Beach described an incident in a Philadelphia restaurant in which a waiter was shot because he refused to keep his mouth shut about a burglary. Although this shooting took place in full view of everyone in the restaurant, no one saw anything, and no one would talk. The victim himself was warned to keep quiet or something might happen to his family.

Use of Corruption

As with monopoly and violence, the threat of émigrés using corruption and collusion to undermine U.S. law enforcement and other government agencies now represents more of a potential than an actual harm. There have been allegations and rumors about police payoffs, but so far no hard evidence has been offered, and no corruption cases have been made. In Miami, where a variety of law enforcement organizations have formed what they call *Operation Odessa,* we interviewed four participants in the operation—two from the U.S. Drug Enforcement Administration and one each from the U.S. Immigration and Naturalization Service and the Broward County Sheriff's Department.[3] Each said that Russian émigrés in their area were involved in corruption—either by paying bribes and payoffs to protect themselves from law enforcement or by attempting to corrupt other public officials or political figures. No specific cases were cited, however, and no charges of this kind have been made.

It would seem that although they have the knowhow and the money, Russian émigré criminals do not yet have the political contacts and the power to influence the legal and political processes in the United States. They have not lived here long enough, and they have not become sufficiently acculturated. Various experts believe, however, that more corruption is inevitable. Given that the individuals involved in criminal activity here are products of a system that is used to buying politicians and government officials, and in which corruption is a way of life, it would be naive to believe that American officials can resist being corrupted by these same individuals.

In the meantime, the pervasive governmental corruption that exists throughout the former Soviet republics creates problems for American law enforcement in collaborating with their counterparts in those countries. For example, attempting to find out whether a suspect now in the United States has a criminal history or is currently under investigation is complicated by a substantial risk that the target will be informed about the inquiry. The Immigration and Naturalization Service indicates that it is often impossible to find out whether a visa applicant has a criminal background. In these and other ways corruption in the former USSR facilitates émigré crime in the United States.

Assessing Harms

The distinctive feature of organized crime that makes it different from other crime is its capacity for harm. To answer the ultimate question of whether Soviet émigré organized crime exists in the United States, we must assess the degree of harm—actual and potential—the Russians inflict on people, institutions, and society itself. As we have stressed, harm manifests itself in a variety of forms that include physical violence, monetary loss, fear, loss of freedom, and the destruction or undermining of economic, political, and legal systems. To address this issue, we use information from three sources: the database developed in conjunction with the Tri-state investigation, the specific criminal indictments that were collected during that investigation, and in-depth interviews with law enforcement authorities (in both the United States and the former Soviet Union) and journalists and writers who have researched Russian crime in this country.

Russian émigrés have been especially linked to such crimes of deception as forgery, counterfeiting, confidence schemes, and tax and insurance fraud. Other criminal activities attributed to Russian émigrés in the United States include such common street crimes as burglary, theft, robbery, prostitution, low-level narcotics trafficking, and arson. They also, however, include crimes that are typically associated with organized crime, such as murder for hire and extortion. Criminals from the former USSR have been associated in various ways with Cosa Nostra organized crime families—including the Bruno/Scarfo family in Philadelphia and the Colombo, Gambino, Lucchese, and Genovese crime families in New York and New Jersey.

While some of the crimes in which Russian émigrés have been involved are the acts of lone individuals, many have involved networks of persons, and some show continuing organization and a degree of specialization. Shoplifting is an example. Although usually a minor offense in itself, the émigré shoplifting incidents identified in our investigation were perpetrated by large rings of individuals engaged in organized shoplifting that included the sale of stolen goods.

Let us briefly look again at three specific types of criminal activity—frauds, fuel-tax scams, and murders or attempted murders—that, because of their frequency and seriousness, are particularly suitable for a harms assessment. The number and diversity of frauds demonstrate the relatively high levels of involvement of ex-Soviet criminals in these types of crimes. As a subset of these frauds, the bootleg gas scams are of special interest because of their sophistication, the collaboration with Cosa Nostra families, and their potential for economic harm. The murders and attempted murders should enable us to best assess their propensity for violence.

Fraud

The database put together by the Tri-state Project contains numerous examples of frauds perpetrated by Soviet émigré criminals. Indeed, fraud of some type is the most common type of crime in the Project's files. Many involve well-known confidence schemes, where in most cases the victims are members of the Russian émigré community, but a variety of frauds were described to us by residents of Brighton Beach. For example, we were told about arranged-marriage scams, in which for $10,000 to $15,000 someone from the former Soviet Union would be married to a U.S. resident who had a "green card," or permanent residence permit. In one such case of particular interest because of the notoriety of the husband, Yelena and Leonard Lev were convicted of arranging the marriage of Vyacheslav Ivankov (Yaponchik) to one Irina Ola, a singer at the Odessa restaurant in Brooklyn. Ola was paid $15,000 by Yaponchik to become his wife so that he could obtain alien residency status in the United States.

These kinds of schemes are not unique to Russian émigrés, nor are they indicative of the presence of organized crime. Even the more sophisticated frauds are similar to those carried out by other persons and groups. What is most important for this analysis is that these crimes do not have the characteristics—monopoly, violence, and corruption—that are the marks of highly developed criminal organizations. The Medicaid frauds are a good example of this.

Medicaid, the giant government health care program for the poor, seems made to order for fraud-oriented former citizens from the Soviet Union who have highly developed skills for bureaucratic maneuvering. Its very large and diffuse bureaucracy manages a multitude of services and procedures and thus provides numerous opportunities for collusion among potential fraud conspirators. That Medicaid is a government program would also presumably add to its attractiveness as fair game for those adept in the black-market and shadow-economy practices of the former Soviet Union.

The most audacious of the medical fraud cases committed by Russian émigrés occurred in California. In a scam that operated from the mid- to late 1980s, a group of individuals from the former Soviet Union masterminded the greatest insurance fraud ever carried out in the United States. This group led by Michael Smushkevich set up phony medical clinics and mobile laboratories and solicited patients with promises of free physical examinations and diagnostic tests. The scam artists then submitted fraudulent bills, supported by falsified medical reports and treatment forms, to insurance companies claiming the clinics had provided medical services prescribed by doctors. The group defrauded California insurance companies of over $50 million. Over 250 medical clinics made fraudulent claims totaling over $1 billion, and illicit proceeds were laundered through 500 different shell companies and foreign banks. As a crime, this sophisticated scheme was highly organized. But it was not organized crime: there was no violence, corruption, or monopolization of the market. The harm, while substantial, was entirely economic. The doctors and other professionals engaged in the scam simply coalesced around a lucrative criminal opportunity. They had no other criminal enterprises or continuing criminal activity.

Counterfeiting is another area in which Russian émigré criminals have been active. Producing fake credit cards, checks, birth certificates, visas, passports, and other documents such as driver's licenses is not unique to this ethnic group but illustrates the continued influence of practices from the Soviet Union. As with the medical frauds, some of the counterfeiting activity is rather sophisticated, and in some instances it has international dimensions. For example, in 1989 four Russians and a Pole were indicted (and subsequently convicted) for manufacturing, possessing, and selling $17 million in counterfeit U.S. currency and $4 million in fraudulent travelers' checks. The money and checks were circulated in New York, Chicago, Los Angeles, and Poland.

In most of the fraud cases noted, the victims are individuals chosen on a seemingly ad hoc basis. There is no evidence of attempts to develop and monopolize an ongoing market in any of these frauds. Even in the cases of immigration documentation, where the potential for market monopoly, at least within the Russian immigrant community, would appear to exist, there are instead many individual criminal entrepreneurs. In keeping with the absence of monopolization, the harms to victims were strictly economic, and with the exception of cases like the Smushkevich medical fraud, the economic loss was not substantial. Consequently, it is our judgment that the frauds that are the most common crime among Russian émigrés, including those committed by groups of individuals, do not result in the kind of harm and do not demonstrate the organizational harm capacity that would qualify them as being organized crime.

Fuel Fraud

As with Medicaid, the motor-fuel frauds were likewise seemingly made to order for a group of former citizens of the Soviet Union who had substantial experience evading government regulations. The modus operandi of these frauds, as was indicated earlier, is quite simple in principle. It takes advantage of the tax procedure. The market price of fuel oil is manipulated (and the market controlled) by the creation of fictitious companies (daisy chains and burn companies) to evade the payment of federal and state excise taxes on gasoline and diesel fuel. The taxes that are charged to retail customers are skimmed, rather than forwarded to the taxing authorities, thus producing the profits from the criminal venture. Then discounted bootleg gasoline is sold to retailers, creating another source of profits. In another variation on the fuel-fraud scheme, waste fuel is mixed with clean fuel and sold as pure.

Besides the fact that they shift the tax burden to other people, fuel tax-evasion cases and the passing off of waste oil as clean product are harmful to the economy because they place honest dealers at a disadvantage and may, ultimately, drive them out of business. Selling contaminated fuel also creates a risk to public health because burning such fuel in schools, hospitals, or elsewhere causes environmental harm that has ripple effects for both individuals and the economy. Violence of this kind to the environment is a special type of harm.

According to one New Jersey investigator, Harvey Borak, the fuel-oil frauds had a negative effect on the business climate across the motor-fuels industry.[4] Initially, mostly the small independent fuel dealers were hurt: small dealers who did not buy from the bootleggers faced unfair competition from the below-market prices charged by competitors who did buy from the bootleggers. But big companies were hurt also. Even after the overall level of motor-fuel fraud had been reduced, major companies like Exxon, Shell, and Mobil were still expressing concern about the problem, which led Borak to speculate that they, too, had felt the impact of the schemes.

The fuel-scam alliance between émigrés and Cosa Nostra crime figures facilitated monopoly control and fed the coffers of traditional organized crime. The Cosa Nostra partners used violence (such as arson, beatings, and extortion) to drive out or control competitors. Such actions represent economic, community, and physical harms.

Borak was one of the lead investigators of the motor-fuel frauds. When we spoke with him, he was the chief investigator of the New Jersey Division of Taxation and had had his first dealings with émigrés in the early 1980s, when he began looking into motor-fuel excise-tax schemes while working for the U.S. Internal Revenue Service in New York and New Jersey. According to Borak, ex-Soviets involved in the motor-fuel frauds resorted to money laundering to take their illegal profits from the excise-tax evasion out of the country. The evidence, he said, points to the investment of illegal profits in Russia. He said that émigrés were also involved in a black market in currency. In some instances they bought goods here with their illegal "dirty" money and then sold these goods in Russia, thus both laundering the money and producing an additional profit. Their capital investment in the motor-fuel tax-evasion scam was sometimes financed with money obtained from previous involvement in the black market in the Soviet Union. They started out with rented trucks, moved up to owning their own trucks, and, in some cases, ended up owning tanker ships. To Borak, this is all evidence that the émigrés in the United States are connected to organized crime in the former Soviet Union.

Borak also believes that those émigrés who are involved in crime are prone to the use of violence. Informants, he said, are terrified of being found out because they fear violent retaliation. The Russians also maintained monopoly control over their territories by the use of force, such as by burning out independent competitors. As was indicated earlier, their Cosa Nostra partners often provided the muscle for this.

Borak saw the Russians as engaging in what he called "a scheme a minute." He said they were simply looking for fast and easy money, such as the kind of money that can be made from various forms of white-collar crime. The particular criminals he investigated were worldly and sophisticated, and most of them viewed Americans as gullible.

It is Borak's opinion that the criminal activities of these Russians constituted a form of organized crime. He offered several arguments to support his contention. He pointed out that a motor-fuel tax scam is a very labor-intensive enterprise that employs a large number of people, conducts most transactions in cash, and uses many offices and bank accounts. His implication is that this structure could not be set up and managed without a considerable degree of organization. One or two individuals working alone—without organization and resources—could not carry out this kind of enterprise. Borak said that people involved in these scams had tremendous assets as evidenced by the fact that the forfeitures arising out of their prosecutions amounted to many millions of dollars.

Borak also characterized the activity of the Soviet émigré criminals and their co-conspirators as being organized crime because, despite the lucrative nature of the business, there was no competition. The latter resulted, he said, from territorial organization and from retaliation against would-be competitors. Fear and an unwillingness to cooperate with law enforcement authorities by potential witnesses or informants connote organized crime to Borak. Further, he argued, some of the same persons participating in the fuel scams were also running gambling operations and handling gambling debts.

Although Borak makes a number of strong points in favor of viewing at least some Soviet émigré crime as organized crime, in our view these arguments are not convincing. For example, it is not clear how or to what extent the fear of retribution felt by potential informers resulted from the actions and reputations of the Russians and how much from their Cosa Nostra partners. It is possible that the reputation of Cosa Nostra was the more important factor. Involvement in multiple criminal enterprises is a characteristic of sophisticated criminal organizations, and the same individuals appeared repeatedly, at times involved in very different activities, which does indicate continuity in their criminal involvement. However, important conceptual and practical differences exist between the repeated involvement of specific individuals and the repeated involvement of a single criminal organization or network in a range of criminal enterprises. Although there is clear evidence of the former, there is little evidence of the latter. The limited scope of the fuel-oil prosecutions reflects this. On the face of the evidence available, the motor-fuel scams were indeed highly organized crimes. At least as far as the Soviet émigré participants were concerned, however, these frauds do not demonstrate that the involved individuals had a sophisticated criminal organization with dominating harm capacity.

Murders and Attempted Murders

Violence, threats, and killings are another hallmark of organized crime. We accept Schelling's view that the difference between ordinary criminal activity—which itself may be highly organized—and organized crime rests in the latter's use of violence to attain and maintain monopoly control.[5] Going back to 1981, many murders and attempted murders have involved Russian émigrés. In almost every case, evidence showed that the killers and the victims were parties to ongoing criminal activity. The victims either were known criminals or had a prior relationship to the person who attacked them or who ordered the attack. In some cases, the victims were attacked as a result of a dispute among individual criminals or groups or in retaliation for an earlier crime, indicating that these were neither random acts of violence nor killings of innocent victims. That evidence could be interpreted as suggesting the use of murder as a tool—as a means to an end. But we have no evidence that the end was the monopoly control of a criminal enterprise.

The nature of the killings is also indicative of the systematic use of violence. The following was the conclusion of the Tri-state report:

> Many of the homicides appear to have been well planned and, in some instances, assassins or "hitmen" were used to commit the crime. Those who carried out the attacks often used distractions, decoys, or other tricks to gain an advantage over the victims. Fifty-three homicides involved the use of guns, including automatic, semi-automatic and silencer-equipped handguns. Victims were often shot either at close range, usually in the head or chest, or from a moving vehicle. One victim, who had been stabbed to death, was found floating in Sheepshead Bay, NY. Another was found frozen stiff in a snow bank at a Morris County, NJ, auto salvage yard, fully clothed in a suit and tie. He had been shot twice in the temple. During the autopsy, bullet wound

scars were discovered on various parts of the deceased's body, indicating he had been the victim of prior shootings.[6]

Clearly, violence is associated with the criminal activities of these Russians, and it is only in their use of violence that we see any close resemblance to organized crime. This evidence, however, does not reflect the systematic use of violence to gain and maintain monopoly control of criminal enterprises that is a defining characteristic of real organized crime.

To go further in our analysis, we need more detailed and specific information that links particular individuals to joint involvement in particular crimes. The indictments are the best source in the Tri-state Project database for looking at this issue. Indictments are not convictions, of course. The charges spelled out have not been proven beyond a reasonable doubt. And in some cases, even when convictions did ensue—as happened in all but one case (it is still pending as of this writing)—not all the charges were sustained against all the defendants named. In some cases defendants pled guilty to reduced charges. The indictments give us the prosecution's picture of a criminal enterprise—a picture that was sufficiently convincing, however, to convince a federal grand jury to find probable cause to believe that crimes had been committed and that the individuals named had committed them.

What Indictments Tell Us About the Harms Caused

During the course of its investigation, the Tri-state Project obtained copies of various indictments that included Russian émigrés as defendants. We cannot generalize from them to describe all Russian émigré criminals, or even all those who have been indicted. The Project was interested in those indictments where the defendants named were of special interest to the investigation or the criminal activity involved bore some marks of organized crime. For example, the crimes enumerated might have been complex and sophisticated, or there was collaboration with Cosa Nostra families, or the defendants were indicted under the Racketeer-Influenced and Corrupt Organizations (RICO) statute. We found eleven indictments and one criminal complaint and arrest warrant in the database. The latter concerned the aforementioned Vyachaslav Ivankov (Yaponchik) and his codefendants and was the basis for their arrests. For our purposes, it is treated as comparable to an indictment.

Table 10.1 portrays the twelve documents in terms of the economic, physical, psychological, and societal harms that the Russian émigré defendants were charged with committing. Economic harm includes the monetary loss of victims, illicit gains to the defendants, and detrimental effects on a legal marketplace. Physical harm includes violence, threats, and killings. Psychological harm refers to charges involving the creation of a climate of fear, intimidation, or cynicism. Societal harm most often means corruption, but we include drug distribution in this category, concluding that its detrimental effects are best classed as a harm against society.

As can readily be seen, the major economic harm was produced by the fuel frauds identified in four indictments (*United States v. Morton Friedberg et al., United States v. Joseph Reisch et al., United States v. Daniel Enright et al.,* and *United States v. Anthony Morelli et al.*). There were considerable monetary losses to the victims, who in these cases turn out indirectly to be all taxpayers. There was also considerable illicit gain to the conspirators. The unpaid gasoline excise taxes ranged from approximately $15 million in the *Friedberg* case up to $140 million in the *Enright* case. The former case involved five defendants, two of whom were Russian émigrés; the latter, twenty-five defendants, including fifteen ex-Soviets. When the *Enright* indictment was announced in August 1995, officials said that the case offered evidence on how "Russian crime" in the United States was evolving. A press release accompanying the indictment emphasized that while émigrés had previously been pulling off mainly petty scams of the street-corner hustling variety, they had now moved up to complicated multilevel conspiracies that involved the creation of dummy corporations and complex accounting.

Of the four fuel-scam indictments, economic harm is the only harm indicated in three of them. According to the indictments, there was no indication of using violence, creating a climate of fear, or corrupting officials. The exception is the *Morelli* case, which involved six ex-Soviet émigrés among its thirteen defendants. Besides charging $60 million in excise-tax evasion, the indictments included nineteen counts of extortion and the gaining of extensions of credit by extortionate means. The latter constitute both a physical and a psychological harm because extortion by definition includes threats and intimidation.

In the other cases where a specific amount of money is identified (*United States v. Ronald Kandel et al., United States v. Peter Cherepinsky,* and *United States v. V. K. Ivankov et al.*), the sums involved are much smaller than the fuel-fraud amounts. The *Kandel* case involved just over $1 million in currency transaction violations, and the *Cherepinsky* case, $200,000 in food stamp violations. In neither of these is there evidence of the presence of a criminal organization. Instead, what we have are individual scam artists. Ivankov (Yaponchik) and his eight fellow ex-Soviet defendants were charged with a $3.5 million extortion, but because no money actually changed hands, there was no monetary loss or gain. In the remaining indictments that charged conspiracy to distribute and distribution of narcotics, we can assume an illicit gain to the defendants, but the amount is unknown.

Four of the indictments were brought under the RICO statute, which is one of the key tools prosecutors use in handling organized crime cases. RICO specifically targets criminal organizations and continuing criminal enterprises and is the preeminent statutory tool for attacking organized crime because of its broad sweep and harsh penalties. RICO permits charging associated defendants who have

Table 10.1 Major Harms Caused by Selected Russian Émigré Defendants

Indictment	Economic	Physical	Psychological	Societal
1. *United States v. Boris Nayfeld** (1 Soviet émigré and "others known and unknown")	Conspiracy to distribute heroin (unknown illicit gain)	Conspiracy to murder Monya Elson; extortion	Extortion	Conspiracy to distribute heroin (health/welfare of society)
2. *United States v. Morton G. Friedberg et al.* (5 defendants, 2 Soviet émigrés)	$14,035,063 unpaid excise taxes			
3. *United States v. Boris Goldberg** (1 Soviet émigré and others)	Narcotics business/ conspiracy; conspiracy to rob; mail fraud/ conspiracy (unknown illicit gain)	Conspiracy to murder Robert Ferrante; conspiracy to murder Evsei Agron; extortion (2 counts); conspiracy to rob	Extortion (2 counts)	Narcotics business/ conspiracy
4. *United States v. David Podlog et al.* (16 defendants, 10 Soviet émigrés)	Distribution of heroin and cocaine (unknown illicit gain)			Distribution of heroin and cocaine
5. *United States v. Boris Nayfeld et al.* (6 defendants, 6 Soviet émigrés)	Distribution of heroin (unknown illicit gain)			Distribution of heroin
6. *United States v. Ronald Kandel et al.* (2 defendants, 1 Soviet émigré)	$1,088,830 currency transaction violations			
7. *United States v. Joseph Reisch et al.* (18 defendants, 5 Soviet émigrés) (known)	$35,098,000 unpaid excise taxes			
8. *United States v. Peter Cherepinsky* (1 Soviet émigré)	$205,300 food stamp fraud			

9. *United States v. V. K. Ivankov et al.* (9 Soviet émigrés)	$3,500,000 extortion money sought	Extortion; threats of violence	Extortion	
10. *United States v. Daniel Enright et al.* (25 defendants, 15 Soviet émigrés)	$140,000,000 unpaid excise taxes			
11. *United States v. Monya Elson** (1 Soviet émigré and others)	Conspiracy to distribute heroin (unknown illicit gain)	Conspiracy to murder Boris Nayfeld; attempt to murder Boris Nayfeld; conspiracy/attempt to murder Vyacheslav Lyubarsky; murder of Vyacheslav Lyubarsky; murder of Vadim Lyubarsky; conspiracy to murder Alexander Slepinin; murder of Alexander Slepinin; conspiracy/attempt to commit arson; conspiracy/extortion (4 counts)	Conspiracy/extortion (4 counts)	Conspiracy to distribute heroin
12. *United States v. Anthony Morelli et al.** (13 defendants, 6 Soviet émigrés)	$60,000,000 excise tax evasion	19 counts of extortion and collection of extensions of credit by extortionate means	19 counts of extortion and collection of extensions of credit by extortionate means	

*RICO indictment.

committed at least two crimes within a ten-year period as having engaged in a pattern of racketeering activity and as investing, maintaining an interest, or participating in a criminal enterprise.[7] Its use
reflects not only the particular facts of a case but also the discretion
of the prosecutor to employ the RICO weapon. Once the decision to
use RICO is made, the indictment has to be drawn to fit the statute.
Thus, we cannot know for certain whether these particular cases look
more like organized crime than the others because they really are
more like organized crime or because of prosecutorial discretion. The
Morelli case reflects this ambiguity because the prosecutors elected
to bring RICO charges in a bootleg gasoline case. In addition to excise-tax evasion and ancillary offenses, they charged the thirteen defendants in that case with racketeering and extortion. The association
formed by the defendants to operate their fuel business was judged to
be a racketeering enterprise.

Of the RICO cases, three most clearly exemplify the harms that
would qualify the culprits as being a criminal organization involved
in organized crime—*United States v. Boris Nayfeld, United States v.
Boris Goldberg,* and *United States v. Monya Elson.* They include
charges of conspiracy and attempts to murder, murder, extortion, and
conspiracy to distribute and distribution of heroin and cocaine. Contrary to our overarching thesis that Russian émigré criminals are principally active in crimes of deception, the crimes charged in these
particular indictments—drugs, extortion, and murder—are very much
like those of traditional organized crime.

Beyond charging criminal harms of all types, these three cases
have several elements in common. Each has only one named defendant, and that person is someone who is from the former Soviet
Union. The other defendants, whether they are known or unknown,
are not named. Two of the defendants—Nayfeld and Elson—are well
known to law enforcement and the media as being associated with the
Russian mafia. They are prominent in the criminal networks we
looked at earlier. This same Boris Nayfeld was also indicted, along

with five Russian codefendants, in a separate case involving the distribution of heroin.

United States v. David Podlog et al. and *United States v. Boris Nayfeld et al.* were narrowly drawn drug cases. Finally, the *Ivankov* criminal complaint is unique because it is not an indictment and because it charges the single crime of extortion. Despite Ivankov's criminal reputation, the complaint reads more like the *Kandel* or *Podlog* indictments in its narrow scope than it does the RICO indictments that one might have anticipated given the aura of organized crime that surrounded Yaponchik.

What do these indictments tell us? They add support to the finding that there is a propensity for crimes of deception among Soviet émigré criminals. And given that their crimes tend to have this particular character, the major harm is economic. Even in the few cases that most resemble organized crime, the criminal organizations involved seem to be more opportunistic (formed to exploit particular criminal opportunities) and more defined by or oriented to one person than is the case with traditional organized crime.

The Mafia Stereotype

Wanting to make familiar what is unfamiliar is a generally acknowledged phenomenon. One result of this is a tendency on the part of some in law enforcement and the media to too readily adopt simplistic, stereotyped perceptions. This has certainly been true in the case of Soviet émigré crime, where the term *Russian mafia* has been loosely applied. As with all stereotypes, this one serves the purpose of simplifying what is otherwise a complex and varied subject. It provides a shorthand characterization that enables law enforcement to communicate among themselves and with the media. The media, in turn, then communicate to the public using this same generally understood term.

Scott Anderson referred to this phenomenon in a 1995 magazine article about Yaponchik. He said that law enforcement, journalists, and gangsters operate in a complexly symbiotic shadow world where it is difficult to separate myth from reality because myth and reality are the same thing. "Ivankov," said Anderson, "was a mafia godfather because it served everyone's interest that he be one. It gave the media a frame, a way to personalize stories about a complex issue. It gave the FBI a symbol to take down, a tool with which to convince the Russian émigré community that justice would prevail."[8] The label *Russian mafia* offers a convenient hook for understanding but at the same time sensationalizes matters so as to peak interest. It thus serves both law enforcement and media interests.

Lydia Rosner offered three answers to why the Russian mafia is sexy.[9] First, she said, there is a need for a substitute in the wake of the fading of the Italian mafia mythology. In addition to the discrediting of the mafia myth,[10] the real Cosa Nostra was badly battered during the past decade,[11] as major figures like John Gotti were sent off to prison. The role played by the Italian mafia myth, if there continued to be such a role, thus had to be assumed by another entity, and the Russians were an attractive alternative. A second answer, Rosner says, is that the lingering "evil empire" image makes it "sexy to read about immigrants from the former Soviet Union who are involved in criminal activities on a grand scale." The cold war and nearly fifty years of competition with the Soviet Union gave Soviets a special status in the eyes of Americans. This special status makes us both more attentive and suspicious of them. Finally, says Rosner, "The sexy Russian Mafia provides journalists and their readers with a relatively unthreatening, European model of crime." By this she seems to mean that just as there was an alien conspiracy belief underlying the Italian mafia myth—a belief that allowed us to attribute our organized crime problem to foreign devils—so too there is now an alien conspiracy belief involving the Russian mafia. According to Rosner, this is a model that is "appealingly seductive, although quite inaccurate." To understand what makes it inaccurate, we go back first to Diego Gambetta.[12] Gambetta offered a very precise and narrowly focused definition of *mafia* that not only distinguishes it from organized crime but clears up a great deal of the confusion about what really constitutes a mafia. He said that a mafia is a specific economic enterprise, "an industry which produces, promotes, and sells private protection."[13] Mafiosi deal in neither legal nor illegal goods. They are not entrepreneurs. Their only product is protection. This protection becomes necessary and desirable in a marketplace where there are "unstable transactions" and where "trust is scarce and fragile."[14]

The mafia protection is a real service, and mafiosi do not merely practice extortion. It is the fact that people who find it in their interest to buy mafia protection may willingly purchase this service that makes it unlike extortion. Honor flows to those mafiosi who have a reputation for supplying credible protection. According to Gambetta, the world is full of violent entrepreneurs, Russians included. Mafiosi, however, are different. "If we confuse them with entrepreneurs, no matter how vicious, engaged in manipulating the market to their own advantage, then the Mafia evaporates, and we are left with nothing to define it except . . . nebulous distinctions."[15]

Gambetta's definition does not fit the criminally active Russians in the United States. As we have shown, the ex-Soviets are criminal entrepreneurs and extortionists. Rather than providing a protection service for market transactions, they are predators in the marketplace. Little honor and respect—except that inspired by fear—are shown to them by members of the émigré community. This is clear from the interviews in and around Brighton Beach.

Russian émigré crime is not a mafia or mafialike because it has not moved beyond simply engaging in crimes that are sometimes well organized. Our conclusion adopts the argument of Schelling and Anderson regarding the difference between highly organized but ordinary criminal activities and true organized crime.[16] Returning to our earlier discussion of the conditions that encourage the development of mafias, it is obvious that these conditions do not prevail in the contemporary United States. Government at the local, state, and federal levels has not abdicated its legitimate power. These governments have not left a power vacuum to be filled by other authority, such as a Russian mafia. Government here is also not excessively bureaucratized or especially prone to corruption. Except for rumors, there is little evidence that Russians are corrupting American officials. In addition, the actual and potential illegal markets available do not lend themselves to domination and monopolization by these Russians. Indeed, in the most lucrative of the illegal markets—drugs and gambling—there is considerable competition from a variety of criminal organizations that are sufficiently powerful to make it impossible for Russian criminals to force them out. We found no evidence that any Russian criminal organization (or organizations) controls drugs, gambling, prostitution, or extortion, in Brighton Beach—where, if anywhere, such control would be most likely. It is our judgment that there is no Russian mafia in the United States.

The Influence of Life in the Soviet Union

Having dispensed with all except one of our propositions, we now address the most difficult one of all—the proposition that the nature of Soviet émigré crime and criminals reflects the peculiarities of life in the former Soviet Union. This idea that Soviet economic contingencies have influenced Russian émigrés who are involved in crime (as was outlined in Chapter 2) is very much at odds with the crooked-ladder theory, as well as with any idealized conceptions of a mafia in which mafiosi are said to be men of honor and respect. Irrespective of the specific ethnic reference, this is a hard thesis to test—much less prove. It demands going beyond personal memoirs and requires comprehensive information about individuals that is neither readily available nor easily attainable. This perhaps explains why it has not yet been done.

To investigate the effect of Soviet attitudes on Russian émigré criminals, for example, we would need, at a minimum, data on their educational backgrounds, training, and work experiences in both the United States and the former Soviet Union and especially detailed information on their criminal histories both there and here. We would want to know about their participation, if any, in the black market and in the shadow or second economies. Unfortunately, there are no reliable sources of such information. Finally, we would need to hear, expressed in their own voices, how the individuals actually involved think about these issues.

Keeping this qualification in mind, observations and opinions from a variety of sources generally support the proposition that the experiences of people under the Soviet system and the attitudes formed there continue to influence their beliefs and behaviors after they emigrate. An example is the comments of an undercover police officer, made to the U.S. Senate Permanent Subcommittee on Investigations that was investigating Russian organized crime in the United States. This officer, born and raised in Russia, reiterated many of the characteristics that we have mentioned and then made this observation: "That mentality, philosophy and upbringing explains why some of the Russian émigrés (many of whom were educated, family people) got involved in white-collar-type criminal activity in the United States."[17]

White-collar crime, organized crime, and corruption are each motivated by a particular form of the "acquisitive urge" we described in Chapter 2. White-collar crime is often defined as occurring in the course of occupational activity and is committed by those with better education and who are seemingly better equipped to earn their living legitimately. Corruption is a form of white-collar crime because it is an occupational abuse requiring an official position. Which of these forms the acquisitive urge manifests itself in depends on the economic, political, and legal environment, as well as the criminal opportunities.

As we explained in Chapter 5, the most highly organized form of crime in the former Soviet Union was white-collar corruption. It was tied to the black market and the shadow economy. Given this tradition, we would expect Soviet émigrés who come to the United States seeking criminal opportunities to have had little involvement in such staples of traditional organized crime as gambling, drugs, and prostitution. Instead, we would expect to find them experienced in crimes of deception. And, indeed, that is what our empirical evidence from the Tri-state Project database and the national law enforcement survey shows. Those data clearly demonstrate Soviet émigrés' involvement in crimes of deception. For example, of those U.S. law enforcement agencies that reported contact with Russians, 53 percent reported fraud crimes, 32 percent reported money laundering, and 31 percent reported drug crimes. Typical organized crimes such as extortion, racketeering, prostitution, and loan sharking were reported by only 19 percent, 17 percent, 12 percent, and 5 percent, respectively. Among these law enforcement agencies there is obviously very limited support for the contention that there is a serious Russian organized crime problem in the United States.

We began this book with a provocative set of premises. Based on all the information available to us, we conclude that the facts do not support the proposition that Soviet émigrés currently constitute an organized crime threat to the United States. Increased immigration and new criminal opportunities may change the nature of émigré crime, but the very nature of these criminal activities may continue to militate against either a need or a desire to adopt a more traditional organized crime structure, such as La Cosa Nostra.

Whatever form or forms may arise, we are confident that they will not constitute a Russian mafia. It is ironic that so many émigrés from the former Soviet Union feel themselves tainted by the stereotype of a Russian mafia that is neither Russian nor a mafia. Most are not opportunists or criminal entrepreneurs wanting only to take advantage of others. But those who are will be the objects of our continuing attention.

APPENDIX A
SAMPLING FOR
THE NATIONAL SURVEY

For the national survey, respondents were chosen from four different mailing lists from organizations involved in law enforcement, including those identified as particularly interested in organized crime:

◆ International Association of Law Enforcement Intelligence Analysts (IALEIA) (Canadian agencies, students, academics, and reporters were removed from this list),
◆ National District Attorneys Association (NDAA) (only jurisdictions with 250,000 people or more were included in our list),
◆ Mid-Atlantic Great Lakes Organized Crime Law Enforcement Network (MAGLOCLEN), and
◆ Law Enforcement Intelligence Unit (LEIU).

Some agencies and individuals were members of more than one of the above organizations. Attempts were made to identify these cases and to remove any duplicates to avoid unnecessary mailings.

This sampling procedure has a number of biases and cannot be considered a scientific sample of all law enforcement agencies within the entire United States. Because mailing lists were used for the selection of cases, agencies could be surveyed only if they belonged to one of the organizations. Efforts were made, however, to ensure that each state was represented in the survey. For example, if one state was not represented in any of the mailing lists, the state police there were contacted, and the survey either was administered by phone or was faxed to the person in charge. Agencies in larger jurisdictions and with a specific interest in organized crime were certainly more likely to be selected than those that were not.

We mailed 750 surveys in the last week of July 1994 to the selected agencies within the United States. Strong efforts were made to receive responses from as many agencies as possible. Repeat mailings, phone calls, and fax attempts were all used to extract responses from agencies that had been delinquent with their responses to the survey. In the end, 484 valid responses were received, an individual-level response rate of 64.5 percent. Our response rate can, however, also be stated on the organizational level. There were cases where several individuals from the same agency received the survey. This means that we have two response rates—one for individuals and one for agencies. If we received one response from any individual from a given agency, that agency may be classified as having responded. Controlling for duplication, 581 agencies were surveyed, from which we received 452 responses for an agency response rate of 77.8 percent.

APPENDIX B
MULTIVARIATE ANALYSIS
OF THE SURVEY

The multivariate analysis of the responses to the survey used a statistical technique called *logistic regression,* which allows us to examine the unique effects of independent variables while controlling for other independent variables. The variables used in the models are listed in Table B.1. The results of the logistic regression analysis of whether agencies had contact with Soviet émigré criminals are given in Table B.2. The results of the analysis of whether those agencies who reported contact with Soviet émigré criminals either defined the émigrés' offenses as organized crime or defined crime by Soviet émigrés as a law enforcement problem are given in Table B.3.

Table B.1 Variable Descriptions

Variable	Definition
Tristate region	Dummy variable indicating whether a state is part of the tristate area comprised of New York, New Jersey, and Pennsylvania
Organizational level	Set of dummy variables classifying the type of law enforcement agency by jurisdictional level
Criminal justice system employees	The total number of people employed by the criminal justice system for each state for 1990 (in 100,000s)
Routine handling	Dummy variable indicating whether agencies have personnel who handle most of the cases involving people from the former Soviet Union
Participation	Dummy variable indicating whether agencies showed an interest in participating in an information exchange program
Obtain information	Dummy variable indicating whether agencies have tried to obtain information from agencies in the former Soviet Union
Russian speaker	Dummy variable indicating whether agencies have a Russian-speaking staff member
Law enforcement problem	Dummy variable indicating whether agencies consider crimes involving persons from the former Soviet Union to be a major law enforcement problem
Number of contacts	Dummy variable classifying agencies by contacts with criminals or suspected criminals who are from the former Soviet Union
Russian population	The population of Russian immigrants in 1992 (in 1,000s)
State population	The state population for 1994 (in 100,000s)

Note: The following crime-type dummy variables indicate the nature of the Russian criminal activity reported by agencies: violent crimes, drug-related crimes, fraud and confidence schemes, money laundering, forgery, prostitution, racketeering, and extortion.

Table B.2 Logistic Regression Model of Whether an Agency Reported Any Contact with Soviet Émigré Criminals

	Coefficient	P value
Intercept	1.043	(.0137)**
Organizational level**		
City	− 1.159	(.0012)**
County	− 1.655	(.0000)**
State	− 1.151	(.0008)**
Federal	—	—
Tristate region	.503	(.0915)*
Russian population	.185	(.0048)**
State population	− 0.000	(.8647)
Criminal justice system employees	− 0.840	(.3127)
Log likelihood test	108.61	(.0000)**

*Significant at .10 level.
**Significant at .05 level.

Table B.3 Logistic Regression Models of Whether Agencies Reporting Contact with Soviet Émigré Criminals Described Their Crimes as Following an Organized Crime Model and Whether Their Crimes Were Termed a Law Enforcement Problem

	Organized Crime Model		Law Enforcement Problem Model	
	Coefficient	P value	Coefficient	P value
Intercept	6.185	(.0022)**	3.132	(.0238)**
Organizational level**				
City	−.716	(.3493)	−1.759	(.0454)**
County	−1.363	(.0649)	−3.022	(.0117)**
State	−.484	(.4720)	−.346	(.6339)
Federal	—	—	—	—
Tristate region	.794	(.1806)	−.260	(.7181)
Russian population	.043	(.7143)	.026	(.8811)
State population	−.003	(.7147)	−.005	(.5354)
Criminal justice system employees	.667	(.6834)	1.291	(.5391)
Number of contacts				
5 or fewer	−.122	(.8435)	−1.297	(.1080)
6 to 20	.004	(.9942)	−.623	(.2729)
Over 20	—	—	—	—
Routine handling	1.052	(.0272)**	.828	(.1241)
Russian speaker	.422	(.3643)	.041	(.9536)
Crime types				
Violent	.393	(.4729)	1.169	(.2394)
Drugs	.076	(.8720)	.217	(.9199)
Fraud	1.446	(.0070)**	.981	(.0507)**
Extortion	1.173	(.0854)*	.468	(.7189)
Prostitution	.648	(.4946)	1.734	(.2294)
Money laundering	.466	(.3625)	.188	(.7197)
Racketeering	2.005	(.0632)*	1.612	(.0608)*
Forgery	.313	(.5910)	1.365	(.1153)
Log likelihood test	147	(.0000)**	166	(.0000)**

*Significant at .10 level.
**Significant at .05 level.

APPENDIX C
NETWORK ANALYSIS

To describe how we used the information on the relationships between individuals, organizations, and other entities in the database described in Chapter 8, it is necessary to step back and explain some of the basic ideas and vocabulary of network analysis. Consider, for example, four of the many possible ways that eight offenders can be connected to each other. In Figure C.1a, all eight know each other, and they exist in a state of maximum connection. This illustrates what is known as a maximally *complete network* because all possible ties are present. In this network it is not possible to distinguish between a central player and a marginal one. If any one actor is removed, the structure remains essentially unaltered.

In Figure C.1b, one of the eight offenders occupies a central position connected to each of the other members of the network, and none of the others is connected to anyone but the center. In this example, it is clear that the person at the center occupies the central role, while those beyond the center are marginal. Remove the central person, and the whole structure falls apart. Remove someone at the margin, and it stays basically the same, although some might be harder to replace than others.

In Figure C.1c, the individuals are organized in a chain, in which each individual is linked to only adjacent persons, except those at either end. Removal of any individual could destroy the chain, but the impact of removal depends on that person's position. Removal of the link between some pairs of individuals might serve to create two identically structured groups of a smaller size. In Figure C.1d, two of the members of a three-person clique are connected to other less central individuals, who may in turn be connected to others. Here again

a.

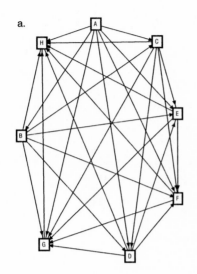

b.

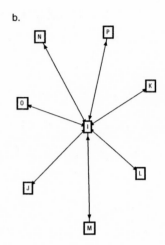

c.

d.

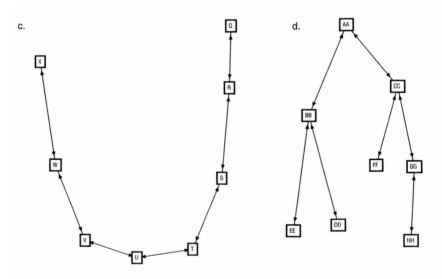

Figure C.1 Four Ways to Arrange Eight Actors in a Network

we see that the removal of some key individuals might lead to the collapse of the network, while the removal of others would not.

Of course, in the real world, few networks are as simple as the four illustrated. Crime networks can take a variety of forms and can be made up in a variety of ways. In some, roles are well defined and highly segmented, while in others the structure is more egalitarian. In some networks not all members have knowledge of all aspects of the crime, while in others they do. In some the members double-cross each other during the crime or in dealing with the authorities, while in others members have strong loyalties to one another. In some crime networks the relationships among co-offenders are ongoing, either criminally or personally, while in others strangers come together for a single crime incident. The representation of organized crime as a set of three hierarchically organized families, each with a single leader who comes together with the leaders of the other families, would be organized as in Figure C.2.

The first step in the transformation of network data into a form that can be analyzed is the creation of a matrix representation of the data. If the population of n individuals[1] makes up the database, then an $n \times n$ matrix is created. Thus the four eight-actor sociograms illustrated in Figure C.1 can be transformed into four eight-by-eight matrices (Figure C.3). A row and a column represent each actor's set of relationships. The presence of a tie (link) between two actors is represented by a 1 and the absence by a 0. An affirmative answer to the question "Is person C tied to person A?" is represented by placing a 1 at the intersection of row A and column C and a second 1 in row C and column A.[2]

Describing the Structure as a Whole

There are a number of different approaches to the description of a network. One important characteristic of a set of relational data is whether it is connected—that is, whether it is possible to get from

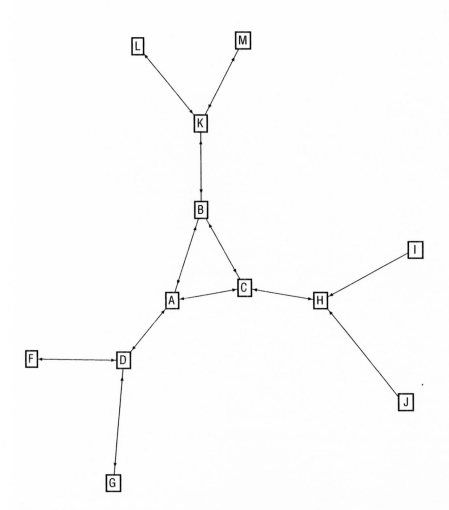

Figure C.2 Center of the Network Implied by Three Organized Crime Families

each member to each other member using the paths or links between network members. A specific pair of actors is called *reachable* if there is a path between them, regardless of how long the path is. It may well turn out that there is not a single connected network but rather several nonoverlapping subgroups or lone individuals within the data.[3] In network analysis, all actors who are directly or indirectly linked to each other are said to form a component. Everyone in a

a.

	1	2	3	4	5	6	7	8
1	–	1	1	1	1	1	1	1
2	1	–	1	1	1	1	1	1
3	1	1	–	1	1	1	1	1
4	1	1	1	–	1	1	1	1
5	1	1	1	1	–	1	1	1
6	1	1	1	1	1	–	1	1
7	1	1	1	1	1	1	–	1
8	1	1	1	1	1	1	1	–

b.

	1	2	3	4	5	6	7	8
1	–	0	0	0	0	0	0	1
2	0	–	0	0	0	0	0	1
3	0	0	–	0	0	0	0	1
4	0	0	0	–	0	0	0	1
5	0	0	0	0	–	0	0	1
6	0	0	0	0	0	–	0	1
7	0	0	0	0	0	0	–	1
8	1	1	1	1	1	1	1	–

c.

	1	2	3	4	5	6	7	8
1	–	1	0	0	0	0	0	0
2	1	–	1	0	0	0	0	0
3	0	1	–	1	0	0	0	0
4	0	0	1	–	1	0	0	0
5	0	0	0	1	–	1	0	0
6	0	0	0	0	1	–	1	0
7	0	0	0	0	0	1	–	1
8	0	0	0	0	0	0	1	–

d.

	1	2	3	4	5	6	7	8
1	–	1	1	0	0	0	0	0
2	1	–	1	1	0	0	0	0
3	1	1	–	0	1	1	0	0
4	0	1	0	–	0	0	1	1
5	0	0	1	0	–	0	0	0
6	0	0	1	0	0	–	0	0
7	0	0	0	1	0	0	–	0
8	0	0	0	1	0	0	0	–

Figure C.3 Matrix Representation of the Networks in Figure 8.2

component is directly or indirectly connected. No one in a component is directly or indirectly connected to anyone in a different component. In our investigation of Soviet émigré crime we were particularly interested in discovering the extent to which actors are directly or indirectly connected to each other. We wished to know whether their organization consisted mainly of small groups or teams acting independently or whether some larger, overarching organization—sometimes labeled the *Organizatsiya*—existed, as has been argued by some analysts. There are a number of ways in which the overall characteristics of a given network can be characterized and compared with other networks. Some of these may be used in any contexts, and others can be used only within a component. To summarize the overall network, a measure called *density* is used. Density is, essentially, the proportion of all possible ties that are actually present. Figure C.1a shows a network with a density of 1; all of the twenty-one possible ties between actors are present.[4] A density of 0 would mean that none of the actors are tied to each other. The organized crime hierarchical structure has a density of .09. The star figure (Figure C.1b) and the chain figure (Figure C.1c) each have the same number of ties and the same number of actors, so their densities are both .333 because seven of the twenty-one possible ties are present. Obviously, density alone is not enough to describe a network because it does not capture the important differences between these two networks.

A second approach measures how tightly tied together the network members are. The shortest route between any two members of a network is called a *geodesic*. To characterize a network, we can look at the longest, shortest, and average geodesics between members of the network. The length of the longest path between any two actors in a network is called the *diameter* of the network. In Figure C.1b (the star), the diameter is two. In Figure C.1c (the chain), it is seven. In the hierarchical organized crime structure (Figure C.2), it is seven. In the study of organized crime, we are particularly interested in understanding the extent to which the structure is hierarchically organized and who is at the center of the network. The measures of centralization provided by network analysis allow us to assess the extent of centralization. If we take Figure C.2 as a model of organized crime that is highly centralized, we can compare other criminal networks to it. Because of the nature of the data we collected, and the large number of actors in the networks, we will rely primarily on measures based on the number of ties and the lengths of geodesics to assess the overall structure of the networks and to identify the central actors.[5]

Identifying Central Actors

Perhaps the most basic of the methods of identifying central actors relies simply on counting the number of ties that are present in the network. For example, important actors in a network may be those who have many ties. The central actor in the star graph has the most ties, for example. The limits of this approach become apparent, however, when the other figures are examined. It is possible that the most important actors in a network—for example, the three family heads in Figure C.2—may not have any more ties than the less important actors.

Another way to identify the central members of a network is to find those actors whose geodesics are small; they are relatively close to everyone else in the network. If we look at each actor and find its longest geodesic—the distance between the actor and the actor from which it is farthest—and then select those actors for whom this longest distance is as small as possible, then that set of actors is called the *Jordan center* of the graph. In the star network, the central actor has a maximum geodesic of 1, while all of the others have a maximum of 2. Therefore, the central actor alone makes up the Jordan center. In the chain network, the two actors in the middle of the chain have a maximum geodesic of 4, and they make up the Jordan center. In the three-family structure, the three central actors have maximum geodesics of 4 and together make up the Jordan center. We found that the Jordan center was useful for identifying important sets of actors.

In our analyses, we looked at overall density and then the connectedness of the overall network. None of the analyses found a single connected network. Instead, they found one large component (or connected network) and many smaller ones. In the subsequent analyses we concentrated on the largest components. Within it we concentrate on measures of density, on measures of centralization and centrality based on the number of ties actors had, and on the path distances (geodesics) between actors.

Describing the Structure of Relationships with Network Data

The approach that is most closely related to the theoretical view of networks as the basic form of social organization describes the structure of the relationships among members of the network. The relationships present in network data and the description of networks can be interpreted using techniques that allow us to summarize data and make it possible to compare two or more groups.[6] These techniques also often serve broader purposes because they allow the analyst to uncover structures within a set of relational data that may not be apparent to the naked eye. An analysis of a network's structure divides the matrix of network data into groups. The structural-equivalence approach groups together individuals who share similar patterns of relationships with third persons. Two actors are structurally equivalent if they send ties to the same other actors and receive the same ties from the same other actors. To carry out this analysis we used a statistical technique known as *cluster analysis* to divide the network matrix into groups of similarly situated actors. In doing this analysis we concentrated on the largest component of actors.[7]

NOTES

Chapter 1

1. Peter Reuter, "Research on American Organized Crime," in *Handbook of Organized Crime in the United States,* ed. Robert J. Kelly, Ko-lin Chin, and Rufus Schatzberg (Westport, Conn.: Greenwood Press, 1994).
2. Lydia S. Rosner, *The Soviet Way of Crime: Beating the System in the Soviet Union and the USA* (South Hadley, Mass.: Bergin & Garvey, 1986).

Chapter 2

1. Thorsten Sellin, "Organized Crime: A Business Enterprise," *Annals of the American Academy of Political and Social Science* 347 (May 1963): 12.
2. Mary McIntosh, *The Organization of Crime* (London: Macmillan, 1975), 3.
3. Donald R. Cressey, *Criminal Organization: Its Elementary Forms* (New York: Harper & Row, 1972).
4. Michael Maltz, *Measuring the Effectiveness of Organized Crime Control Efforts,* UIC Office of International Criminal Justice Monograph, no. 9 (Chicago: University of Illinois at Chicago, 1990).
5. Cressey, *Criminal Organization.*
6. Gaia Servadio, *Mafioso: A History of the Mafia from Its Origins to the Present* (New York: Stein and Day, 1976).
7. Dwight C. Smith, Jr., *The Mafia Mystique* (New York: Basic Books, 1975).
8. Diego Gambetta, *The Sicilian Mafia: The Business of Private Protection* (Cambridge, Mass.: Harvard University Press, 1993).
9. Anton Blok, *The Mafia of a Sicilian Village 1860–1960: A Study of Violent Peasant Entrepreneurs* (New York: Harper & Row, 1974), 6.
10. Pino Arlacchi, *Mafia, Peasants and Great Estates* (Cambridge: Cambridge University Press, 1983), 111.
11. Raimondo Catanzaro, *Men of Respect* (New York: Free Press, 1988), 26.
12. Judith Chubb, *The Mafia and Politics: The Italian State Under Seige,*

Center for International Studies, Western Societies Program Occasional Paper, no. 23 (Ithaca, N.Y.: Cornell University Press, 1989), 18.

13. Adolfo Beria di Argentine, "Conclusions," in *Mafia Issues,* ed. Ernesto U. Savona (Milan, Italy: ISPAC, 1993), 256.

14. Annelise Anderson, "Organised Crime, Mafias and Governments," in *The Economics of Organised Crime,* ed. Gianluca Fiorentini and Sam Peltzman (Cambridge: Cambridge University Press, 1995), 33.

15. Ibid., 35.

16. Blok, *Mafia of a Sicilian Village.*

17. Anderson, "Organised Crime, Mafias and Governments," 35.

18. Pino Arlacchi, *Mafia Business: The Mafia Ethic and the Spirit of Capitalism* (London: Verso, 1986), 221.

19. Report (Milan: International Scientific Programme Advisory Committee, 1996), 23.

20. Ibid.

21. Gus Xhudo, "Men of Purpose: The Growth of Albanian Criminal Activity," *Transnational Organized Crime* 2(1) (Spring 1996): 1–20.

22. Personal communication with Professor Menachim Amir, Institute of Criminology, Faculty of Law, Hebrew University, Jerusalem, July 17, 1996.

23. Daniel Bell, "Crime as an American Way of Life," *The Antioch Review* 13 (June 1953), reprinted in *The Sociology of Crime and Delinquency,* 2d ed., ed. Marvin E. Wolfgang, Leonard Savitz, and Norman Johnston (New York: Wiley, 1970); Francis A. J. Ianni, *Black Mafia: Ethnic Succession in Organized Crime* (New York: Simon & Schuster, 1974); James M. O'Kane, *The Crooked Ladder: Gangsters, Ethnicity, and the American Dream* (New Brunswick, N.J.: Transaction, 1992).

24. Bell, "Crime as an American Way of Life," 166.

25. Ibid.

26. Francis A. J. Ianni, *A Family Business: Kinship and Social Control in Organized Crime* (New York: Russell Sage Foundation, 1972); Ianni, *Black Mafia.*

27. O'Kane, *Crooked Ladder.*

28. Arlacchi, *Mafia Business.*

29. Reuter, "Research on American Organized Crime," 112.

30. Humbert S. Nelli, *The Business of Crime: Italians and Syndicate Crime in the United States* (Chicago: University of Chicago Press, 1976), 103–105.

31. See, for example, Harry Elmer Barnes and Negley K. Teeters, *New Horizons in Criminology,* 3d ed. (Englewood Cliffs, N.J.: Prentice-Hall, 1959); Stephen Fox, *Blood and Power: Organized Crime in Twentieth-Century America* (New York: Morrow, 1989); Peter Lupsha, "Individual Choice, Material Culture, and Organized Crime," *Criminology* 19(1) (May 1981): 3–24; Peter Lupsha, "American Values and Organized Crime: Suckers and Wiseguys," in *American Social Character,* ed. Rupert Wilkinson (New York: HarperCollins, 1992); Peter Lupsha, "Transnational Organized Crime Versus the Nation-State," *Transnational Organized Crime* 2(1) (Spring 1996): 21–48.

32. Lupsha, "Individual Choice," 15.

33. Becker, among others, has pointed out a pattern of hostility to those not engaged in deviance among those who are involved. See Howard Becker, *The Outsiders: Studies in the Sociology of Deviance* (New York: Free Press, 1966).

34. Elin Waring, David Weisburd, and Ellen Chayet, "White Collar Crime and Anomie," *Advances in Criminological Theory* (6) (1995): 207–225.

35. Arlacchi, *Mafia, Peasants and Great Estates,* 121.

36. Ianni, *Family Business,* 61.

37. Barnes and Teeters, *New Horizons in Criminology,* 12–16.

38. Ibid., 14.

39. Ibid., 15.

40. This need for both lack of constraints against crime and facilitation of specific crimes has been used in the examination of many different types of crime. For example, Hirschi and Gottfredson argue that low self-control combines with opportunity for specific offenses to produce criminal activity. Michael Gottfredson and Travis Hirschi, *A General Theory of Crime* (Stanford: Stanford University Press, 1990).

41. Lupsha, "American Values and Organized Crime," 298.

42. See Gresham Sykes and David Matza, "Techniques of Neutralization: A Theory of Delinquency," *American Sociological Review* 22 (1957): 664–670.

43. Lupsha, "American Values and Organized Crime," 300.

44. Ibid., 302.

45. Lupsha, "Transnational Organized Crime," 34.

46. Fox, *Blood and Power,* 76.

47. Frederic D. Homer, *Guns and Garlic: Myths and Realities of Organized Crime* (West Lafayette, Ind.: Purdue University, 1974).

48. Rupert Wilkinson, ed., *American Social Character* (New York: Harper-Collins, 1992), 308–309.

49. Thomas A. Firestone, "Mafia Memoirs: What They Tell Us About Organized Crime," *Journal of Contemporary Criminal Justice* 9(3) (August 1993): 202.

50. George Anastasia, *Blood and Honor: Inside the Scarfo Mob—The Mafia's Most Violent Family* (New York: Morrow, 1991), 32–33.

51. Vincent Teresa and Thomas C. Renner, *Vincent Teresa's Mafia* (New York: Doubleday, 1975), 5–6.

52. Firestone, "Mafia Memoirs," 202.

53. Nicholas Pileggi, *Wiseguy* (New York: Simon & Schuster, 1985), 38–39.

54. Firestone, "Mafia Memoirs," 204.

Chapter 3

1. Moses Rischin, *The Promised City: New York's Jews 1870–1914* (Cambridge, Mass.: Harvard University Press, 1962), 19–20.

2. Ibid., 19–31. Others disagree, for example, Arthur Hertzberg, *The Jews in America: Four Centuries of an Uneasy Encounter* (New York: Simon & Schuster, 1989), 153.

3. See Stephen Castles and Mark Miller, *The Age of Migration: International Population Movements in the Modern World* (Hampshire, England: Macmillan, 1993), for a summary of the push-pull approach to the analysis of migration and a discussion of its limitations.

4. Hertzberg, *Jews in America,* 242–244.

5. "Report of the Duma Commission on the Bialystok Massacre," in *The American Jewish Year Book 5667,* ed. Henrietta Szold (Philadelphia: Jewish Publication Society of America, 1906), 70–89.

6. "From Kishineff to Bialystok: A Table of Pogroms from 1903–1906," in Szold, *American Jewish Year Book 5667,* 34–69.

7. Hertzberg, *Jews in America,* 157–158.

8. Kate Holladay Claghorn, "The Foreign Immigrant in New York City," *Reports of the Industrial Commission 15* (Washington, D.C.: U.S. Government Printing Office, 1901), 465–492.

9. Ibid.

10. Ibid.

11. Jacob Riis, *How the Other Half Lives* (New York: Dover, 1971), 85.

12. Ibid., 98.

13. "In Defense of the Immigrant," *The American Jewish Year Book 5671,* ed. Herbert Friedenwald (Philadelphia: Jewish Publication Society of America, 1910), 19–98.

14. Claghorn, "The Foreign Immigrant."

15. Jenna Weissman Joselit, *Our Gang: Jewish Crime and the New York Jewish Community, 1900–1940* (Bloomington: Indiana University Press, 1983), 24.

16. Claghorn, "The Foreign Immigrant."

17. Ida Van Etten, "Russian Jews as Desirable Immigrants," *Forum* 15 (1893): 172–182.

18. Steve Birmingham, *"Our Crowd": The Great Jewish Families of New York* (New York: Harper & Row, 1967), 342–344, 149.

19. Ibid.

20. Joselit, *Our Gang,* 23–24.

21. Quoted in Joselit, *Our Gang,* 24.

22. Quoted in Irving Howe, *World of Our Fathers* (New York: Harcourt Brace Jovanovich, 1976), 98. The original source is William McAdoo, *Guarding a Great City* (Chicago: Harper, 1906).

23. Quoted in Joselit, *Our Gang,* 6.

24. Ibid., 19.

25. Howe, *World of Our Fathers,* 101.

26. Quoted in Joselit, *Our Gang,* 29.

27. Howe, *World of Our Fathers,* 98.

28. Riis, *How the Other Half Lives,* 90.

29. Howe, *World of Our Fathers,* 98. See also Joselit, *Our Gang,* 29–30.

30. Howe, *World of Our Fathers,* 16.

31. Van Etten, "Russian Jews."

32. "In Defense of the Immigrant," 25.
33. Joselit, *Our Gang,* 32.
34. Ibid., 35.
35. Ibid., 56.
36. Ibid., 55.
37. Robert Lacey, *Little Man: Meyer Lansky and the Gangster Life* (Boston: Little, Brown, 1991), 31–33.
38. Ibid., 40–42.
39. Jacob Riis, "The Jews of New York," *Review of Reviews* 13 (1896): 58–62.
40. Quoted in Joselit, *Our Gang,* 15.
41. Ibid., 158.
42. Ibid., 162.
43. Ibid., 54; also Howe, *World of Our Fathers,* 98.
44. A variety of sources to this effect are quoted in Edward Bristow, *Prostitution and Prejudice: The Jewish Fight Against White Slavery 1870– 1939* (New York: Schoken Books, 1983), 147–148.
45. The two-thirds figure is from Turner as quoted in Joselit, *Our Gang,* 46; lower figures are provided at 47–48.
46. "In Defense of the Immigrant," 21.
47. Bristow, *Prostitution and Prejudice,* 158–159, quotes contemporary accounts to this effect.
48. Ibid., 35–47.
49. Ibid., 46.
50. Quoted in Joselit, *Our Gang,* 52.
51. Ibid.; Bristow, *Prostitution and Prejudice,* 173.
52. Bristow, *Prostitution and Prejudice,* 224.
53. Ibid., 284.
54. Joselit, *Our Gang,* 108.
55. Ibid., 110.
56. Ibid., 36–37.
57. Riis, *How the Other Half Lives,* 91.
58. Joselit, *Our Gang,* 38.
59. Ibid., 5.
60. Ibid.

61. Ibid., 45.

62. Bristow, *Prostitution and Prejudice,* 146–148.

63. Alfred Fried, *The Rise and Fall of the Jewish Gangster in America* (New York: Columbia University Press, 1993), 93.

64. Joselit, *Our Gang,* 94.

65. Lacey, *Little Man,* 50.

66. Ibid., 50.

67. Fried, *Rise and Fall of the Jewish Gangster,* 94.

68. Ibid., 111–114.

69. Ibid., 123–124.

70. Ibid.

71. Joselit, *Our Gang,* 149.

72. Ibid., 150.

73. Deborah Dash Moore, *At Home in America* (New York: Columbia University Press, 1981).

74. Howe, *World of Our Fathers,* 555–638.

Chapter 4

1. See, for example, Natan Sharansky, *Fear No Evil* (New York: Random House, 1988), and Andrei Sakharov, *Memoirs* (New York: Knopf, 1990), for discussions of Soviet immigration policy as influenced by the Jackson-Vanik amendment to U.S. law requiring most-favored-nation trading status to be dependent on more liberal emigration.

2. New York State Organized Crime Task Force, New York Commission of Investigation, New Jersey State Commission of Investigation, "An Analysis of Russian Émigré Crime," *Transnational Organized Crime* 2(2–3) (Summer-Autumn 1996): 181–185.

3. Of course, immigration laws in New York and Philadelphia are the same.

4. Mike Mallewe, "From Russia with Guns," *Philadelphia Magazine* (May 1983), 104.

5. Ibid., 147.

6. Alan Jaffe and Bryna Paston, "Is There a Soviet-Jewish Mafia in the United States?," *Baltimore Jewish Times,* February 24, 1984.

7. Daniel Burstein, "The 'Russian Mafia': A New Crime Menace Grows in Brooklyn," *New York* (November 24, 1986): 38–43.

8. Ibid.

9. Rosner, *Soviet Way of Crime.*

10. In an interview (May 2, 1997), two vice ministers in the Ministry of State Security in Tbilisi, Georgia (one of whom had served in the KGB's central office in Moscow), vehemently denied any knowledge of KGB involvement in infiltrating criminals into the United States in the 1970s and 1980s. They stated that crime knows no country, that Soviet criminals could have certainly emigrated, but that they were not assisted in doing so by the KGB.

11. Stephen Handelman, personal interview, June 30, 1994.

12. Smith, *Mafia Mystique;* Dennis J. Kenney and James O. Finckenauer, *Organized Crime in America* (Belmont, Calif.: Wadsworth, 1995).

13. An example of Russian anti-Semitism is the infamous *Protocols of the Elders of Zion,* a work fabricated in 1904 by the Russian czar's secret police (the Okhrana) with the purpose of turning the Russian people's anger with their conditions away from the czar and onto the Jews.

14. Vladimir Uvanudze, "Russian Shadow on New York," *Novoye Russkoye Slovo* 24 (December 1996): 20, 28.

15. Nathan M. Adams, "Menace of the Russian Mafia," *Reader's Digest* (August 1992): 33–40.

16. Uvanudze, "Russian Shadow on New York."

17. Adams, "Menace of the Russian Mafia," 34.

18. Uvanudze, "Russian Shadow on New York," 20.

19. William Kleinknecht, *The New Ethnic Mobs: The Changing Face of Organized Crime in America* (New York: Free Press, 1996), 271–272. The cattle prod stories appear in nearly all accounts of Agron and his activities, and the cattle prod seemed to be his favorite implement.

20. Adams, "Menace of the Russian Mafia," 34–35.

21. Tim Cronwell, "Russian Mafia," unpublished report.

22. Robert I. Friedman, "Brighton Beach Goodfellas," *Vanity Fair* (January 1993), 26.

23. Ibid.

24. Ibid., 36.

25. Uvanudze, "Russian Shadow on New York," 22.

26. United States v. Anthony Morelli et al., in the U.S. District Court for the District of New Jersey, Criminal No. 93-210 (1995).

27. Ibid., 23.
28. Testimony of FBI Director Louis J. Freeh, U.S. Senate, Permanent Sub-committee on Investigations of the Committee on Governmental Affairs, *Hearings on Russian Organized Crime in the United States,* 104th Cong., 2d Sess. (May 25, 1994).
29. Rosner, *Soviet Way of Crime;* Kleinknecht, *New Ethnic Mobs.*
30. Reuter, "Research on American Organized Crime."
31. Victor Ripp, *From Moscow to Main Street* (Boston: Little, Brown, 1984), 154–155.
32. Alexander Zinoviev, *Homo Sovieticus* (Boston: The Atlantic Monthly Press, 1985).
33. Gaileviciute spoke at a seminar, sponsored by the Thorolf Rafto Foundation for Human Rights. The seminar was part of a ceremony to honor Palermo Anno Uno, a grassroots citizens' group organized to combat the Sicilian Mafia. It was held in Bergen, Norway, October 31 to November 4, 1996.
34. Konstantin M. Simis, *USSR: The Corrupt Society,* trans. Jaqueline Edwards and Mitchell Schneider (New York: Simon & Schuster, 1982), 248–249.
35. "Crime," *World Affairs* 152(2) (Fall 1989): 109.
36. Stanislav Govorukin, "The War Against Crime," *World Affairs* 152(2) (Fall 1989): 115–116.
37. Vladimir Shlapentokh, *Public and Private Life of the Soviet People: Changing Values in Post-Stalin Russia* (New York: Oxford University Press, 1989), 212–213.
38. Alec Nove, "An Economy in Transition," in *Chronicle of a Revolution,* ed. Abraham Bramberg (New York: Pantheon Books, 1990), 51.
39. Hedrick Smith, "The Russian Character," *New York Times Magazine* 28 (October 1990), 62.
40. Ibid., 145.
41. Valery Chalidze, *Criminal Russia: Crime in the Soviet Union,* trans. P. S. Falla (New York: Random House, 1977).
42. Simis, *USSR,* 248–249.
43. Ibid., 252.
44. Ibid., 299.

45. Louise Shelley, "The Second Economy in the Soviet Union," in *The Second Economy in Marxist States,* ed. Maria Los (London: Macmillan Press, 1990), 19.

46. Boris Z. Rumer, *Soviet Central Asia: "A Tragic Experiment"* (Boston: Unwin Hyman, 1989).

47. Gordon B. Smith, *Soviet Politics: Struggling with Change* (New York: St. Martin's Press, 1992), 247.

48. Edward A. Hewett, *Reforming the Soviet Economy: Equality Versus Efficiency* (Washington, D.C.: Brookings Institution, 1988), 36.

49. Lydia S. Rosner, "The Sexy Russian Mafia," *Criminal Organizations* 10(1) (Fall 1995): 29.

50. Doina Chiacu, "Established Immigrants Balk at Post-Communist Newcomers," *Island Packet,* January 4, 1995, p. 11-A.

51. Our sources of information about Andrei Kuznetsov include Robert Cullen, "Comrades in Crime," *Playboy Magazine* (April 1994): 70–72, 130, 160–163; a personal interview with Cullen; interviews with law enforcement authorities in California; U.S. Senate, *Hearings on Russian Organized Crime in the United States* (May 15, 1996).

52. Cullen, "Comrades in Crime," 161.

53. Ibid.

54. U.S. Senate, *Hearings on Russian Organized Crime in the United States,* 190.

Chapter 5

1. Stephen Handelman, *Comrade Criminal: Russia's New Mafiya* (New Haven: Yale University Press, 1995).

2. Sergey Avdienko, "Organized Crime in the Former Soviet Union," Paper presented at the Thorolf Rafto Foundation's Seminar on Organized Crime: The New Threat to Human Rights, INTERPOL, Bergen, November 1, 1996.

3. R. T. Naylor, "From Cold War to Crime War: The Search for a New National Security Threat," *Transnational Organized Crime* 1(4) (Winter 1995): 37–56.

4. Avdienko, "Organized Crime in the Former Soviet Union," 4.

5. Naylor, "From Cold War to Crime War," 48.

6. Chalidze, *Criminal Russia.*

7. William A. Clark, *Crime and Punishment in Soviet Officialdom: Combating Corruption in the Political Elite 1965–1990* (Armonk, N.Y.: Sharpe, 1993), 38.

8. Letter from Acton to Creighton, April 3, 1887, quoted in *Life and Letters of Mandell Creighton* (1904), http://www.acton.org/actonbio.html, April 22, 1998.

9. Arkady Vaksberg, *The Soviet Mafia* (New York: St. Martin's Press, 1991), 200; Alexander S. Nikiforov, "Organized Crime in the West and in the Former USSR: An Attempted Comparison," *International Journal of Offender Therapy and Comparative Criminology* 37(1) (1993): 5–15.

10. Nikiforov, "Organized Crime in the West and in the Former USSR," 11.

11. Z, "To the Stalin Mausoleum," *Daedalus: Journal of the American Academy of Arts and Sciences* 119(1) (Winter 1990): 304.

12. Simis, *USSR,* 72.

13. Ibid., 73.

14. Ibid., 80–81.

15. Ibid., 94–95.

16. Vaksberg, *Soviet Mafia,* 19.

17. Ibid., 20.

18. Lev Timofeyev, *Russia's Secret Rulers: How the Government and Criminal Mafia Exercise Their Power* (New York: Knopf, 1992), 61.

19. Ibid., 63.

20. Rumer, *Soviet Central Asia,* 151.

21. Ibid.

22. Joseph D. Serio and Vyacheslav Stephanovich Razinkin, "Thieves Professing the Code: The Traditional Role of *Vory v Zakone* in Russia's Criminal World and Adaptions to a New Social Reality," CJ Europe Online Web document: http://www.acsp.uic.edu/oicj/pubs/cje/050405_1.htm, 1997.

23. Vyacheslav Afanasyev, "Organized Crime and Society," *Demokratizatsiya: The Journal of Post-Soviet Democratization* 2(3) (Summer 1994): 438.

24. A. I. Gurov, *Professional Crime: Past and Present* (Moscow: Iuridicheskaia Literatura, 1990).

25. Handelman, *Comrade Criminal,* 31.

26. Gurov, *Professional Crime.*

27. Ibid.

28. Mikhail Dyomin, *The Day Is Born of Darkness: A Personal Account of the Soviet Criminal Underworld,* trans. Tony Kahn (New York: Knopf, 1976), 124.

29. Arkady G. Bronnikov, "Telltale Tattoos in Russian Prisons," *Natural History* (November 1993): 50–58.

30. Ibid., 53.

31. Serio and Razinkin, "Thieves Professing the Code." This same kind of linking of political insurgents with professional criminals is alleged to have taken place more recently in the former Soviet Republic of Georgia. When Georgia became independent after the collapse of the Soviet Union, a nationalist leader named Gamsakhurdia was chosen as its new president. For a variety of reasons, some in the world community (including the United States) subsequently became disenchanted with Gamsakhurdia, and—as alleged by Georgian nationalists and Gamsakhurdia supporters—the United States then became instrumental in engineering a coup to overthrow the president. He was to be replaced by former Soviet Foreign Minister (and former Communist Party and KGB boss in Soviet Georgia) Eduard Shevardnadze. It is further alleged that to provide muscle and firepower for this coup, the top-ranking thief-in-law in the country (who happened to be in prison) was released to round up his some 5,000 followers and to take up arms to fight the Gamsakhurdia administration. Following the coup's success, the *vor* was rewarded with a major government post and became a Shevardnadze advisor. Later, however, when his services were no longer needed, and perhaps when he was an embarrassment (again according to sources), the old *vor* was reimprisoned. It would seem that the tradition lives on. Georgi Glonti, personal interview, Tbilisi, April 1997.

32. Aleksandr I. Solzhenitsyn, *The Gulag Archipelago 1918–1956: An Experiment in Literary Investigation* (New York: Harper & Row, 1973), 445.

33. Yuri Brokhin, *Hustling on Gorky Street: Sex and Crime in Russia Today,* trans. E. B. Kane and Yuri Brokhin (New York: Dial Press, 1975).
34. Chalidze, *Criminal Russia,* 48.
35. Serio and Razinkin, "Thieves Professing the Code."
36. These criminal communes are not to be confused with crime families in the sense of Italian mafia families. The latter are relatively small—having anywhere from fewer than a hundred to up to several hundred members. They also have continuing, fairly well-defined hierarchical structures, with Italian or specifically Sicilian ethnicity being a prerequisite for membership. The criminal commune of a *vor,* on the other hand, can involve hundreds and even thousands of participants from a variety of backgrounds. Membership is loosely defined. The grouping is also less well structured and much flatter in its hierarchy. The *vor* in the thieves' world is more like a first among equals than like the Italian capo or boss of a crime family.
37. Brokhin, *Hustling on Gorky Street.* Questions and some intervening comments have been removed from this and other quotations from this interview. Brokhin was himself a fascinating character. A Ukrainian Jew, he emigrated to New York in 1972. Daniel Burstein, "Death of a Hustler: Was Émigré Writer Yuri Brokhin Murdered by the 'Russian Mafia'?," *New York* (May 2, 1983): 24–29. Brokhin was intelligent, well educated, and ambitious. Although educated as a mining engineer, he became a hustler in the Soviet Union—gambling, selling record albums, pickpocketing, running illegal casinos, and working the black market. He came to the Big Apple looking for quick success by making big money, and as one of his friends said, "The means of doing it were not important." Some people, according to Burstein's account, saw Brokhin as the personification of the Soviet system of corruption—corruption that Brokhin had documented in his book. This was the system that forced even those like Brokhin, who seemingly had the ability and education to do well legitimately, to resort instead to deception, bribery, and black-market dealing. Brokhin's story ended violently when he was shot and killed on December 5, 1982, in his apartment in New York City. The killer or killers have never been found: according to rumors, they were either the KGB or the ubiquitous Russian mafia.

38. Ibid., 115.
39. Andrei Kruzhilin, "An Iron Hand Without Arms or Money," *Literary Gazette International* (December 1990): 15.
40. Serio and Razinkin, "Thieves Professing the Code."
41. Kruzhilin, "An Iron Hand Without Arms or Money," 15.
42. Serio and Razinkin, "Thieves Professing the Code."
43. Handelman, *Comrade Criminal,* 260.
44. Gene Mustain and Jerry Capeci, "Infamous from Moscow to N.Y.," *New York Daily News,* April 20, 1997, p. 7.
45. United States v. Vyacheslav Kirillovich Ivankov et al., U.S. District Court Eastern District of New York, Complaint and Affidavit in Support of Arrest Warrants (June 6, 1995).
46. *Novoye Russkoye Slovo,* July 19, 1995, p. 7.
47. Handelman, *Comrade Criminal,* 261.
48. Ibid.; United States v. Vyacheslav Kirillovich Ivankov et al.
49. Ibid.
50. Handelman, *Comrade Criminal.*
51. Interview with Alexander Grant, August 9, 1994.
52. Kleinknecht, *New Ethnic Mobs,* 284.
53. Claire Sterling, *Thieves' World: The Threat of the New Global Network of Organized Crime* (New York: Simon & Schuster, 1994), 16.
54. Mustain and Capeci, "Infamous from Moscow to N.Y."
55. *Novoye Russkoye Slovo,* April 24, 1997, p. 6.

Chapter 6

1. Such official statistics would include the Uniform Crime Reports and the National Crime Victimization Survey.
2. A. I. Dolgova, "Organized Crime in Russia," trans. Alexander S. Nikiforov, unpublished report, 1997.
3. Alexander S. Nikiforov, "What Shall We Have to Do with Organized Crime?," unpublished, 1997.
4. Joseph Serio, "Threats to the Foreign Business Community in Moscow," *Transnational Organized Crime* 2(2–3) (Summer-Autumn 1996): 89.
5. Nils H. Wessell, "Criminal Russia: From City Streets to Kremlin Offices," *Russian Politics and Law* 33(4) (July-August 1995): 29.

6. Considered a serious crime, banditry is a crime (or crimes) that is committed by a group and that involves theft or robbery. An equivalent in the United States would be mugging when committed by a group.

7. Avdienko, "Organized Crime in the Former Soviet Union."

8. Ibid.; Yuri A. Voronin, "The Emerging Criminal State: Economic and Political Aspects of Organized Crime in Russia," *Transnational Organized Crime* 2(2–3) (Summer-Autumn 1996): 53–62.

9. Timur Sinuraja, "Organized Crime in the Economic and Financial Sectors of Russia and Its Impact on Western Europe," unpublished report, 1996, 28–29.

10. Guy Dunn, "Major Mafia Gangs in Russia," *Transnational Organized Crime* 2(2–3) (Summer-Autumn 1996): 63.

11. Wessell, "Criminal Russia," 13.

12. Voronin, "Emerging Criminal State."

13. Personal interview, May 6, 1997.

14. Avdienko, "Organized Crime in the Former Soviet Union"; Dolgova, "Organized Crime in Russia."

15. See, for example, Andrian Kreye, "Mafia Capitalism in Moscow," unpublished paper, 1994.

16. Ibid., 3.

17. Dolgova, "Organized Crime in Russia."

18. Avdienko, "Organized Crime in the Former Soviet Union."

19. Phil Williams, "Introduction: How Serious a Threat Is Russian Organized Crime?," *Transnational Organized Crime* 2(2–3) (Summer-Autumn 1996): 12.

20. Dunn, "Major Mafia Gangs."

21. Ibid., 65.

22. Ibid., 68.

23. Ibid., 70.

24. Williams, "How Serious a Threat Is Russian Organized Crime?," 14.

25. Sinuraja, "Organized Crime in Economic and Financial Sectors of Russia," 22.

26. Dolgova, "Organized Crime in Russia."

27. Louise Shelley, "Post-Soviet Organized Crime: A New Form of Authoritarianism," *Transnational Organized Crime* 2(2–3) (Summer-Autumn 1996): 124–126.

28. Ibid., 136.

29. Wessell, "Criminal Russia," 24.

30. Kreye, "Mafia Capitalism."

31. Wessell, "Criminal Russia," 33.

32. Dolgova, "Organized Crime in Russia"; Ol'ga V. Kryshtanovskaia, "Illegal Structures in Russia," *Russian Social Science Review* 8 (1995): 44–64.

33. Wessell, "Criminal Russia," 29.

34. Joseph D. Serio, "Organized Crime in the Former Soviet Union" (master's thesis, University of Illinois at Chicago, 1993).

35. Avdienko, "Organized Crime in the Former Soviet Union," 4.

36. Patricia Rawlinson, "Russian Organized Crime: A Brief History," *Transnational Organized Crime* 2(2–3) (Summer-Autumn 1996): 51.

37. Joseph L. Albini et al., "Russian Organized Crime: Its History, Structure and Function," *Journal of Contemporary Criminal Justice* 11(4) (December 1995): 214–215.

38. Frederico Varese, "What Is the Russian Mafia?," *Low Intensity Conflict and Law Enforcement* 5(2) (Autumn 1996): 129–138.

39. Anderson, "Organised Crime, Mafias and Governments"; Gambetta, *Sicilian Mafia;* Frederico Varese, "Is Sicily the Future of Russia? Private Protection and the Rise of the Russian Mafia," *Archives Européennes de Sociologie* 35 (1994); Varese, "What Is the Russian Mafia?"

40. U.S. Senate, *Hearings on Russian Organized Crime in the United States.*

41. Voronin, "Emerging Criminal State," 54.

42. Igor Ilynsky, "The Status and Development of Youth in Post-Soviet Society," in *Young People in Post-Communist Russia and Eastern Europe,* ed. James Riordan, Christopher Williams, and Igor Ilynsky (Aldershot, Eng.: Dartmouth, 1995), 14.

43. Ibid., 14–15.

44. I. A. Dvoimennyi, "The Social-Psychological Characteristics of Juvenile Delinquents," *Russian Education and Society* 38(1) (1996).

45. Ibid., 8.

46. Celestine Bohlen, "A New Russia: Now Thrive the Swindlers," *New York Times,* March 17, 1994, p. 1.

47. Christopher J. Ulrich, "The New Red Terror: International Dimensions

of Post-Soviet Organized Crime," *Low Intensity Conflict and Law Enforcement* 5(1) (Summer 1996): 7.

48. International Organization for Migration, *Newsletter* (1996): 1–2.
49. United Nations General Assembly, "Measures to Combat Alien-Smuggling," Crime Prevention and Criminal Justice, Report of the Secretary-General, August 30, 1994.
50. Information on the Russian problem in Israel was obtained from Israeli criminologist Menachem Amir.
51. International Organization for Migration, *Newsletter* (1994).
52. U.S. Senate, *Hearings on Russian Organized Crime in the United States.*
53. Ulrich, "The New Red Terror," 36.
54. U.S. Senate, *Hearings on Russian Organized Crime in the United States,* 10–17.
55. Ibid., 15–17.

Chapter 7

1. Robert I. Friedman, "The Organizatsiya," *New York* 27(44) (November 7, 1994): 50–58; Robert I. Friedman, "Brighton Beach Goodfellas," *Vanity Fair* 56(1) (January 1993): 26–41; Scott Anderson, "Looking for Mr. Yaponchik," *Harper's* 291(1747) (December 1995): 40–51; Ronald K. Noble, "Russian Organized Crime: A Worldwide Problem," *Police Chief* 62(6) (June 1995): 18–21; Selwyn Raab, "Influx of Russian Gangsters Troubles F.B.I. in Brooklyn," *New York Times,* August 23, 1994, sec. A, p. 1, col. 5.
2. New York State Organized Crime Task Force et al., "Analysis of Russian Émigré Crime in the Tri-State Region."
3. The sample is discussed in detail in Appendix A.
4. See, for example, Friedman, "Brighton Beach Goodfellas"; Anderson, "Looking for Mr. Yaponchik"; Friedman, "The Organizatsiya"; Raab, "Influx of Russian Gangsters"; Jennifer Gould, "The Russian Mob's Submarine Scheme: Cosa Nostra's Rival Is Savagely Smart," *Village Voice,* March 4, 1997, pp. 32–33.
5. To do this we use multivariate statistical techniques, the details of which are discussed in Appendix B. These techniques allow us to evaluate the impact of many possible factors simultaneously.

6. Complete details of this analysis are given in Appendix B.

7. The fact that some federal agencies, such as the FBI, had initiated projects investigating Soviet organized crime may have influenced federal agencies to be particularly aware of these issues.

8. New Jersey State Commission of Investigation, "Motor Fuel Tax Evasion" (February 1992), 23.

9. Ibid., 15.

10. Alan A. Block, "Racketeering in Fuels: Tax Scamming by Organized Crime," in *Space, Time, and Organized Crime*, 2d ed., ed. Alan A. Block (New Brunswick, N.J.: Transaction Books, 1994).

11. Ianni, *Black Mafia;* Kleinknecht, *New Ethnic Mobs.*

12. Ashley Craddock and Mordecai Lawrence, "Swoop-and-Squats," *Mother Jones* 18(5) (September 1993): 16–20.

13. Block, "Racketeering in Fuels," 162–164; Richter H. Moore, Jr., "Motor Fuel Tax Fraud and Organized Crime: The Soviet and the Italian-American Mafia," in *Contemporary Issues in Organized Crime,* ed. Jay Albanese (Monsey, N.Y.: Criminal Justice Press, 1995), 189–200.

14. U.S. Senate, *Hearings on Russian Organized Crime in the United States.*

15. New York State Organized Crime Task Force et al., "Analysis of Russian Émigré Crime in the Tri-State Region."

16. Ibid., 220–226.

17. "New Comrades of Crime," [Trenton] *Times,* August 14, 1995, p. A1.

18. Guy Dunn, "Major Mafia Gangs in Russia," in *Russian Organized Crime: The New Threat?* ed. Phil Williams (London: Frank Cass & Company, 1997), 65–67.

19. Rosner, "The Sexy Russian Mafia"; Roy Surrett, "Remarks," Paper presented at the First International Law Enforcement Sharing Conference on Russian Organized Crime, September 19–23, 1994.

20. Walter W. Powell and Laurel Smith-Doerr, "Networks and Economic Life," in *The Handbook of Economic Sociology,* ed. Neil Smelser and Richard Swedborg (Princeton: Princeton University Press, 1994).

Chapter 8

1. Elin Waring, James Finckenauer, and Emmanual Barthe, "The Impact of Data Sources on the Study of White-Collar Crime: An Examination

of the Biases in a Study of Russian Émigré Crime," Paper presented at the Forty-Eighth Annual Meeting of the American Society of Criminology, Chicago, November 1996, 3.

2. Walter W. Powell, "Neither Market nor Hierarchy: Network Forms of Organization," in *Research in Organizational Behavior,* vol. 2, ed. Barry M. Staw and L. L. Cummings (Greenwich, Conn.: JAI Press, 1990).

3. Peter M. Blau, *The American Occupational Structure* (New York: Wiley, 1967); Howard Aldrich, *Organizations and Environments* (Englewood Cliffs, N.J.: Prentice-Hall, 1979); Oliver E. Williamson, *Markets and Hierarchies, Analysis and Antitrust Implications: A Study in the Economics of Internal Organization* (New York: Free Press, 1975).

4. Williamson, *Markets and Hierarchies.*

5. In the case of some offenses, especially those committed by organized crime, formal organization may be present. Yet this organization usually acts more as a disguise meant to create the appearance of legitimacy than as a true hierarchical structure. Often these offenses take place in market settings, but the crime involves undermining the legitimate operation of the market. See Powell, "Neither Market nor Hierarchy."

6. Richard Sparks, Alexander Greer, and Sally Manning, "Crimes as Work: An Illustrative Example," in *Theoretical Studies: Final Report* (Rutgers, N.J.: Center for the Study of the Causes of Crime for Gain, School of Criminal Justice, Rutgers University, undated), 9, explores the similarities and differences between the search for an employee in the legitimate marketplace and the search for a crime partner.

7. See, e.g., Cressey, *Criminal Organization,* 51–52; Mark Granovetter, "Economic Activity and Social Structure: The Problem of Embeddedness," *American Journal of Sociology* 91 (1985): 491–493. Another alternative is a group structure. A true group structure—defined by small size, fixed relationships, and well-defined boundaries—is rarely found in natural settings. Williamson, *Markets and Hierarchies,* 42–45, introduces the concept of peer groups, but these are seemingly anachronistic structures that appear as an intermediate form during the process of a market relationship being replaced by a firm.

8. Powell, "Neither Market nor Hierarchy," 324.

9. Ibid., 325.

10. Derek B. Cornish and Ronald V. Clarke, *The Reasoning Criminal: Rational Choice Perspectives on Offending* (New York: Springer-Verlag, 1986); Michael Gottfredson and Travis Hirschi, *A General Theory of Crime* (Stanford, Calif.: Stanford University Press, 1990).

11. Although this goal may exist, it may often not be achieved.

12. Powell, "Neither Market nor Hierarchy," 326; Granovetter, "Economic Activity and Social Structure"; Stuart Macaulay, "Non-Contractual Relations in Business: A Preliminary Study," *American Sociological Review* 28 (1963): 55–67.

13. Powell, "Neither Market nor Hierarchy," 326.

14. E.g., Ianni, *Family Business;* Ianni, *Black Mafia;* Albert J. Reiss, Jr. and David P. Farrington, "Advancing Knowledge About Co-Offending: Results from a Prospective Longitudinal Survey of London Males," *Journal of Criminal Law and Criminology* 82(2) (1991): 360–395. Of course, that actors select individuals similar to themselves may be a result of limited conventional or criminal contact with people who are different.

15. See Granovetter, "Economic Activity and Social Structure," 12. This trust may, of course, be misplaced. Offenders may hedge their trust in various ways—for example, by skimming money from the take or developing an informant relationship with the authorities.

16. Powell, "Neither Market nor Hierarchy," 324–327.

17. See Donald R. Cressey, *Theft of a Nation: The Structure and Operations of Organized Crime* (New York: Harper & Row, 1969).

18. For exceptions see J. Jackson et al., "Examining Criminal Organizations: Some Possible Methodologies," *Transnational Organized Crime* 2(4) (Winter 1996): 83–105, and R. H. Davis, "Social Network Analysis: An Aid in Conspiracy Investigations," *FBI Law Enforcement Bulletin* 50(12) (1981): 11–19.

19. The figures were prepared using the Krackplot software package. See David Krackhardt, J. Blyth, and C. McCratch, "Krackplot 3.0: An Improved Network Drawing Program," *Connections* 17 (1995): 53–55. Some network analyses were performed with the UCINET software package. See Stephen Borgatti, Martin Everett, and Linton Freeman, *UCINET IV* (Columbia, S.C.: Analytic Technologies, 1994). The re-

mainder were performed with custom-written procedures using the SAS software package. See SAS Institute, *SAS/STAT Software: Version 6,* 4th ed. (Cary, N.C.: SAS Institute, 1990).

20. For more complete definitions and explanations of network analysis terminology, see Appendix C and the sources it cites.

21. These measures included degree, mean geodesic, and maximum geodesic distance. See Appendix C for details.

22. For an illustration and discussion of the network properties of the organized crime family model, see Appendix C.

23. The analysis is carried out on a matrix like those shown in Appendix C. A brief explanation of the reasons for choosing the k-means approach can be found in Stanley Wasserman and Katherine Faust, *Social Network Analysis: Methods and Applications* (Cambridge: Cambridge University Press, 1994), 679–708.

24. The number of clusters was determined using the CCC and the pseudo F statistic. See SAS Institute, *SAS/STAT Software,* 97–99. The solutions we regarded as viable were indicated by both of these. We examined possible solutions of up to thirty-five clusters. It is possible that with more clusters some of the "important" individuals in the large cluster would be separated out. For each of the approaches there were also viable solutions with smaller numbers of clusters. These indicated a structure similar to those in the solutions we describe.

25. Although the other components were smaller, their size did not detract from their potential importance and relevance for other analyses.

26. U.S. Senate, *Hearings on Russian Organized Crime in the United States,* 50.

Chapter 9

1. These statistics are based on the 11235 zip code. U.S. Bureau of the Census, "1990 U.S. Census Data," Database STF3B "Kings County (pt.): 11235: Ancestry," http://venus.census.gov/cdrom/lookup/885095675, May 5, 1998.

2. Some examples of this coverage are Chris Hedges, "Where Soviet Émigrés Finally Let Loose," *New York Times,* August 11, 1990, p. A27, col. 3; Eleanor Randolph, "In Brighton Beach, Savoring the Pleasures of Russia, Without Pain," *Washington Post,* April 16, 1995, p. E1, col. 4;

Nancy Reckler, "Gone Knishin': When So Many Russian Jews Settle in a Small Seaside Corner of Brooklyn, Something Is Cooking," *Washington Post,* March 15, 1995, p. B9, col. 1; Abby Goodnough, "The Furs of Brighton Beach," *New York Times,* February 19, 1995, sec. CY, p. 3, col. 1.

3. Cal McCrystal, "Under the Gun," *Independent Magazine,* May 30, 1992, 36–43; Roger Rosenblatt, "From Russia, with Hope and Fear," *New York Times Magazine,* November 20, 1994, 70–78; Pierre Briancon, "Russian Mob Scene," *World Press Review* 42(10) (October 1995): 28–29; "Russia's New Export: The Mob," *Washington Post,* June 24, 1990, sec. C, p. 1, col. 4; Bruce Frankel, "Extortion Now the Least of Its Illegal Activities," *USA Today,* September 1, 1995, sec. A, p. 1, col. 3.

4. Before its current notoriety, Brighton Beach may have been best known outside New York for Neil Simon's series of plays based on his life, including *Brighton Beach Memoirs.*

5. For example, in fiscal year 1992 the Soviet Union was the fourth-largest country of birth for immigration (following Mexico, Vietnam, and the Philippines), and Russia was the seventh-largest country of last residence. Immigration and Naturalization Service, "Immigration Fact Sheet," http://www.ins.usdoj.gov/stats/299.html, May 5, 1998. In fiscal year 1996 Ukraine was the eighth-largest country of birth of immigrants, and Russia was the ninth. Immigration and Naturalization Service, "Immigration to the United States in Fiscal Year 1996," Table 5, Immigrants Admitted by Region and Selected Country of Birth: Fiscal Years 1994–96, http://www.ins.usdoj.gov/stats/annual/fy96/1005.html, May 5, 1998.

6. We reassured them of this by reading them this statement: "Now I want to ask you some questions about crime and especially about organized crime. We are not asking you these questions because we suspect that you are involved in any way in this crime. Rather, we are simply seeking the views and concerns of people in the community—such as yourself—about whether they think organized crime is or is not a problem in Brighton Beach."

7. Joe Sexton, "The Cold War in Brighton Beach: Police and Russian Émigrés Share an Uneasy Relationship," *New York Times,* January 17, 1995, p. B1.

8. U.S. Bureau of the Census, "1990 U.S. Census Data," Database C90STF1A "Brooklyn County, Tables: Persons, Detailed Race, Hispanic Origin by Race," http://venus.census.gov/cdrom/lookup/870799276, May 5, 1998.

9. Craig Wolff, "Five Youths Arrested in Rape of Coney Island Jogger," *New York Times,* April 14, 1994, sec. B, p. 1, col. 2; Craig Wolff, "Rape Sounds Alarm on Gangs on Coney Island's Boardwalk," *New York Times,* April 11, 1994, sec. B, p. 3, col. 1.

Chapter 10

1. Interview with Vladimir Knyazev, June 16, 1994.

2. Interview with Bryant and Stanny, May 25, 1994.

3. Interview with law enforcement officials in Miami, June 14, 1995.

4. Interview with Harvey Borak, October 27, 1994.

5. Thomas C. Schelling, "What Is the Business of Organized Crime?," *Journal of Public Law* 20 (1971): 33–165.

6. New York State Organized Crime Task Force et al., "Analysis of Russian Émigré Crime in the Tri-state Region," 192.

7. Kenney and Finckenauer, *Organized Crime in America,* 320.

8. Anderson, "Looking for Mr. Yaponchik," 51.

9. Rosner, "Sexy Russian Mafia," 32.

10. Kenney and Finckenauer, *Organized Crime in America.*

11. James B. Jacobs et al., *Busting the Mob* (New York: New York University Press, 1994).

12. Gambetta, *Sicilian Mafia.*

13. Ibid., 1.

14. Ibid., 17.

15. Ibid., 85.

16. Schelling, "What Is the Business of Organized Crime?"; Anderson, "Organised Crime, Mafias and Governments."

17. U.S. Senate, *Hearings on Russian Organized Crime in the United States.*

Appendix C

1. Other units of analysis, such as organizations, can also be used and are used in this study. All of the descriptions that follow can also be applied to other units of analysis.

2. Including both 1s in the matrix means that we are creating a symmetrical network. It is not required that both 1s be included, and in some situations it is more appropriate not to do so. However, the type of data that we had available made it appropriate to treat the relationships between actors as symmetrical.

3. The discovery that there are isolates who are not connected to any other members of the population of study is often one of the most intriguing results of a network analysis. David Knoke and James H. Kuklinski, *Network Analysis* (Beverly Hills, Calif.: Sage, 1982), 39. If a network is not connected, then raising the network matrix to the power of $n - 1$ will still produce a matrix with 0 cells.

4. There are $n^2 - n$ potential nondiagonal ties in a size n network; the number of ties present is equal to the number of 1s in the matrix representation. Formally, the formula is (n = number of observations, i = row number, j = column number):

$$\frac{\sum_{i=1}^{n} \sum_{j=1}^{n} X_{ij} - n}{n^2}$$

5. Other approaches to the overall description of a structure are available. Wasserman and Faust, *Social Network Analysis,* 169–219; Knoke and Kuklinski, *Network Analysis,* 50–53. Because of the size of our networks and the nature of the information coded, particularly the lack of directional information, these were not used.

6. Unlike these conventional descriptive statistics, in most instances no generally accepted tests of statistical significance allow inferences to be made.

7. There are many different mathematical approaches to cluster analysis. We used the one known as *k*-means. To carry out the analyses we used the PROC FASTCLUS procedure from the SAS/STAT software package. SAS INSTITUTE, *SAS/STAT Software,* 823–850.

INDEX